BIOGRAPHY AND CRITICISM

General Editors
A. NORMAN JEFFARES
R. L. C. LORIMER

9

E. M. FORSTER'S OTHER KINGDOM

Denis Godfrey is Professor of English Literature
at the University of Alberta, Canada. He is
a regular contributor to scholarly journals and
periodicals, and is well-known as the author
of such novels as *No Englishman Need Apply,
When Kings Are Arming,* and *The Bridge
of Fire.*

DENIS GODFREY

E. M. FORSTER'S OTHER KINGDOM

OLIVER & BOYD
EDINBURGH
LONDON
1968

OLIVER AND BOYD LTD

TWEEDDALE COURT
EDINBURGH I

39A WELBECK STREET
LONDON W I

FIRST PUBLISHED 1968

05 001631 8
PRINTED IN GREAT BRITAIN

BY OLIVER AND BOYD LTD

EDINBURGH

SCOTLAND

Not where the wheeling systems darken,
And our benumbed conceiving soars!—
The drift of pinions, would we hearken,
Beats at our own clay-shuttered doors.

FRANCIS THOMPSON

Acknowledgements

F OR permission to quote from the novels and short stories of E. M. Forster, thanks are due to the publishers of the following works : *Where Angels Fear to Tread*, *The Longest Journey*, *A Room with a View*, and *Howards End* (Edward Arnold (Publishers) Ltd., and Alfred A. Knopf Inc) ; *Two Cheers for Democracy* and *A Passage to India* (Edward Arnold (Publishers) Ltd., and Harcourt, Brace and World Inc) ; *The Collected Tales of E. M. Forster* (Alfred A. Knopf Inc).

Contents

I

Introduction—"The Impact of the Unseen"

WRITING of E. M. Forster in 1935, Cyril Connolly pro-
phesied that the future would increasingly neglect him,
finding his very excellence "inconvenient".[1] Thirty
years of steadily accumulating criticism and appreciation would
seem to have refuted this prophecy, and yet a consideration of
that body of criticism, of its general emphasis and direction,
would certainly suggest at least one aspect of Forster's excellence
that the critics have found it inconvenient to pursue; his concern namely with what he chooses frequently to refer to as the
"unseen". The existence of this "unseen" factor, of a mystical
quality informing the author's novels and stories, has of course
been the subject of critical comment and conjecture, but as yet
without a sufficient realisation of its essential importance. It is
one thing to say, as many critics do, and quite correctly, that
the novels of E. M. Forster abound in spiritual implications,
that they are fundamentally concerned with the relation
between the seen and unseen worlds, it is quite another however
to take that relationship seriously, to accept as a fact rather
than a hypothesis the reality of the spiritual world in terms of
which the visible everyday world is being presented to us.
Many critics, it is to be suspected, if confronted with the
transcendent reality about which they write in connexion with
Forster, would be as embarrassed as the eminent zoologist who
found waiting for him one morning, not the manuscript of his
work on the lion, but—a lion!

Some critics, while recognising the mystical element in
Forster, tend simply to deplore it, to feel that his books would
be greater if it were not there. Edward Marsh, for example,

[1] *The Condemned Playground*, p. 103. London (Routledge) 1945.

considers *A Passage to India* a masterpiece, but finds it rather spoilt for him by its "strain of occultism" which leaves him baffled.[2] Roger Fry also qualifies his admiration of the same book in much the same way:

> I think it's marvellous texture—really beautiful writing. But Oh Lord I wish he weren't a mystic, or that he would keep his mysticism out of his books. ... I'm certain that the only meanings that are worth anything in a work of art are those that the artist himself knows nothing about. The moment he tries to explain *his* ideas and *his* emotions he misses the great thing.[3]

Nevertheless the mysticism is there, together, at least by implication, with the author's personal endorsement behind it. Moreover within Forster's creative work it is basic, the determining factor in his interpretation of human character and of every aspect of human life. To ignore it, or to take it insufficiently into account is indeed to extract the Prince of Denmark from *Hamlet*.

Among recent extended studies of Forster, that by James McConkey, *The Novels of E. M. Forster*, may perhaps be singled out for the emphasis it places on the occult element in Forster's writings, for its appreciation of the importance within them of the impact of the unseen upon the seen:

> The portion of Forster's novels [he writes] which deals essentially with the world of human relationships, the world of human reality, is not difficult to analyze; and it is indeed an important element in his fiction. That it is but a portion, however, and that the world of human reality is ever contrasted with another reality any reader of him is aware. Forster's interest in both the human and transcendent realities accounts for what his friend G. Lowes Dickinson has termed his kind of "double vision", a sense of "this world, and a world or worlds behind". These "worlds behind" cannot be ignored or given a minor position by the critic, for in Forster the sense of the transcendent realm consistently affects and colors the physical realm.[4]

---

[2] Leonard Woolf, *Sowing, an Autobiography of the years 1880-1904*, pp. 171-2. London (Hogarth) 1960.

[3] Virginia Woolf, *Roger Fry*, pp. 240-1. London (Hogarth) 1940.

[4] James McConkey, *The Novels of E. M. Forster*, p. 3. Ithaca (Cornell) 1957.

This is promising, but McConkey immediately goes on from this point to insist that Forster is at pains in all his creative writings to keep these two contrasting realms distinct from each other, that his human protagonists do not embody any transcendent principle, that he postulates in fact an unbridgeable gulf between the seen, about which it is possible to verbalise, and the unseen which may be experienced in feeling but never made known in words. On the basis of such an insistence, McConkey's book, despite the gestures it continues to make towards the "worlds behind", becomes just one more study of Forster in terms of human reality. Forster himself, in particular through a personal observation in *A Passage to India* to which reference will later be made, has done something to encourage the almost universal tendency of his critics to perceive in his works this alleged disassociation between the seen and the unseen. Further encouragement in the same direction has also been offered by the curious fact that in his critical works and essays he has confined himself almost exclusively to the human level and refrained from any direct personal endorsement of the belief in the unseen to which the novels bear witness. Yet the witness is there, an insistence by statement and implication not only on the existence of an underlying spiritual reality that may be mystically experienced, but also on the various manifestations of that reality at the human level. Critical appreciation of Forster, by conceiving of the unseen as existing in total isolation from the seen, has so far underestimated or even ignored the way in which, in the novels, the unseen is presented as interpenetrating the seen by contriving and controlling events within it, and by influencing and revealing character. This underestimation is particularly evident in the interpretation that has been accorded two of Forster's most complex and significant characters, Mrs Wilcox and Mrs Moore. Here, it will be remembered, in *Howards End* and *A Passage to India* respectively, are two elderly and remarkable ladies whose influence on others, moderate in their lifetimes, becomes far reaching and decisive only after their deaths. With one notable exception, Ernest Beaumont in an article "Mr E. M. Forster's Strange Mystics", critics have either passed over the nature and extent of the posthumous influences involved, or have interpreted them

simply in terms of human memory. Ernest Beaumont, while
disapproving on orthodox Christian grounds of the implications
he detects, does at least detect them, does at least realise that
Mrs Wilcox and Mrs Moore are being presented to us as continuing to exist spiritually after death, and as exerting from out
of the unseen a controlling influence upon events and people.

The spiritual influences of the dead, as implied in the last
two novels, is of course only one of the many unseen forces
manifesting at the human level to which Forster directs our
attention throughout his work, and whose identification and
analysis has yet to receive adequate critical recognition. The
purpose of this study is to accord that recognition, to present the
evidence within the novels and short stories for that "other
world" whose ultimate nature may not be fully communicated
but whose presence may certainly be inferred in terms of its
effect on human character and activity.

Inevitably Forster's mysticism, his postulation of a transcendent reality, has raised the question of the relationship of that
world to this one, of the unseen to the seen, and this may in part
account for the intense preoccupation of so many critics with
the author's use of symbolism. That symbols of various kinds
have been deliberately introduced, especially into the novels, is
clear enough: for example, the division of *A Passage to India*
into three sections entitled, Mosque, Caves, Temple respectively. Also on occasion a particular event may be endowed
intentionally with symbolic significance; as when in *Howards
End* Leonard Bast lies dead beside the Schlegels' bookcases, and
the books that have done so much to destroy him fall over him
in a shower. Symbolism again, has legitimately been detected
in the author's imagery, and in his rhythmic, or repetitive use
of particular images. Criticism, in so far as it has confined itself
to the identification of symbols obviously intended by the
author, has contributed much to our appreciation of Forster
especially as a literary technician, for the provision of symbolic
or metaphorical images within a work of literature, is essentially
a matter of invention, of technique. The quest for symbols,
however, in the works of Forster, has tended in recent years to
go far beyond any objective determination of the author's
intentions, and to impose on events and objects within the

novels significance of a highly subjective kind. It is difficult for instance to accept or to see much point in the alleged discovery that each of the rooms in Howards End symbolises a member of the Wilcox or Schlegel family,[5] or that—another extreme example—the "pomper, pomper, pomper" sound of the train in *A Passage to India* carrying the party to the Marabar caves, constitutes a travesty of the Hindu invocation to the three-in-one, A U M.[6] The quest for symbols in the novels of Forster has been carried too far, become an end in itself, a critical exercise in intellectual ingenuity. Various attempts have of course been made to get beyond the mere collection of symbols for their own sake, and to fit them into some larger pattern of interpretation applicable to a particular novel, or to the novels as a whole. Such wider interpretations however have tended to be in humanistic or realistic terms, in terms of the seen rather than the unseen, or—which amounts to the same thing—in terms of an unseen conceived of as existing on its own in isolation from the seen. To be adequate, however, interpretation must go deeper than this, must concern itself more intimately than has so far been the case with the exact nature of the alleged "realism" that Forster presents to us. The realism is certainly there, to the point that we do not hesitate to discuss the author's characters as though they were real people. We could not do this however, nor would their reality convince us so overwhelmingly, did they not also partake in the artistic principle of universality. In this connexion it is instructive to recall the Goethean concept of the artist as one whose function is "through semblance to give the illusion of a higher reality".[7] Semblance, according to Goethe, mere realistic imitation, though always necessary to provide the artist with a point of departure, must never be persisted in too long. To begin with, as he says with reference to painting, the artist must "faithfully and devotedly follow nature's pattern in the detail"; but, "in the higher regions of artistic activity, where actually a picture becomes a picture", there he has "free play and may even

[5] George H. Thomson, "Theme and Symbol in *Howards End*", in *Modern Fiction Studies*, VII, No. 3 (1961), p. 232.
[6] Wilfred Stone, *The Cave and the Mountain*, fn. p. 341. London (Oxford) 1966.
[7] *Dichtung und Wahrheit*, III, 40.

proceed to fiction".[8] In Forster's work the initial subordination to nature, the starting point in realism, is abundantly evident. So much so that criticism, as we have seen, has tended to come to rest within it, to find in the novels no more than the representation of a visible human world set apart from and essentially independent of any higher form of reality. The higher spiritual reality, however, referred to by Goethe, is nevertheless present, not only in the form of direct references to the mystical experience of the divine, but also, by implication, within the objects and processes of everyday human life. This sense, conveyed to us through the novels, of a higher reality penetrating and to some extent transfiguring the material fabric of existence, has been noted in particular by a personal friend of Forster's, herself a novelist, Virginia Woolf. She notes the intention even while concluding that it does not succeed:

> At certain moments [she writes] on the Arno, in Hertfordshire, in Surrey, beauty leaps from the scabbard, the fire of truth flames through the crusted earth; we must see the red brick villa in the suburbs of London lit up. But it is in these great scenes which are the justification of the huge elaboration of the realistic novel that we are most aware of failure. For it is here that Mr. Forster makes the change from realism to symbolism; here that the object which has been so uncompromisingly solid becomes, or should become, luminously transparent. He fails, one is tempted to think, chiefly because that admirable gift of his for observation has served him too well. He has recorded too much and too literally. He has given us an almost photographic picture on one side of the page; on the other he asks us to see the same view transformed and radiant with eternal fires.[9]

Such a criticism by so eminent a writer must be taken seriously, for it is always possible that realism, correct as a starting point, may be persisted in too far. Again as Goethe points out, a "false effort" results when the artist retains "the semblance so long within reality, that finally a common reality

[8] Eckermann, *Gespräche mit Goethe*, III, 106.
[9] Virginia Woolf, *The Death of the Moth*, p. 108. London (Hogarth) 1942.

[is] left".[10] However, the purpose of this study is to suggest and demonstrate that Virginia Woolf and those who think like her, while not altogether wrong, may perhaps have failed to detect within the realism the full transfiguring range of the author's spiritual implications. The very fact that his realism is so convincing, the illusion to which he compels us to succumb so complete, is in itself a sign that a higher not a common reality has after all been created. At no point in fact, as we shall attempt to show, is the realism so photographic, so opaque, that we may not with sufficient insight observe the spiritual forces at work within it, endowing it with a higher degree of reality than is to be found in actual life. Thus the world that Forster creates for us is not this world, nor is it a symbol of the spiritual world; it is this world universalised, irradiated by the spirit, raised up, as man for ever seeks to raise himself, towards the divine.

It is possible, as Roger Fry indicates, for the artist, simply to present us with his higher, universalised world impersonally, in ignorance of his own achievement and intention. The modern artist, however, finds it increasingly difficult to create in this way. He needs to know what he is doing and why, to observe and understand his own creative processes. He may not always succeed, may find, as Forster himself does, that creativity is for him both a conscious and a subconscious process. In a passage in his essay "The Raison d'Être of Criticism in the Arts" he defines the creative state from such a point of view:

> What about the creative state? In it a man is taken out of himself. He lets down as it were a bucket into his subconscious, and draws up something which is normally beyond his reach. He mixes this thing with his normal experiences, and out of the mixture he makes a work of art. It may be a good work of art or a bad one—we are not here examining the question of quality—but whether it is good or bad it will have been compounded in this unusual way, and he will wonder afterwards how he did it. Such seems to be the creative process. It may employ much technical ingenuity and worldly knowledge, it

---

[10] *Dichtung und Wahrheit*, III, 40. A summary of Goethe's aesthetics will be found in the writer's "Imagination and Truth—Some Romantic Contradictions", in *English Studies* (Amsterdam), XLIV, No. 4 (1963), pp. 260-3.

may profit by critical standards, but mixed up with it is this
stuff from the bucket, this subconscious stuff, which is not
procurable on demand. And when the process is over, when
the picture or symphony or lyric or novel (or whatever it is) is
complete, the artist, looking back on it, will wonder how on
earth he did it. And indeed he did not do it on earth.[11]

An element then of the instinctive, the subconscious may
well be at work in creating the higher reality that confronts us
in a work of art. The artist himself may not be aware that the
reality thus created *is* a higher one, may not even be conscious
of the transfiguring spiritual implications with which the bucket
of the subconscious has provided him. Yet in the case of Forster
those implications are certainly there, and only in terms of
them can his created world and the events and characters within
it be adequately interpreted. The transfiguring spirituality is
there, as we shall find, in the implications of decisive invisible
influences emanating from such entities as "Italy", "nature",
the "English soil". It is present also in a sense of the fateful
ordering of events, in the evidences of superstition, in the
dispositions within the present of the ancestral past and in the
ministrations of the dead. It is present finally in the consistent
assessment of character in terms of its sensitivity to the unseen
as such, and to its various manifestations within the physical
world. Sometimes Forster seems to be aware of his own
spiritual implications, sometimes, as in his references to the
"unseen" and to the mystical experience of the divine, he is
being spiritually specific: occasionally however, in the analysis
now ahead of us, we shall be identifying spiritual implications
of which the author himself may be unconscious. But the
extent of the author's deliberation will not affect the ultimate
result, the creation of a higher reality—higher because within it
the spiritual powers and forces informing and transfiguring the
everyday world may be observed more extensively and openly
at work, and in greater freedom.

[11] *Two Cheers for Democracy*, p. 121. Harmondsworth (Penguin) 1965.

II

The Short Stories

It will be appropriate to begin our assessment of Forster's writings, our interpretation of them in terms of what we may conveniently call "the impact of the unseen", with the short stories—written at various times before 1914, and collected in the two volumes, *The Celestial Omnibus* and *The Eternal Moment*. Although the stories accompanied rather than preceded the writing of the first four novels, it is possible to consider them collectively, to see them, in relation to the novels, as preparatory. In 1946, in an introduction to a collected edition, Mr Forster refers to the stories as fantasies, and such for the most part they are. In the most typical of them, fantasy, usually an occurrence of a supernatural kind, is made to erupt in the midst of, and in defiance of everyday reality, and the characters in accordance with the degree of their spiritual sensitivity react to it. An examination of three of the best known of the tales, beginning with "The Story of a Panic", will show the process at work.

The panic in question is, in the classical tradition, the unreasoning contagious terror inspired in mortals by the presence of the god Pan. The great god Pan, as Mr Sandbach the curate points out, died with the Birth of Christ; and yet here he is among the chestnut woods and slopes above Ravello in Italy once more in full manifestation, to the great discomfiture of a group of prosaic British tourists. From the supernatural presence of the god suggested by no more than a catspaw of wind and a terrible silence, the conventional tourists flee in mindless terror down the hillside. Only Eustace a boy of fourteen, moody, unsatisfactory and not given to healthy exercise, is unaffected. The others return from their panic flight to find Eustace stretched serenely on the ground

and when some goat prints, presumably of the god, are observed
in the moist earth he rolls on them "as a dog rolls in dirt".
From this point the boy, strangely transfigured, behaves with a
bewildering eccentricity, racing through the woods, capturing
a hare, kissing an old Italian peasant woman on the cheek.
That night in the hotel, he escapes from his room, capers madly
about the garden and is overheard addressing, with an extraordinary eloquence, a song of praise and blessing to the "great
forces and manifestations of Nature".[1] The uncomprehending
adults close in to capture him, but the story ends with the
shouts and laughter of the boy "escaping" down the valley to
the sea. The other characters involved in this curious, whimsical blending of the real and the fantastic have reacted
variously, but each in strict accordance with the degree of his
or her spiritual sensitivity. Eustace, a maladjusted, much
disapproved of boy of fourteen, has revealed in actual contact
with the unseen a presence of mind, an insight that lifts him far
above his disapproving elders. Only in the simple, also much
disapproved of Italian waiter, Gennaro, does he find a kindred
spirit, one who knows what has happened on the hillside, and
exactly what it involves. Over against the inspired, the
sensitive, have been set the spiritually obtuse, including those,
like the artist Leyland and the clergyman Mr Sandbach,
professionally committed to a belief in the unseen. In particular there has been the narrator, Mr Tytler, one whose every
word gives him away, reveals him as in fact the antagonist of
his own sententiously professed ideals. Measured in terms of
their initial panic reaction to the manifestation of the unseen,
and of their subsequent behaviour towards Eustace, and also
towards Gennaro, all three stand condemned. The unseen in
which they profess to believe, has challenged them and found
them out. Especially revealing has been the obtuseness of the
smugly British Mr Tytler towards Gennaro, in whom, as in all
simple Italians, there resides—or so we are required to
assume—a kind of superior wisdom deriving from an instinctive
communion with the unseen.

[1] *The Collected Tales of E. M. Forster*, p. 28. New York (Knopf) 1947. All
subsequent page references will be taken from this edition, henceforth cited as,
C.T.

The pattern, the formula, established by "The Story of a Panic", is to be repeated in essence and with only surface variations in both "The Celestial Omnibus" and "Other Kingdom". In the first of these, we again have a boy, younger even than Eustace, whose imaginative sensitivity is mocked and suppressed by uncomprehending elders. Again the unseen is made to erupt right in the heart of everyday suburban reality, this time in the form of a mysterious omnibus in which the boy is conveyed skywards into the realm of the imagination, escorted and welcomed thither by some of the creators of great literature and their created characters—Dante, for example, and Sir Thomas Browne, Mrs Gamp, the great Achilles. Obtuseness, spiritual insensitivity is here contributed by Mr Septimus Bons, president of the local Literary Society, an expert on Dante, and possesser of no less than seven copies of the works of Shelley. Mr Bons committed to the unseen through the medium of literature also makes the journey with the boy in the celestial omnibus; but while the boy is set in spiritual triumph on the shield of Achilles, Mr Bons, confronted at last with the reality of the literature he had theorised about so long and so glibly, panics and falls.

In "Other Kingdom" the supernatural event (a girl turns into a tree) occurs only at the end of the story and is thus less an instigator of events than a conclusion. However we are constantly being prepared for it, and again as in "The Story of a Panic" through the medium of the classics. "Other Kingdom" in fact begins with the classics, with the characters, under the eye of a tutor, Mr Inskip, translating the line from Vergil, "Quem fugis, ah demens, habitarunt di quoque silvas"—which in turn leads to a discussion on the classical habit of investing nature, woods in particular, with gods. The metamorphosis of mortals into laurels, into reeds is also touched on. So when a small wood of beech trees called "Other Kingdom" is introduced by the pompous Harcourt Worters as a gift for Miss Beaumont, his intended bride, we are already prepared for its endowment with unseen attributes, for its use as a spiritual touchstone for character. Most sensitive, most attuned to the invisible is Miss Beaumont herself, patronisingly picked out of Ireland by Mr Worters, despite her lack of money and connexions, and now in process of being moulded intellectually to become his wife. From the first she rejoices extravagantly in her Other Kingdom, arranges a picnic there and takes formal possession chanting a humorous translation of the line from Vergil "Ah you silly ass gods live in woods". Almost at once the wood raises between herself and Harcourt Worters the issue of the unseen; for Harcourt, like Mr Tytler before him, is one whose every word and action reveals him as the antagonist of his professed ideals. Hostile to the genuine spirituality he senses in Miss Beaumont, he seeks to control and destroy it, symbolically by fencing in Other Kingdom and linking it to his architecturally deplorable mansion by an asphalt path. Allied to Miss Beaumont in her battle for the spiritual, is the young Jack Ford, dependent on Harcourt Worters who is his guardian, and yet uncompromisingly aware of his falsity. Ford, a matured version of Eustace and of the boy in "The Celestial Omnibus", is both spiritually sensitive, fully initiated into the mystery of Other Kingdom, and at the same time dangerously dedicated to truth. In between the antagonists, and involved despite himself in the spiritual entanglement, is the narrator, Mr Inskip, dependent also in his capacity of tutor on the favour of Mr Worters. Unlike Ford, however, he is an equivocator, cynically aware of the side on which his bread is buttered. Seeing it all, and with the falsity of his employer as clear to him as to Ford, he yet stays obsequiously in line, ends up as Harcourt's private secretary.

Other Kingdom therefore, abode of gods, and ultimate refuge for Miss Beaumont through her metamorphosis into a tree, issues its challenge to integrity, to imagination, to character. Only to Ford, accused by Harcourt of abducting Miss Beaumont, is the ultimate truth revealed: that she has escaped "absolutely, for ever and ever, as long as there are branches to shade men from the sun".

Thus, in three of the most typical of the collected stories, the unseen is dominant, precipitating events, revealing character. To the three should also be added a lesser fourth "The Curate's Friend", in which a clergyman is saved from his own superficiality by an encounter with a faun on a down in Wiltshire. In each story a supernatural event is, as it were, postulated. We are not being asked to believe in it, or even to "suspend our disbelief", but rather to go along with it whimsically, for the sake of argument. Actual supernatural happenings—visions, the appearance of ghosts, hallucinations—are a part of human experience and acceptable as such in literature, but the occurrences in the four stories we have touched on are not of this order. Their whimsicality is most evident in "The Celestial Omnibus" where the seen and the unseen are so irrationally combined, that Mr Bons's fall from the celestial height to which the omnibus has transported him, becomes a literal fall through space and his body is found later in a "shockingly mutilated condition in the vicinity of the Bermondsey gas works". Such irrationality is of course intentional, part of the joke. As Mr Forster has himself confessed elsewhere,

> I like that idea of fantasy, of muddling up the actual and the impossible until the reader isn't sure which is which, and I have sometimes tried to do it when writing myself.[2]

What counts, in other words, in the stories, is not the impossible events but the reactions of the characters to them. These, assessed with an almost mathematical exactitude in terms of their sensitivity or insensitivity to a spiritual challenge, stand before us with an extraordinary vividness and reality. The method of assessment, the provision however whimsically of a spiritual touchstone, clearly justifies itself in the field of characterisation.

Next of the tales to be considered are those in which the unseen continues to be manifest, but less incongruously, less openly in defiance of our daily experience. In "The Point Of It" the seen and the unseen are kept conventionally apart, as we follow Michael first through a summary of his earthly career and then, fancifully, through a series of after-death experiences. The after-life, presented somewhat satirically in Christian terms, is also the setting for "Mr Andrews". In "Co-ordination" the seen and the unseen are once more blended, but humorously, with the shades of Napoleon and Beethoven comically and uncomprehendingly presiding over the curri-

[2] From the essay, "A Book That Influenced Me", in *Two Cheers for Democracy*, p. 226.

culum of a girls' school. After death experiences also feature to
some extent in the purely allegorical "The Other Side of the
Hedge", where the dusty highway of life is fenced in by brown
crackling hedges through which, nevertheless, one can force
one's way at will into the pastoral paradise beyond. The dead,
it is made clear, belong in this paradise, but the living also may
penetrate to it, substitute its spiritual values for those obtaining
along the dusty road. It cannot be said in any of these fantasies
that the nature of man's after-death experience is being at all
seriously postulated; at the most, humorously or allegorically,
some aspects of what that experience may turn out to be are
being speculated upon. However, preoccupation with the
unseen is still there, basic to all four stories.

The unseen again, as conceived of this time in superstitious
folk-lore, appears in "The Story of the Siren", related to us,
or rather to the narrator, by a simple Sicilian boatman. Once
more, as in "The Story of a Panic" a group of British tourists
are involved, but their presence is perfunctory, and the narrator
alone, poised on a rock with the boatman above the blue depths
of the Mediterranean, hears what happens to those to whom the
Siren has appeared. The boatman's story, an account of the
dire supernatural consequences attendant on having seen the
siren, is told with such matter-of-fact conviction that the
narrator despite himself is moved, and in part persuaded:

> The story . . . for all its absurdity and superstition, came nearer
> to reality than anything I had known before. I don't know why,
> but it filled me with desire to help others—the greatest of all
> our desires, I suppose, and the most fruitless.[3]

To this extent, in respect that is to the effect of the boatman's
story on the narrator, and by implication on the author as well,
"The Story of the Siren" goes beyond "The Story of a Panic",
where the supernatural event, despite its matter-of-fact
acceptance by the simple Gennaro, is too obviously a device,
whimsically presented. Meanwhile in "The Story of the Siren"
our attention is again being drawn to the special spiritual
sensitivity of the simple Italian: an instinctive sensitivity that
issues forth in an attitude to life, in values to which the sophisti-

[3] *C.T.*, p. 254.

cated, the intellectual, as represented by the British tourists, can no longer attain.

"The Machine Stops", a long science-fiction fantasy of the future, might seem to belong in a category of its own, to be ignoring the unseen altogether. And yet, by implication, through the mere fact of its being denied, the significance of the unseen is constantly being impressed upon us. For the scientific Utopia envisaged by the author, is one from which not only the unseen itself but all values derived from it have been ruthlessly eliminated. Living underground in a totally artificial machine-made and controlled environment, the world's inhabitants exist in impersonal isolation exchanging their limited machine-conditioned ideas. Especially significant is the rejection by all devotees of the "Machine" of nature. When Vashti is compelled to travel by air-ship to visit her son, the rebellious, heretical Kuno, she observes the surface of the earth, even the might of the Himalayas, with disdain, and screens off the view with a metal blind. And when Kuno makes his escape from underground, it is to nature, the unseen in nature, that he finds himself mysteriously attracted. The hills he sees above ground are low and colourless, but yet vivid and alive:

> I felt that those hills had called with incalculable force to men in the past, and that men had loved them. Now they sleep—perhaps for ever. They commune with humanity in dreams. . . .[4]

Over against the Machine, and the desolation of mechanical ideas, is thus set the mysticism of nature already suggested to us, for example, by the panegyric of the boy Eustace and by the whimsical peopling of nature in story after story with classical divinities. Explicitly in fact, as well as by implication, the unseen is omnipresent in "The Machine Stops", and basic to it. And again we should note the antagonism brought against the unseen in this story by "ideas", by an intellectualism, a sophisticated rationality such as we have already encountered in Mr Tytler, in Inskip and Harcourt Worters, in Mr Bons. This barren rationality, so clever and plausible on the surface, so outwardly cultured and humane, is already being identified

for the dangerous enemy that it will turn out to be in the
novels, an arch-destroyer of the human soul.

Two stories, essentially different from those touched on so far
still remain—"The Road from Colonus" and "The Eternal
Moment". In both of them the unseen, or rather forces from
out of the unseen, are manifest, but now realistically, in terms,
so to speak, of everyday life. So far the unseen has been
presented to us on the level of fantasy, whimsically, humorously,
allegorically, or through the medium of naïve superstition. We
have not been invited to accept it as indeed operating actually
and literally in real life. Now, fantasy is to be set aside, and the
actual impact of the unseen, at least by implication, demonstrated.

Mr Lucas, the Oedipus figure of "The Road from Colonus",
is on a visit to Greece, and in common with the Oedipus of
legend is growing very old. He has lost interest in people and
their affairs, and seldom listens when they speak to him. The
dream of his life, a visit to Greece, is being realised, but with
none of the magic to which he had confidently looked forward
for forty years. Then beside a tiny Khan, or country inn,
surrounded by magnificent trees, a transfiguring moment
awaits him. One of the great trees is hollow, and from out of it
there gushes, to his amazement, an impetuous spring coating
the bank with fern and moss and flowing on to create a fertile
meadow beyond. The simple country folk paying "to beauty
and mystery such tribute as they could" have cut a shrine in the
rind of the tree and adorned it with native offerings to the
"presiding Power". With a curious sense of companionship, Mr
Lucas approaches, spreads out his arms and leans back against
the tree:

> His eyes closed, and he had the strange feeling of one who is
> moving, yet at peace—the feeling of the swimmer, who, after
> long struggle with chopping seas, finds that after all the tide
> will sweep him to his goal.[5]

Aroused at length by the shock of some kind of arrival, he opens
his eyes to find that "something unimagined, indefinable, had
passed over all things, and made them intelligible and good".
Meaning and beauty have flowed back into life, transfiguring

[5] *C.T.*, p. 130.

the commonplace, and in a single moment of experience Mr Lucas has "discovered not only Greece, but England and all the world and life". He has a passionate longing to prolong his ecstasy, to spend a night, perhaps a week in the Khan among the gracious, kind-eyed country people, but his companions, arrogantly practical, intellectual and insensitive, soon arrive to ridicule the suggestion. He fights back, fortified by the word-less appeal directed to him from the simple Greeks, and because in that place and with those people he knows that "a supreme event was awaiting him which would transfigure the face of the world".[6] But in vain. Losing patience with the tiresome old man, his companions hoist him onto his mule and lead him away, pursued by the execrations and stones of the instinctively percipient villagers. Mr Lucas accepts his fate, reverts to his former, dessicated self and deteriorates further. We see him next in England, in loveless companionship with his daughter Ethel, a querulous old man testily preoccupied with trivialities. And when a Greek newspaper arriving by chance informs them of a rural tragedy, a tree blown down killing the occupants of a village Khan, and Ethel, translating it out loud, checks the date and the locality and is promptly aghast with realisation, the old man babbles on with his grievances uninterested, indeed unhearing. Ethel perceives the delivering hand of Providence, but the reader knows that death in the Khan would have been for Mr Lucas a fulfilment, that in fact at the Khan he had already died.

"The Eternal Moment", last and most considerable of the tales, has much in common with "The Road from Colonus". For again the unseen is operative, as the title suggests, by influencing though without intruding upon a sequence of everyday events. In fact the surface happenings are here more consistently commonplace than in the "Road from Colonus", where the contrived coincidence of the ending, the destruction of the Khan, is an intrusion somewhat difficult to accept. Even the "Eternal Moment" itself, Miss Raby's romantic encounter on the mountain side with the Italian guide, Feo Genori, is already twenty years distant in the past, and we are to be concerned only with its sequel.

[6] *C.T.*, p. 137.

B

Returning, after twenty years, to the Alpine village of Vorta, Miss Raby finds herself haunted by a sense of betrayal. For thanks to her, to her portrayal of it in a successful novel, Vorta has become known and fashionable, blossoming forth into a vulgar and prosperous tourist resort. Famous, in the evening of her life, and accompanied by the prosaic Col Leyland, she must now confront the spiritual devastation for which she has been responsible.

The reality surpasses her fears. Fleeing in disgust from the pretentious Hotel des Alpes, she returns to the Albergo Biscione, the simple, gracious inn of her first visit, only to find it a pathetic survival, excluded from the new order, the new prosperity. She visits the ailing, aged proprietress, the aristocratic Signora Cantù, who can talk of nothing now but her grievances, especially against her son, the proprietor of the infamous Hotel des Alpes. Listening to her and perceiving all the degradation for which she has been to blame, Miss Raby experiences a kind of death:

> It seemed to her that with this interview her life had ended. She had done all that was possible. She had done much evil. It only remained for her to fold her hands and to wait, till her ugliness and her incompetence went the way of beauty and strength.[7]

Yet one hope, one person remains—Feo Genori. Perhaps through him, through the shared recollection of their eternal moment together, her craving for atonement can be appeased. But the meeting with Feo, now the fat and unattractive *concierge* at the Hotel des Alpes, is a total catastrophe. He does not recognise her, and when, recklessly, she forces him to remember, he panics, fearing blackmail. Col Leyland appears and the misunderstandings multiply, become grotesque. Hearing that Feo now has three children, Miss Raby pursues her quest for atonement by desperately offering to adopt one. But Feo, after some mercenary calculations, declines. His wife is too sharp, and might find out about his past indiscretion. The scandal spreads through the hotel, and the situation is saved only by the intervention of Col Leyland who enters into a

[7] *C.T.*, p. 288f.

secret, vulgar pact with Feo. They will explain that Miss Raby is not responsible, not quite right in the head.

Her defeat is total, her attempt at atonement repudiated, and yet Miss Raby finds herself not altogether forsaken:

> In that moment of final failure, there had been vouchsafed to her a vision of herself, and she saw that she had lived worthily. She was conscious of a triumph over experience and earthly facts, a triumph magnificent, cold, hardly human, whose existence no one but herself would ever surmise.[8]

The eternal moment on the mountain side, the remembrance of which had spiritually irradiated all her subsequent life, had not after all been invalidated. Always it had been to her a source of power and inspiration, "just as trees draw vigour from a subterranean spring";[9] and so now it enables her to go beyond experience and earthly facts, to accept her own and the tragedy of Vorta, and the coming of age. "I suppose this is old age," she thought. "It's not so very dreadful."

In the short stories then, in a variety of ways, the workings of the unseen have been suggested: through fantasy, classical mythology and superstitious folklore, through the implication of spiritual forces manifesting in nature, in the instincts of simple, especially Italian, people, and in the events of everyday life. On the whole fantasy has predominated, a whimsical fantasy which the author invites us not to take too seriously. Yet the unseen, fantastic or otherwise, has been the common basic factor in all the stories, and will continue to be basic in the novels. Observable also in the stories has been a certain progress away from the whimsical, the equivocal towards a concept of a literal unseen actually at work with its forces within everyday reality. And again, even in those tales where the unseen is manifestly fantastical, it has always been presented as a precipitator of significant events, a touchstone for the judgement of character. The novels will lead more deeply into human experience, into far more subtle interpretations of events and people, but in one respect at least they will not go beyond the stories. Consistent in the novels as in the stories will be the author's interpretation of life and people in terms of an invisible underlying reality.

[8] *C.T.*, p. 307. [9] *C.T.*, p. 300.

III

Where Angels Fear to Tread

THE setting of Mr Forster's first novel, *Where Angels Fear to Tread*, is in part Italy, in part an English suburb of London to which he gives the name of Sawston. The theme of the novel is the involvement of a number of English characters, two in particular, with Italy. Through their experience of Italy and the Italians, they are to be brought up against unseen forces they can neither understand nor control, and which will bring them despite themselves through the catharsis of tragedy. In the short stories, for example in "The Story of a Panic", "The Story of the Siren" and "The Eternal Moment", the special nature of the English involvement with Italy has already been touched on; but now in the first novel it will be explored further, with all its explosive potentiality for both good and evil, in detail and in depth. And, as in "The Eternal Moment", the exploration will be a realistic one, consistently at the level of everyday life.

Entirely actual and everyday are the English characters introduced to us as the story opens, leading their acquiescent lives in suburban Sawston. Perhaps only two, Mrs Herriton and her daughter Harriet, are represented as fully acquiescent, as having come to terms with their respectable, spiritless environment; and these two, significantly, show either indifference or hostility towards Italy. Philip Herriton on the other hand, the clever son of the family, has already been to Italy and come under its disrupting spell, and has preserved ever since a cynical, if somewhat theoretical detachment from the conventions of Sawston. Now, as the story opens, the complex and fateful involvement of the Herritons with Italy is about to begin again through Lilia, Philip's widowed sister-in-law. Lilia who is high spirited, not out of the same top drawer as the Herritons and unconventional in the wrong way,

has been causing social embarrassment and is in consequence
being sent off for an extended tour of Italy in the protective
custody of the staid and sensible Miss Caroline Abbott. Philip,
seeing the pair off at Victoria Station, is full of enthusiastic
advice on his favourite theme. They are not to think of Italy
simply as a museum of antiquities and art, but to " 'love and
understand the Italians, for the people are more marvellous
than the land' ".[1] Confident of his theory that Italy purifies
and ennobles all who visit her, half attracted and half repelled
by the thought of his vulgar sister-in-law journeying to places
he loves and reveres, he returns with his mother and sister to
Sawston, where they settle down to a quiet winter. Then in the
spring the news comes that Lilia, taking her brother-in-law's
advice to love the Italians, has done precisely that and is now
engaged to be married to one of them. The information
received by the Herritons is guarded and incomplete, the Italian
in question a native of Monteriano, a minute provincial town.
Obviously the marriage is undesirable, and Philip, summarily
dispatched by his outraged mother, must go out to prevent it.
He who for years has sung the praises of Italy, used it as a
weapon against the standards of Sawston, must now serve and
uphold those standards, and rescue Lilia from the very Italy
in which he had professed to believe. He goes reluctantly, "as
for something commonplace and dull". The remembered
charm of Italy surrounds him but he cannot respond to it, and
when he reaches Monteriano and finds out that Gino Carella,
Lilia's choice, is totally unsuitable, the son of a dentist, he gives
a cry of personal disgust and pain:

> A dentist! A dentist at Monteriano. A dentist in fairyland!
> False teeth and laughing gas and the tilting chair at a place
> which knew the Etruscan League, and the Pax Romana, and
> Alaric himself, and the Countess Matilda, and the Middle Ages,
> all fighting and holiness, and the Renaissance, all fighting and
> beauty! He thought of Lilia no longer. He was anxious for
> himself: he feared that Romance might die.[2]

---

[1] *Where Angels Fear to Tread*, p. 7, henceforth cited as *W.A.F.T.* All page
references to this and subsequent novels are to the Pocket Edition, London
(Edward Arnold) 1947.
[2] *W.A.F.T.*, p. 32.

Romance however, as the author steps in to point out, dies only
with life; and what Philip is losing now, what is going from
him with the cry of pain, is only what had been spurious in his
former love of Italy, unable to resist the unexpected, the
incongruous, the grotesque. Indeed he is better without it.
However, it is a temporarily weakened Philip who must go on
to face the squalid crisis ahead, the discovery that Lilia and
Gino are married already. Humiliated by Gino who laughs at
him, topples him over backward on a bed, he returns in anger
and disgust to Sawston. In a matter of months the tragedy of
the marriage is consummated in the death of Lilia in child-
birth, and Philip's disillusion with Italy is completed:

> She had no power to change men and things who dwelt in her.
> She, too, could produce avarice, brutality, stupidity—and,
> what was worse, vulgarity. It was on her soil and through her
> influence that a silly woman 'had married a cad. He hated
> Gino, the betrayer of his life's ideal, and now that the sordid
> tragedy had come, it filled him with pangs, not of sympathy,
> but of final disillusion.[3]

Philip's repudiation of Italy, more emotional than final, cannot be equated with the prejudice and indifference of his mother
and sister, which have never wavered. For Mrs Herriton,
a capable and sensible woman devoid of imagination, Italy has
been simply a place on a map and a disrupting influence.
When Philip came back from his first visit, full of passion for
everything Italian and ridicule for Sawston and its ways, she
had simply taken steps to deal with him. " 'Let Philip say what
he likes, and he will let us do what we like' ", is the memorable
formula she evolves to keep the peace between her son and
daughter. For Harriet, deeply, indeed fanatically religious, is
virulently opposed to Italy which she has never visited, and is
provoked by Philip's taunting praises of it, and especially his
tolerance of its Catholicism, almost to the point of open rupture.
That Philip's eventual disillusion with Italy is less complete
than he suspects is shown some time after the news of Lilia's
death, when he meets Miss Abbott on the train to London and
she reveals to him in the course of their conversation hitherto

[3] *W.A.F.T.*, p. 79f.

unsuspected depths and qualities. Formerly he would have looked for the source of these new qualities in Miss Abbott's Italian experience, and though he does not do so now, he still cannot restrain his admiration.

When she denounces the idleness, the stupidity, the petty unselfishness of Sawston, he attempts to correct her. Surely petty *selfishness* is what she means. But no:

> "Petty unselfishness," she repeated. "I had got an idea that everyone here spent their lives in making little sacrifices for objects they didn't care for, to please people they didn't love; that they never learnt to be sincere—and, what's as bad, never learnt how to enjoy themselves. That's what I thought—what I thought at Monteriano."[4]

At once Philip is delighted with an insight into Sawston that exceeds his own. And though he must still insist sadly that society, Sawston, is invincible, he is inspired despite himself to go on and remind Miss Abbott in something of his former Italian manner that her own life is the real one:

> "There is no power on earth that can prevent your criticising and despising mediocrity—nothing that can stop you retreating into splendour and beauty—into the thoughts and beliefs that make the real life—the real you."[5]

A new relationship, based on their mutual recognition of mediocrity, now becomes possible between Philip and Miss Abbott and endures rather than progresses for some seven months. Then a little incident, a postcard from Monteriano for Lilia's child by her first marriage, Irma, brings it to a close. Once more Italy is about to erupt on the Sawston scene.

Irma has been told of her mother's death, but not of the existence of a far away little brother. Now through the medium of two postcards sent, without any sinister intention, by Gino, she hears about him and in due course bubbles out with the news to her schoolfellows who happen to be going through an acute phase of baby-worship. One girl tells her mother and the secret is out. From this point on the behaviour of Miss Abbott becomes increasingly enigmatic and emotional. She too, like Philip, appears to have turned violently against Italy. In her

[4] *W.A.F.T.*, p. 87.   [5] *W.A.F.T.*, p. 89.

imagination, and especially since Lilia's death, Monteriano
has become

> a magic city of vice, beneath whose towers no person could
> grow up happy or pure. Sawston, with its semi-detached
> houses and snobby schools, its book teas and bazaars, was
> certainly petty and dull; at times she found it even con-
> temptible. But it was not a place of sin. . . .[6]

And so she is now resolutely determined that in Sawston and
not in Monteriano, Lilia's baby shall grow up. It must be
adopted, by herself or the Herritons, and transferred to Sawston. The child, she insists, came into being through her
negligent supervision of Lilia. Her sacred duty now is to ensure
its moral welfare. Threatened with scandal, and determined
that if any adopting is to be done the Herritons will do it, Mrs
Herriton is forced to get in touch with Gino, who surprises
everyone by refusing to surrender the child. The matter seems
disposed of, but Miss Abbott, by now frenzied and wholly
unaccountable, refuses to acquiesce and prepares to leave for
Monteriano.

Such behaviour, it is clear, cannot be rationally explained,
and the reasons Miss Abbott gives for it, to herself and to others,
are inadequate. The outer happenings, the postcards to Irma,
the comings and goings of the various protagonists for this
reason or that, clearly conceal rather than reveal a deeper
motivation. Italy, sounding from afar her imperious summons,
has again intervened, and the machinery, trivial only on the
surface, has been set in motion. Miss Abbott possessed with
moral frenzy, the Herritons running in frightened circles, even
Irma bubbling out with news of her little brother, are simply
putting their hands to the wheel. Philip, revolted at being sent
on a second rescue mission to an Italy which he now "hates", is
inspired into partial realisation. If Miss Abbott wants to mess
with Italy by herself, well let her. Let her meddle with what
she doesn't understand and involve herself again with Gino:

> ". . . (he) will marry her, or murder her, or do for her somehow.
> He's a bounder, but he's not an English bounder. He's
> mysterious and terrible. He's got a country behind him that's
> upset people from the beginning of the world."[7]

---

⁶ *W.A.F.T.*, p. 99.   ⁷ *W.A.F.T.*, p. 104.

And so, in a mood of cynical indifference, Philip goes, gathering up the inflexible Harriet in the Tyrol on his way. It is August and terrifyingly hot, and everything is beastly. However, the irresistible charm of Italy begins to work, and presently Philip senses that he is to blame for the beastliness and that a slight influx of virtue would have a transfiguring effect:

> For there was enchantment, he was sure of that; solid enchant-ment, which lay behind the porters and the screaming and the dust. He could see it in the terrific blue sky beneath which they travelled, in the whitened plain which gripped life tighter than a frost, in the exhausted reaches of the Arno, in the ruins of brown castles which stood quivering upon the hills. . . . There was nothing pleasant in that journey to Monteriano station. But nothing—not even the discomfort—was common-place.[8]

Increasingly relaxed, not caring one straw about the baby he has come to buy, Philip approaches his destination in the spirit of a cultivated tourist. He means to do his duty by his mother, to negotiate honestly, and thinks he will be successful. Gino, who would have given up Lilia for a thousand lire had he not married her already, will obviously part with his child for less. Harriet, on the other hand, detecting her brother's indifference, becomes ever more strident and fanatical. Italy, in her eyes, is irredeemably horrible, Gino a straightforward incarnation of wickedness. Arrived at the hotel in Monteriano, she insists that Philip go at once "to the Italian", and when he refuses, she creates a scene. Utterly single-minded, erecting an iron screen between herself and Italy, Harriet is grotesque, but also, as the author has to concede, a straight, brave woman.

At the hotel, the *Stella d'Italia*, the presence of "un altra signorina" is made known to them. Miss Abbott—supposedly on holiday at the time in Normandy—has preceded them. Distrusting Mrs Herriton, who is only pretending to want Gino's child, she has come as a spy. As she explains to Philip: "If you are here to get the child, I will help you; if you are here to fail, I shall get it instead of you." In theory the old, the Sawstonian attitude has not altered. In her own quiet way Miss

[8] *W.A.F.T.*, p. 108f.

Abbott is no less determined than Harriet. But soon it becomes
all too apparent that upon her, as upon Philip, the splendour
and beauty, the essential mystery of Italy, is beginning once
again to have its inevitable effect. At Sawston she had shut her
mind against it as pernicious, proceeding out of evil; but now,
with the ancient towers of Monteriano rising about her, witness
to a past that was full of violence and wickedness certainly, but
also of magnificence and life, she finds the edge of her determination starting to turn. In spite of herself she must des-
pairingly acknowledge the complexity of life, the tangle of
"beauty, evil, charm, vulgarity, mystery" in which she is
involved. " 'I wish I was Harriet,' " she exclaims, "throwing
an extraordinary meaning into the words."[9]

Because this is Italy, and because in any case you cannot
rehearse life, the best laid schemes of the Herritons soon begin
to go astray. Philip calls on Gino, primed for a decisive interview, and finds him out. Then a somewhat reckless decision is
taken to spend an otherwise empty evening at the local opera,
and here of course is the execrable Gino, in a box, hailing
Philip with voluble affection, dragging him up by the arms to
stand beside him and introducing him to his friends. Philip,
though duly horrified by this development, soon ceases to care,
surrenders himself to the intoxication of the opera. By civilised
standards, it has been deplorable: not badly sung perhaps, but
makeshift and in a setting of overwhelming vulgarity. Nothing
however has mattered but the vitality of the performance, the
communion between stage and audience, the violent waves of
excitement sweeping round the theatre. Harriet alone has
remained impervious, grimly disapproving throughout. But
Miss Abbott, emerging from the theatre in a daze of music and
emotion, bathed in beauty within and without, cannot sleep for
happiness.

> Had she ever been so happy before? Yes, once before, and
> here, a night in March, the night Gina and Lilia had told her
> of their love—the night whose evil she had come now to undo.[10]

And undo it she still must. The very next morning, quite
untaught by the transfiguring happiness of the night before, she

[9] *W.A.F.T.*, p. 125.   [10] *W.A.F.T.*, p. 138.

sets firmly out to do battle with the powers of evil—stealing a march in the process on Philip, whose resolution she has every reason to doubt. That Miss Abbott does not understand herself or her motives is by now all too apparent, but the author still remains content with hints to this effect and implications. The full truth about Miss Abbott is only to become clear to us as it becomes clear to herself. Nevertheless we are sure enough already that the impending interview with the incalculable Gino is not going to conform in any way to Miss Abbott's expectations. And indeed it does not. Gino is again out, and she must wait for him in the hideous unused parlour sacred to the memory of the dead Lilia. He returns, not noticing her, and she must watch him unseen in the next room, eerily talking to some unknown person. A wreath of smoke from his cigar envelopes her and she screams, faints, has to be revived with wine. Then with Gino all solicitude and herself hopelessly at a disadvantage, she must encounter for the first time that object, for a month past, of all her own and the Herritons' abstract schemings—the baby. And here it is, a real baby, asleep on a dirty rug:

> . . . so much flesh and blood, so many inches and ounces of life—a glorious, unquestionable fact, which a man and another woman had given to the world.[11]

Strangely moved and disconcerted, she begins to falter, recovers her self-esteem, her high-principled resolve only with deliberate effort. Then she hears that Gino is about to marry again, a loveless marriage, and indignation comes to her rescue. He explains that he is marrying for the child's sake, and she sees her opportunity. Since, evidently, he is tired of the baby. . . .

At once she perceives her terrible mistake, and Gino pretends courteously that because of the foreign language she must have expressed herself wrongly. But the issue has now been wordlessly settled, and the depth and fixity of Gino's relationship to his child overwhelmingly established. The reader is not unprepared for this. Lilia too in the last days of her life had grasped the mystical tenacity of Gino's passion for

[11] *W.A.F.T.*, p. 145.

fatherhood, his one great immortal longing to "continue" through his son. Now in a flash of insight Miss Abbott has learned it too. Not yet however can she bring herself to renounce her duty. The baby must still be rescued, even though she now knows herself to be in the presence of something greater than right and wrong. Domestic trivia complete her downfall. The baby must be given a bath, and she takes charge with the impersonal competence acquired as a district visitor in Sawston; but when Gino holds out to her the naked child, "a little kicking image of bronze", the wrong kind of tears come hurrying to her eyes. The man, transfigured by paternal love, is majestic, a part of Nature. She bathes the child, and Gino to get a better view kneels beside her, so that Philip, entering at this moment perceives, to all intents and purposes, a picture—the Donor with Virgin and Child. Philip's arrival however, reminding her ruthlessly of what she had intended and failed to do, proves too much for Miss Abbott. In sudden agony she raises her hands to her mouth, bursts into tears and departs weeping bitterly. All but the final truth, of her own love for Gino, has now come home to her.

Philip talks business with Gino, discovers in him a "certain affection" for his child, and, lacking Miss Abbott's insight still believes that a deal is possible. In a long interview which takes place in the church of Santa Deodata where he finds her (of all things!) praying, she attempts to persuade him of the truth, that Gino will never part with the child, and confesses that on the issue of adoption she has now changed sides. That afternoon he has a last friendly meeting with Gino, and Miss Abbott is proved right. Not caring very much, only dreading what he may have to put up with from his mother, he arranges their departure. Miss Abbott does the same. But meanwhile the betrayed and maddened Harriet has kidnapped the child.

In Italy nothing, and least of all tragedy, ever happens by halves. The ensuing melodramatic events, the reckless overturning of the carriage, the death of the baby, Gino's murderous acts of vengeance on the already injured Philip, though unthinkable in Sawston, here in Italy, where all feeling is immediately passion, come charged with a logic of their own. And with an equal logic, because this is Italy, the passion of evil can presently transform itself, like a sunlit tower rising out of darkness, into an equivalent passion of good. Miss Abbott, a goddess inspired, steps in and stops the frenzy of deterioration, sets in motion the counteracting powers, and Gino, distracted from torturing Philip to death, becomes his perfect friend. "I never was so completely forgiven," he explains later to Miss Abbott:

> "Ever since you stopped him killing me, it has been a vision of perfect friendship. He nursed me, he lied for me at the inquest, and at the funeral, though he was crying, you would have thought it was my son who had died."[12]

Italy, its purpose accomplished, can now withdraw. Philip and Harriet and Miss Abbott are allowed to go. Only upon Harriet has no lasting impression been made. After a short bout of illness and remorse, she has returned to her normal, impervious self: is already speaking of "this unlucky accident" and "the mysterious frustration of one's attempts to make things better". For Philip and Miss Abbott however, standing together in the corridor of the train rising to the St Gotthard tunnel, all the wonderful things are now over. Yet it is obvious that neither of them will ever again be the same. For Philip there had come an actual moment of conversion when, saved from death at the hands of Gino by the intervention of Miss Abbott, he had become aware of her greatness:

> He was happy; he was assured that there was greatness in the world. There came to him an earnest desire to be good through the example of this good woman. He would try henceforward to be worthy of the things she had revealed. Quietly, without hysterical prayers or banging of drums, he underwent conversion. He was saved.[13]

The last word however is still with Italy: Miss Abbott's revelation, when Philip is on the point of declaring his love for her, that her own was and had long been for Gino. With this admission Miss Abbott discovers and reveals herself, becomes for the first time wholly consistent and intelligible. Philip,

[12] *W.A.F.T.*, p. 194.   [13] *W.A.F.T.*, p. 192.

momentarily shattered by the knowledge, goes on to perceive its beauty:

> To such a height was he lifted, that without regret he could now have told her that he was her worshipper too. But what was the use of telling her? For all the wonderful things had happened.[14]

Italy, a country that has upset people from the beginning of the world, has played its part, convulsing a handful of English souls, subjecting them to forces of which they might otherwise have had no experience in all their lives. Obviously in the light of what has happened, of events precipitated, thoughts and emotions violently aroused, Italy has been presented to us as more than an empty abstraction, more than a literary symbol of certain qualities that certain people do or do not possess. Italy in *Where Angels Fear to Tread* is an overwhelming reality, a *presence*, in the Wordsworthian sense, undefined and invisible, yet objectively and continuously there. So far we have observed it in terms of its impact on a group of English characters. At its bidding we have seen them act and react, seek to understand and explain what they are required to undergo. Now we must go deeper than action and conscious motive to the source of both: in particular to what we can learn of Italy through the one Italian character presented to us in any detail, Gino Carella. But first what of Italy itself, the land of Italy? Of this much has been stated, more implied. Philip, even when he was in no mood for it, has had to acknowledge it, to recognise the solid enchantment of the terrific blue sky, the whitened plain, the castles quivering upon the hills. This enchantment however has always had its disturbing side, a suggestion, especially for the northern traveller, of the mysterious, the terrible. Lilia, in the early days of her marriage, and thinking in terms of English country walks, confronts the vast slopes of olives and vineyards, the chalk-white farms about Monteriano, and in the distance other slopes with more olives and more farms, in dismay:

> "I don't call this country," she would say. "Why, it's not as wild as Sawston Park!" And, indeed, there was scarcely a

---

[14] *W.A.F.T.*, p. 204.

touch of wildness in it—some of those slopes had been under cultivation for two thousand years. But it was terrible and mysterious all the same, and its continued presence made Lilia so uncomfortable that she forgot her nature and began to reflect.[15]

And the cultivated Philip arriving unwillingly on his first mission to Monteriano feels the same, feels himself in an enemy's country where

everything—the hot sun, the cold air behind the heat, the endless rows of olives, regular yet mysterious—seemed hostile to the placid atmosphere of Sawston in which his thoughts took birth.[16]

As with the land, so with its people: on the one hand enchantment, a charm and grace of manner and movement, on the other an ever-present latency of the terrible, the mysterious, needing but a touch to spring to life. And that this has always been so, the tremendous panorama of Italian history is there to witness: the Middle Ages, "all fighting and holiness", the Renaissance, "all fighting and beauty"—everywhere the strange commingling of sweetness and barbarity, the sunlit towers arising from the dark. So it is inevitably, by right of inheritance, with Gino Carella. On the surface the charm, the agreeable manners, so characteristic of the inhabitants of Monteriano as to be noted by Baedeker, and underneath the mysterious, frightening latency. Philip again, at their first luckless meeting, though repelled by Gino's superficial grossness, his utter unpresentability from the Sawston point of view, nevertheless sees before him the face he had seen and loved a hundred times before in Italy: a face not merely beautiful, but with the charm that is "the rightful heritage of all who are born on that soil". Gross, capable of acts of unpremeditated brutality—as when he flings a starving cat away from him by the paw—and equally of acts of an extraordinary kindness and sensitivity, Gino is above all an individual who does not understand or even seek to understand himself. Possessed now by this feeling, now by that, or else submitting without question to an

[15] *W.A.F.T.*, p. 65.   [16] *W.A.F.T.*, p. 28.

extreme conventionality, he goes his instinctive way. Miss
Abbott and the Herritons, knowing little of the truth, assumed
that Lilia in the months before her death had been subjected by
Gino to the utmost brutality. But in fact, as the author notes,
she had received no unkind treatment at all, and few unkind
words. He had simply treated her conventionally, as any other
Italian in his position would have treated a wife. Social life in
Italy, as Lilia soon discovered, though free and democratic and
altogether delightful if you happened to be a man, made no
corresponding provision for the freedom, or indeed the involvement of women. Excluded from all her husband's activities,
unvisited, virtually a prisoner in her own home and allowed
nothing but the consolations of an alien religion, she comes to
realise how free and easy by comparison had been the despised
social amenities of Sawston. Distressed by his wife's all too
apparent misery, and quite unable to understand it, Gino can
only suppose that with patience and time and a little kindness
and firmness on his part, she will presently settle down and
become indistinguishable from all the other acquiescent wives
of his and his friends' experience. Only by standards other than
his own could his behaviour, and even his eventual casual
infidelity, have been looked upon as in any way brutal or out of
the ordinary. And yet quite clearly the latent brutality,
counterpart of the spontaneous charm and sensitivity, is all the
time there. And once, by threatening to cut off supplies of
money, Lilia touches it to life. The effect is horrifying:

> As she said to Perfetta afterwards, "None of his clothes seemed
> to fit—too big in one place, too small in another." His figure
> rather than his face altered, the shoulders falling forward till
> his coat wrinkled across the back and pulled away from the
> wrists. He seemed all arms. He edged round the table to
> where she was sitting, and she sprang away and held the chair
> between them, too frightened to speak or move. He looked at
> her with round expressionless eyes, and slowly stretched out his
> left hand.[17]

The timeless moment of terror, of possession, passes, but the
return from it is to be no less terrifying. For Gino also has been
badly frightened. Lying at her feet he implores her pardon,

[17] *W.A.F.T.*, p. 67.

murmuring "It was not I", striving to define the incomprehensible. For three days he stops in the house, ill with physical collapse. Nothing this time, no fulfillment of violence had resulted: the possession had been interrupted just in time. Nevertheless we have been clearly warned, and when the baby is stolen and killed and Philip must confront Gino with the news, we are not surprised at what happens. Again the uncanny, the impersonal supervenes. Again the movements become instinctive—the touching of the furniture, the floor, the walls, the final slow stretching forward of the left hand. But this time possession culminates in action, in a kind of diabolism, with Gino reaching back to the skill of his ruffian ancestors in torturing a man to death. The death of Philip is averted through the intervention of Miss Abbott, and again with "a loud and curious cry—a cry of interrogation" Gino returns to his conscious self:

> A great sob shook the whole body, another followed, and then he gave a piercing cry of woe, and stumbled towards Miss Abbott like a child and clung to her.[18]

No less extreme in its way, no less of a possession is the reaction that follows, with the passion of hatred passing over into an equally instinctive passion of love. We would like to feel that the Gino forcing an "almost alarming intimacy" on Philip, and utterly reconciled even to Harriet, is indeed the true Gino; but it is clear that the true, the individual Gino is a shadowy, colourless, unstable entity with a perpetual tendency to lose itself, to become submerged in emotional extremes. Philip and Miss Abbott take away with them from Italy the recollection of goodness, of a capacity for selfless love that far transcends their own; but neither can forget the obverse of that capacity and Miss Abbott can only mock herself for a love that is physical rather than spiritual:

> "He's not a gentleman, nor a Christian, nor good in any way. He's never flattered me nor honoured me. But because he's handsome, that's been enough. The son of an Italian dentist, with a pretty face."[19]

And yet it is evident that Miss Abbott's mockery is directed

---

[18] *W.A.F.T.*, p. 191f.   [19] *W.A.F.T.*, p. 202.

finally more against herself than Gino. Gino, though gross and uneducated, though compounded of irreconcilable extremes, is presented to us as in some essential way a superior being— superior to Philip and Miss Abbott even at their enlightened best. Gino's faults are manifold and at times terrible, but something, a mystical something, redeems them, makes them in the last analysis of no account. For Gino is an Italian, with a country behind him that has provided for centuries the spiritual impulses of the Western world. And even in such as Gino those impulses are still manifest in an instinctive genius for feeling, in what we might call "a mysticism of the heart".

Brought into contact with this mysticism, product of the unseen Italy, the English character in *Where Angels Fear to Tread* is shown as tending to lose its stability, to respond with a passion either of acceptance or repudiation. The Englishman, traditionally reserved and unemotional, is one nevertheless capable of feeling. In an important essay "Notes on the English Character" Forster has dealt with this potential emotionality in explicit detail. If the English nature is cold, he argues, how is it that it has produced a great literature, and one moreover particularly great in poetry? To illustrate the complexity and depth of the English character he develops the metaphor of the sea, level and of one colour and obviously without such creatures as fish:

> But if we look into the sea over the edge of a boat, we see a dozen colours, and depth below depth, and fish swimming in them. That sea is the English character—apparently imperturbable and even. The depths and the colours are the English roman- ticism and the English sensitiveness—we do not expect to find such things, but they exist. And—to continue my metaphor— the fish are the English emotions, which are always trying to get up to the surface, but don't quite know how. . . . Now and then they succeed and we exclaim, "Why, the Englishman has emotions! He actually can feel!" And occasionally we see that beautiful creature the flying fish, which rises out of the water altogether into the air and the sunlight. English literature is a flying fish. It is a sample of the life that goes on day after day beneath the surface; it is a proof that beauty and emotion exist in the salt, inhospitable sea.[20]

---

[20] *Abinger Harvest*, p. 17. Pocket Edition, London (Edward Arnold) 1947.

Also in the same essay Forster faces the accusation often brought against the English of spiritual insensitivity and indifference, of a disbelief in the unseen, and again argues against it:

> That facile contrast between the spiritual East and the material-
> istic West can be pushed too far. The West also is spiritual.
> Only it expresses its belief, not in fasting and visions, not in
> prophetic rapture, but in the daily round, the common task.
> An incomplete expression, if you like. I agree. But the argu-
> ment underlying these scattered notes is that the Englishman
> is an incomplete person. Not a cold or an unspiritual one. But
> undeveloped, incomplete.[21]

In *Where Angels Fear to Tread*, the English characters find themselves through their involvement with Italy challenged to achieve completeness. The challenge is essentially mystical, an appeal to the heart, and they respond passionately, whether in acceptance or repudiation. But some degree of acceptance, some movement at least towards completeness, is clearly being demanded of them by the author, and by the extent of that acceptance they are being estimated as individuals and strictly judged.

Particularly severe, for example, is the judgement pro-nounced upon Mrs Herriton, whose repudiation of Italy and, by implication, of the unseen, is not so much passionate, as automatic and unwavering, the product of an absolute incapa-city to imagine or to feel. As the author notes when he shows her looking up Monteriano in the atlas, "the map left a good deal to the imagination, and she had not got any". As a result even her good qualities, her intelligence and efficiency, her deft handling of Lilia's child Irma, her social tact and competence, the fact that she keeps her servants for years, are all suspect— loveless devices finally for getting her own way, for serving and maintaining her position in Sawston society. Sawston is her kingdom, her substitute for the unseen. To it, and to her pride in it all and everybody must be sacrificed. Philip, revolted by her insincerity over the adoption of Gino's baby, perceives the full truth:

[21] *Op. cit.*, p. 19.

> Her ability frightened him. All his life he had been her puppet.
> She had let him worship Italy, and reform Sawston—just as she
> had let Harriet be Low Church. She had let him talk as much
> as he liked. But when she wanted a thing she always got it.
>
> And though she was frightening him, she did not inspire
> him with reverence. Her life, he saw, was without meaning.
> To what purpose was her diplomacy, her insincerity, her
> continued repression of vigour? Did they make anyone better
> or happier? Did they even bring happiness to herself? Harriet
> with her gloomy peevish creed, Lilia with her clutches after
> pleasure, were after all more divine than this well-ordered,
> active, useless machine.[22]

Seldom does the author permit himself so complete a
denunciation as this, and because Mrs Herriton is not un-
deserving at times of at least a qualified admiration, its
completeness tends to take us by surprise. Yet the severity is
ultimately justified. Worse in fact than outright opposition, is
unawareness, indifference to the unseen, and Mrs Herriton's
sheer lack of interest in Italy and in her son's enthusiasm for it,
reveals her as without aspiration, a permanently lost soul.
Imagination, the gateway to the unseen, is closed for her and
she must proceed without it, a cold-hearted manipulator of
human beings whom she cannot love.

Harriet by contrast, peevish, graceless, unlovable and
unloving, is presented to us with a certain sympathy. For
Harriet, unlike her mother, has some concept of an unseen
however distorted and conventional, and cares about it
passionately. Confronted by the challenge of the greater unseen
that is Italy, with its extreme potentialities for both good and
evil, she recoils instinctively and in blinkered opposition sees
only the evil side. In the end, her whole Italian experience is
shrugged off as if nothing untoward had happened, and she
returns ostensibly to her former self. But this shutting of the
mind against the unthinkable, this obsession with the evil side of
Italy, has had in Harriet's case one curious outcome. By a
strange irony, Harriet who could see nothing but evil in the
genius of Italy, becomes herself evil, yielding to an impulse,
inconceivable in Sawston, to kidnap a child. Under the impact

[22] *W.A.F.T.*, p. 98.

of Italy Harriet makes no progress towards completeness, becomes ever more rigidly her narrow and limited self. Yet the redeeming capacity for feeling is always with her, and deriving from it, as even Philip had to concede, such virtues as courage and integrity. As a comprehensive human being Harriet fails, presumably with finality. However, her rejection of the unseen power that could have saved her is redeemed, at least to some extent, by its vehemence and passion.

Failure, a final inability to rise to the challenge of the unseen, must also be recorded against Lilia. Yet Lilia comes closer to completeness than Harriet, and once in her life may even be said to have achieved it. Common rather than commonplace, and devoid of inner resources, she is at least a constant thorn in the side of the Herritons, a reckless defier of the respectability, the stuffiness of Sawston. Defiance carries her too far, into the pathos and tragedy of her marriage to Gino, and Philip is justified in accusing her of clutching greedily at pleasure. But her excesses are at least the product of a redeeming virtue, of a genuine zest for life. Lilia, blowsy, high-spirited, and vulgar, is also most emphatically alive. What could be more expressive of vigour and life than her denunciation of Philip who had come to Monteriano to "rescue" her from Gino!

> "For once in my life I'll thank you to leave me alone. I'll thank your mother too. For twelve years you've trained me and tortured me, and I'll stand it no more. Do you think I'm a fool? Do you think I never felt? Ah! when I came to your house a poor young bride, how you all looked me over—never a kind word—and discussed me, and thought I might just do; and your mother corrected me, and your sister snubbed me, and you said funny things about me to show how clever you were! And when Charles died I was still to run in strings for the honour of your beastly family, and I was to be cooped up at Sawston and learn to keep house, and all my chances spoilt of marrying again. . . . But, thank goodness, I can stand up against the world now, for I've found Gino, and this time I marry for love!"[23]

Thus equipped, open at all events to the influx of life itself, Lilia comes under the liberating spell of Italy and instinctively

[23] *W.A.F.T.*, p. 42f.

responds to it. Her letters to Sawston though vulgar and
commonplace reveal enthusiasm, and Philip who had hoped so
much from the influence of the country declares that she is
improving. He is particularly gratified when she begins to take
his advice about visiting small places off the tourist track, and
her letter from Monteriano concludes "with a not unsuccessful
description of the wonderful little town". A simple extrovert,
incapable of sensing the mystery of Italy, she nevertheless rises
to an awareness of the unspoiled charm and simplicity of the
Italian nature and responds to it in Gino with spontaneous love.
This, the response to Gino, is the greatest moment of Lilia's life,
the closest she is ever to come to completeness. Miss Abbott,
sharing in the moment, was to look back on it with astonishment, seeing both herself and Lilia as raised above their daily
selves, possessed by an intoxication of happiness never again to
be surpassed. "We were mad—" she explains to Philip later,
"drunk with rebellion. We had no common sense."[24]

Under the impact of Italy, Lilia achieves a limited and
fleeting fulfilment and thereafter reverts to her original self.
The glow of rebellion, so intoxicating to begin with, soon fades.
Her new status, she discovers, that of a married woman in a
small Italian provincial town, far from conferring freedom, is
subjecting her to a tyranny, a paralysis of convention such as she
had never before known. When Gino suggests that her
daughter, Irma, should come out and live with them, she
experiences a spasm of terror at the thought of any English
child being educated at Monteriano. And in the last unhappy
days before her death it is to Sawston that her mind returns in a
passion of nostalgia:

> It was September, Sawston would be just filling up after the
> summer holidays. People would be running in and out of each
> other's houses all along the road. There were bicycle gymkhanas,
> and on the 30th Mrs. Herriton would be holding the annual
> bazaar in her garden for the C.M.S. It seemed impossible that
> such a free, happy life could exist.[25]

Lilia, trapped by Italy, by an overwhelming reality she
cannot begin to understand, is subjected to a fate, or so it would
seem, quite beyond her deserving. Even the Italian child she

[24] *W.A.F.T.*, p. 88.   [25] *W.A.F.T.*, p. 71.

bears at the sacrifice of her life, is marked down for an eventual pointless destruction. For her single moment of happiness and fulfilment Lilia must pay, because of her intellectual incapacity, a seemingly disproportionate price. Fools, it seems, must indeed not rush in where angels fear to tread.

Less disproportionate, by reason of their greater inner resources, are the penalties and sufferings exacted from Miss Abbott and Philip Herriton for their reckless and foolish meddling with the Italian unseen. Although Philip, we should remember, came close enough to losing his life. Alone among the book's characters these two are shown to develop, to achieve through the catharsis exacted by Italy a state of salvation. Philip when we first encounter him, though intelligent, cultivated, and imaginatively inspired by his experience of Italy, is still only potentially capable of salvation through spiritual completeness. And there was always the very real danger that he would never attain it:

> His face was plain rather than not, and there was a curious mixture in it of good and bad. He had a fine forehead and a good large nose, and both observation and sympathy were in his eyes. But below the nose and eyes all was confusion, and those people who believe that destiny resides in the mouth and chin shook their heads when they looked at him.[26]

The threat of failure, of spiritual deterioration, is already suspended over him. He is, as he realises, his mother's puppet, and though he can criticise her, perceive her as Sawston incarnate, he believes that he can never rebel against her, that he will probably go on doing her bidding to the end of his days.

The same threat of dullness and mediocrity, of ultimate deterioration hangs over Miss Abbott, who when we first meet her is good, quiet and amiable, young only because she is twenty-three, and with nothing in her appearance to suggest the fire of youth:

> All her life had been spent at Sawston with a dull and amiable father, and her pleasant, pallid face, bent on some respectable charity, was a familiar object of the Sawston streets.[27]

---

[26] *W.A.F.T.*, p. 78.   [27] *W.A.F.T.*, p. 27.

And yet, as with Philip, the imaginative potentiality is there, and though she sees herself as "John Bull to the backbone", she can still aspire to the reported marvels of Italy and demand to have her fling at them, if only that she may have them to think and talk about for the rest of her life. Italy, however, produces the tragedy of Lilia, and she experiences a revulsion against it. Sawston, with all its limitations, is henceforth to be preferred. As a result, deterioration, incompleteness again threaten, and a further, climactic involvement with Italy is needed that salvation may be secured.

The exact nature of the salvation achieved by Philip and Miss Abbott is implied rather than stated. Miss Abbott interrupting by her sheer presence and comprehension Gino's impersonal frenzy of vengeance and summoning him back to himself, appears to Philip as a goddess inspired:

> All through the day Miss Abbott had seemed to Philip like a goddess, and more than ever did she seem so now. Many people look younger and more intimate during great emotion. But some there are who look older, and remote, and he could not think that there was little difference in years, and none in composition, between her and the man whose head was laid upon her breast. Her eyes were open, full of infinite pity and full of majesty, as if they discerned the boundaries of sorrow, and saw unimaginable tracts beyond.[28]

Philip looks away from her, "as he sometimes looked away from the great pictures where visible forms suddenly became inadequate for the things they have shown to us". But he is happy, assured once more of the existence of greatness in the world. As a result, there comes to him that earnest desire to be good, worthy of the greatness which this good woman has revealed. Quietly, he undergoes conversion and is saved.

Perhaps we are satisfied. The salvation conferred by Italy on Philip and Miss Abbott, their achievement of completeness, is clearly an absolute thing and will endure for a lifetime. The catharsis of the emotions, that made salvation possible is in the past. All the wonderful things, as they both realise, have happened. They will return—Miss Abbott to Sawston and work and the care of her tiresome father: Philip, who is free to

[28] *W.A.F.T.*, p. 192.

break with Sawston, to work in London. But there is no doubt
that a sustaining, transfiguring power will accompany them.
A power, strong enough, in Philip's case to surmount the shock
and disappointment of Miss Abbott's rejection of his love, his
discovery that she is in love with Gino.

Perhaps we are satisfied, persuaded that the great gift of
completeness conferred by Italy has been worth so tragic a price.
Italy, the mysterious and terrible impact of the Italian unseen,
has proved at least for Philip and Miss Abbott finally beneficial. Even so the medium of salvation, what we have called
the mysticism of the heart, cannot but inspire us with a great
deal of misgiving. Gino is its exponent, a man the obverse of
whose very charm and emotional spontaneity is the capacity for a
degree of malevolence that Sawston at least, with all its limitations, will never produce. Also Italy itself, the Italy made in
Gino's image, though it is presented to us with a humorous
indulgent sympathy, can be accepted only with considerable
reserve. There is something atavistic, for example, finally
unacceptable, in a society organised by men for men, and in
which women are callously, almost slavishly, relegated to a
subordinate position. This primitivism of the dominant male
reaches mystical intensity in Gino's longing for a son. When
Lilia is pregnant he becomes utterly distracted:

> His one desire was to become the father of a man like himself,
> and it held him with a grip he only partially understood, for it
> was the first great desire, the first great passion of his life.
> Falling in love was a mere physical triviality, like warm sun or
> cool water, beside this divine hope of immortality.[29]

And it is of course this primitivism that the Herritons and Miss
Abbott come up against so unexpectedly in their negotiations
for Gino's child.

Italy, we must conclude, for all that it has to offer in the life
of the feelings, cannot by itself, any more than Sawston by
itself, confer completeness. While Sawston has developed the
intellect at the expense of the feelings, Italy develops emotions,
at least in such as Gino, that the intellect can neither compre-
hend nor control. Gino, for better and for worse, is a creature

[29] *W.A.F.T.*, p. 76f.

of instinct, subconsciously rooted in the Italian past. That past has certainly been glorious, the very fountain head of Western civilisation, but nevertheless here too we must recognise that "all the wonderful things are over". Monteriano though still a crumbling witness to the past, to the glories of Renaissance and Middle Ages, has long ceased to produce anything on its own account except in the worst of taste. The author is amused by the current bad taste of Italy, whimsically diverted by its very blatancy and vigour. Philip, visiting the opera house at Monteriano is so appalled by the interior decoration, in the "tints of the beetroot and the tomato", that he can scarcely suppress a cry. However, he is moved to excuse it:

> There is something majestic in the bad taste of Italy; it is not the bad taste of a country which knows no better; it has not the nervous vulgarity of England, or the blinded vulgarity of Germany. It observes beauty, and chooses to pass it by. But it attains to beauty's confidence. This tiny theatre of Monteriano spraddled and swaggered with the best of them, and these ladies with their clock would have nodded to the young men on the ceiling of the Sistine.[30]

We are certainly disarmed by this defence, and by the extenuations offered in due course for the tasteless aspects of the operatic performance, but in cold retrospect are we altogether persuaded? The Italian heritage though still productive of the emotional charm and spontaneity so badly needed by Sawston, is clearly productive of nothing else. The ruffianism, the mindless malevolence of the past, still terrifyingly manifest in Gino, is no longer counterbalanced by any continuing greatness of spiritual or artistic achievement. The unseen spirit of the past is still manifest in the Italy of *Where Angels Fear to Tread*, but the mysticism of the heart proceeding from it is compounded even more, it would seem, of darkness than of light. For there comes always a decisive point in history when the old must yield to something new if it is not to become a source of decadence and corruption.

Philip Herriton and Miss Abbott are saved by the Italian unseen, but only because they can harmonise the primitive

[30] *W.A.F.T.*, p. 131f.

mysticism of the heart with the moral and intellectual achievements of Sawston. And with scrupulous fairness from time to
time the author allows us to see the better side of Sawston, the
degree of its enlightenment. Lilia's spasm of horror at the
thought of an English child being brought up in Monteriano, is
certainly shared by the reader. Even so, there is something
ultimately unsatisfying, something over-particularised and even
far fetched in the means of salvation offered to us through Philip
and Miss Abbott in *Where Angels Fear to Tread*. Obviously not
all English men and women can embroil themselves with Italy
for the sake of their immortal souls! Is there then no other way,
no means by which the English character unaided and within
its own environment can rise to completeness? Is Sawston really
England, or has England within itself spiritual resources that
Sawston cannot deny? In his next novel, *The Longest Journey*,
Forster addresses himself to this problem, firmly confining
himself in the process to the English scene. That he did so with
some deliberation is indicated by what he has since told us of the
composition of this novel and of its successor, *A Room With a
View*, in which the influence of Italy on a number of English
characters is again to be the issue. In an article published in
1958 Forster points out that he had in fact drafted the Italian
section of *A Room With a View*, before deciding to set it aside in
favour of *The Longest Journey*.[31] The problem of spiritual
salvation is still basic in both of these novels, but in *The Longest
Journey* the English characters are being required to dispense
with external influences, to find or lose themselves solely upon
English ground.

[31] "A View Without a Room", in *The Observer*, 27 Jul. 1958, p. 15.

IV

The Longest Journey

ENGLAND, the England once again of Sawston, but with extensions into Cambridge and Wiltshire, must now take up the challenge, provide an environment within which, unassisted by Italy, an aspiring character may pursue salvation and succeed or fail. Such a character is Rickie Elliot, and it should be noted that, like his predecessor Philip Herriton, he is very much aware of Italy, "the spiritual fatherland of us all", and hopes to visit it eventually and to find it marvellous.[1] Again and again he is on the point of going there, but he never does go, and so remains dependent from first to last upon his own resources and upon such support for them as England can contrive. The support in his case does not prove adequate, and in terms of its central character *The Longest Journey* is a record of defeat, of spiritual deterioration. However, there are others in the novel who do not deteriorate, and for whom the impact of the English unseen in its various manifestations suffices. Thus the tragedy of Rickie Elliot is not an inevitable one. The adverse forces in his environment, especially those of Sawston, prove too much for him; however, other beneficent forces, in particular those emanating from Wiltshire, are available, and so England in the matter of his defeat is not entirely to blame. That defeat and its origins in the character of Rickie Elliot himself and in the influences brought to bear upon him, is the central theme of *The Longest Journey*, and with its delineation we must begin.

Rickie, first encountered in the friendly, congenial atmosphere of Cambridge, has already had much to contend with. His upbringing in a London suburb had been Sawstonian:

---

[1] *The Longest Journey*, p. 146, Pocket Edition. Henceforth cited as *L.J.*

He had opened his eyes to filmy heavens, and taken his first walk on asphalt. He had seen civilization as a row of semi-detached villas, and society as a state in which men do not know the men who live next door. He had himself become part of the grey monotony that surrounds all cities.[2]

Driven in upon himself by a lonely, unhappy childhood and by the hereditary defect of lameness, bullied at a great public school, he had crept cold and friendless to Cambridge, praying as a highest favour to be left alone. Cambridge however,

had not answered his prayer. She had taken and soothed him, and warmed him, and had laughed at him a little, saying that he must not be so tragic yet awhile, for his boyhood had been but a dusty corridor that led to the spacious halls of youth.[3]

And here we find him, happy, relaxed, surrounded by friends, and in overreaction against the bleak past, maintaining that everyone is likeable "that one can like many more people than one supposes".[4] No less emotional at the time is his concept of the unseen, to which he gives expression in little stories reminiscent of Forster's own. In them also nature is peopled with divinities in the Greek manner; and in one, as in "Other Kingdom", a girl is metamorphosed into a tree. In daily life as well we find Rickie endowing nature, in particular a secluded dell of fir trees, with mystical attributes. Coming upon the place, an abandoned chalk pit, at a time when his own life was expanding, he allowed it to become for him,

a kind of church—a church where indeed you could do anything you liked, but where anything you did would be transfigured. Like the ancient Greeks, he could even laugh at his holy place and leave it no less holy. He chatted gaily about it, and about the pleasant thoughts with which it inspired him; he took his friends there; he even took people whom he did not like. "*Procul este, profani!*" exclaimed a delighted aesthete on being introduced to it. But this was never to be the attitude of Rickie. . . . If the dell was to bear any inscription, he would have liked it to be "This way to Heaven," painted on a signpost by the high-road, and he did not realize till later years

---

[2] *L.J.*, p. 29.   [3] *L.J.*, p. 10.   [4] *L.J.*, p. 27.

that the number of visitors would not thereby have sensibly increased.[5]

Thus precariously equipped, fortified by a concept of the unseen at once emotional and ill-defined, Rickie is soon called upon to encounter the different reality of the Pembrokes, Herbert and Agnes, Sawstonian intruders upon his Cambridge Eden. The term "reality" in application to the Pembrokes is fiercely rejected by Stewart Ansell, Rickie's philosopher friend, who on being introduced to Agnes pays absolutely no attention, and ever after insists that she has no objective existence, simply is not there. The philosophical problem of reality is one that recurs throughout *The Longest Journey* and the book opens with its discussion at a gathering presided over by Ansell in Rickie's rooms—a discussion which, characteristically, Rickie cannot follow. Challenged over his rudeness to the "non-existent" Agnes, who has interrupted the discussion, Ansell explains:

> "Did it never strike you that phenomena may be of two kinds: *one,* those which have a real existence . . .; *two,* those which are the subjective product of a diseased imagination, and, which, to our destruction, we invest with the semblance of reality? If this never struck you, let it strike you now."[6]

Rickie's involvement with the "unreal" Pembrokes is, at this stage, somewhat peripheral, for Agnes is engaged to be married. However, in the vacation he visits the Pembrokes at Sawston School, where Herbert is a master, and where cataclysmic events await him. To begin with he must undergo the ordeal of meeting Gerald Dawes, Agnes's fiancé, a boorish athlete whom he remembers too well, for Gerald had been with him at School and had horribly bullied him. But he comes upon the lovers in each other's arms and the moment, which might well have disgusted him, in fact shines forth with a transcendent radiance. It is as though, suddenly, a light had been held behind the world. While he must listen to the prosaic conversation of Herbert Pembroke, a riot of fair images throngs his mind:

> They invaded his being and lit lamps at unsuspected shrines. Their orchestra commenced in that suburban house, where he

---

had to stand aside for the maid to carry in the luncheon. Music flowed past him like a river. He stood at the springs of creation and heard the primeval monotony. Then an obscure instrument gave out a little phrase. The river continued unheeding. The phrase was repeated, and a listener might know it was a fragment of the Tune of tunes.[7]

Thus, for Rickie, Agnes and Gerald had transcended the commonplace; they had achieved heaven, and would never get out of it again.

Exalted, and appalled that the lovers cannot marry at once because of money, Rickie greatly offends Gerald by offering him some of his own. But the indignation is short lived, for that afternoon Gerald is broken up in a football match and dies. Under the impact of this supreme event, Rickie's dreaming sensitivity, his hitherto imprecise emotional intuitions of things unseen, suddenly harden, crystallise for the first and last time in his life into certainty. When he finds Agnes disposed to bear up against sorrow, to slide past the absoluteness of what has happened, he insists with extraordinary vehemence that she shall face the truth and mind it:

> "It's your death as well as his. He's gone, Agnes, and his arms will never hold you again. In God's name, mind such a thing, and don't sit fencing with your soul. Don't stop being great; that's the one crime he'll never forgive you."[8]

Exhorted with such unquestionable authority, Agnes allows herself to break down completely. And Rickie will not comfort her:

> "I did not come to comfort you. I came to see that you mind. He is in heaven, Agnes. The greatest thing is over."[9]

Unsurprisingly, Agnes can hardly recognise the Rickie whose meagre face now shows as a seraph's, speaking the truth and forbidding her to evade it:

> "I don't know you," she said tremulously. "You have grown up in a moment. You never talked to us, and yet you understand it all."[10]

---

[7] *L.J.*, p. 49. [8] *L.J.*, p. 63.
[9] *L.J.*, p. 64. [10] *L.J.*, p. 64f.

It puzzles her too that Rickie "who could scarcely tell you the time without a saving clause, should be so certain about immortality".[11]

He cuts short his visit to Sawston, and returns to Cambridge, with a sigh of joy re-entering the haven of his beloved rooms. But he is no longer the same Rickie. The horrors and splendours of the world, the transcendent reality of love and death have fallen upon him, setting a barrier even between himself and Ansell who could discuss love and death admirably, but somehow "would not understand lovers or a dying man". He begins to wonder whether Cambridge also and its dons, who dealt with so much and had experienced so little, would understand them any better. Was it possible, for all that it had done for him idealistically, that he would ever come to think of Cambridge as limited and narrow? He re-reads one of his little stories, full of fantasy and the supernatural, and rebels against it. "But what nonsense! When real things are so wonderful, what is the use of pretending?" And so he deflects his enthusiasms:

> Hitherto they had played on gods and heroes, on the infinite and the impossible, on virtue and beauty and strength. Now with a steadier radiance, they transfigured a man who was dead and a woman who was still alive.[12]

The greatness, the spiritual radiance which Rickie has detected in Agnes, is of course no longer there. He continues to believe in it, however, and presently and fatally to fall in love. At this point the author steps in with the observation that love may be entered into through the desires or through the imagination, and whereas the former method is inferior, at least it will not breed a tragedy quite like Rickie's. Absurdly young, not yet twenty-one, he has no knowledge of the world, not even the theoretical toughness of such as Ansell to protect him. He thinks, for example,

> that if you do not want money you can give it to friends who do. He believes in humanity because he knows a dozen decent people. He believes in women because he has loved his mother. And his friends are as young and as ignorant as himself. They

are full of the wine of life. But they have not tasted the cup—
let us call it the teacup—of experience, which has made men of
Mr. Pembroke's type what they are.[13]

Tragedy for Rickie, via his marriage to Agnes, his involvement through Herbert with Sawston School, is already
imminent and unavoidable. Ansell, intellectually ruthless as
usual, can see it all:

> "She wants Rickie, partly to replace another man whom she
> lost two years ago, partly to make something out of him. He is
> to write. In time she will get sick of this. He won't get famous.
> She will only see how thin he is and how lame. She will long
> for a jollier husband, and I don't blame her. And, having made
> him thoroughly miserable and degraded, she will bolt—if she
> can do it like a lady."[14]

Correct as ever, Ansell begins to fight back, to declare openly
that the engagement must be broken off. Rickie, he insists, is
unfitted for marriage in body and in soul; his need is to
like many people, not attach himself to one. But Rickie, in love
and convinced that Agnes loves him in return, that she also
wants him to have friends, work and spiritual freedom, will not
listen. For him the light continues to shine from behind the
world. Agnes, enquiring enthusiastically into his little stories
and refusing to accept his belittlement of them, urging him to
believe in himself, to seek publication, is surely faultless, the
emissary of that practicality he so badly needs. And then there
is Herbert, the embodiment of paternal kindliness, securing his
appointment to Sawston School at a generous salary, tempering
his naïve enthusiasms with much needed advice. But the reader,
unlike Rickie, is left in no doubt as to what is really happening:
that in fact a process of spiritual destruction is already being
directed against him, a process that his fragile connexion with
the unseen will be unable to resist.

Sawston School now begins to exercise its pernicious sway,
an establishment setting out to ape the Public School tradition,
and in which Herbert Pembroke is the coming man. Rickie,
with occasional reservations and misgivings, accepts the school
as he finds it, bows to Herbert's superior knowledge and

[13] *L.J.*, p. 72.   [14] *L.J.*, p. 94.

D

experience. Only to find soon enough that by sure degrees the edge of his idealism and eventually of his integrity is being blunted. He had hoped for example to be friends with his pupils, to kindle in them an enthusiasm for beauty, to share their problems. But Herbert soon persuades him of the unwisdom of all this, of the need to preserve detachment and authority, and he lets it all slide. In the class-room he becomes a martinet:

> It is so much simpler to be severe. He grasped the school regulations, and insisted on prompt obedience to them. He adopted the doctrine of collective responsibility. When one boy was late, he punished the whole form. "I can't help it," he would say, as if he was a power of nature. As a teacher he was rather dull. He curbed his own enthusiasms, finding that they distracted his attention, and that while he throbbed to the music of Virgil the boys in the back row were getting unruly.[15]

Overshadowed and overpowered by Herbert, Rickie is nevertheless being offered by implication an alternative in the amiable classical enthusiast and scholar, Mr Jackson, who even at Sawston has managed to preserve his integrity. Jackson however is a lone non-conformist, indifferent to organisation and opposed to "progress". Put in charge of the unnecessary house established for the day boys, he merely tells them, "Well, I don't know what we're all here for. Now I should think you'd better go home to your mothers."[16] So next term Mr Pembroke has to take over. Left to himself, Rickie might well have responded to the humane friendliness of the Jacksons, husband and wife, and there are opportunities for this to occur. The Jacksons are visited by one of his Cambridge friends, and eventually by Ansell. But the contempt of Herbert, the virulence of Agnes, deter him, and the tenuous alternative, the life-line reached towards him from out of the unseen by the Jacksons is allowed to drop away.

The tragedy of Rickie, swiftly intensifying, is seldom to take him wholly by surprise. Not the least of its distressing aspects, is the fact that he can perceive so much of its progress with open eyes. Already before his marriage, before his arrival at Sawston he was praying to be delivered from "the shadow of unreality that had begun to darken the world".[17] Now the marriage, the crown of life, is behind him, and the alleviation, the spiritual transfiguration from love so confidently expected has not come. Perhaps it is not too late. Italy at this point is thought to be imminent, and there, perhaps, at Easter the delayed infinities of love will emerge. But love, as the author now reminds us, has shown him its infinities already:

> Neither by marriage nor by any other device can men insure themselves a vision; and Rickie's had been granted him three years before, when he had seen his wife and a dead man clasped in each other's arms. She was never to be so real to him again.[18]

Easter comes and Italy remains unvisited. Pupils have to be tutored and he must go instead to Ilfracombe.

Perceptive, at least to some extent, of what is happening to him, Rickie can also estimate and judge those whose influence he is so powerless to resist. Always he had known, for instance, that something was amiss with Herbert, and after some experience of him at Sawston, he could begin to formulate what it was. Herbert, with his "round rather foolish face", had many excellent qualities. He was kind, unselfish, charitable and it gave him real pleasure to give pleasure to others:

> He was, moreover, diligent and conscientious: his heart was in his work, and his adherence to the Church of England no mere matter of form. He was capable of affection: he was usually courteous and tolerant. Then what was amiss? Why, in spite of all these qualities, should Rickie feel that there was some-thing wrong with him—nay, that he was wrong as a whole, and that if the Spirit of Humanity should ever hold a judgement he would assuredly be classed among the goats?[19]

Rickie's conclusion, endorsed by the author, is that Herbert is stupid, that his whole life is coloured by a contempt for the intellect. Rickie himself, as he recognises and admits, is some-what defective intellectually, more imaginative than logical in his approach to problems. This defect however, gives him no satisfaction, and he does what he can to overcome it, admiring

[17] *L.J.*, p. 173.   [18] *L.J.*, p. 189.   [19] *L.J.*, p. 187f.

the intellectual efforts of others more gifted than himself. And
so Herbert's fundamental contempt for all such efforts revolts
him:

> He saw that for all his fine talk about a spiritual life he had but
> one test for things—success: success for the body in this life or
> for the soul in the life to come.[20]

Under no illusions about Herbert, Rickie is somewhat
slower to perceive the full truth about Agnes, even after their
marriage. Cheerful, positive and handsome, practical in a slap-
dash manner, she yet has and eventually reveals such "terrible
faults of heart and head" as to alienate all sympathy. By the
time the mild and cultured Jackson has come to describe her as
one of the most horrible women he has ever seen, a "Medusa in
Arcady", we can only silently agree. Already she has revealed
her contempt for everything of spiritual value in Rickie's life,
his idealism, his Cambridge friendships, his little stories, in fact
his essential self. Worst of all has been her determination to
alter him, to deny him the freedom of his own soul. Certainly
she is ambitious for him, anxious that he should succeed as a
writer and in the teaching profession she has helped force upon
him. But, like Herbert, she can envisage no success other than
the practical and the material, no aim beyond the social standing which his success will ensure for her. Here in the making is
another Mrs Herriton, a ruthless and purposeless manipulator
of other people's lives. Limited, and spiritually defective, one
from whom the inner life eventually withdraws, she can yet lay
claim in some degree to tragedy, to that single moment of
greatness, detected by Rickie, which preceded her decline—the
moment of her love for Gerald:

> She belonged to the type—not necessarily an elevated one—
> that loves once and once only. Her love for Gerald had not
> been a noble passion: no imagination transfigured it. But
> such as it was, it sprang to embrace him, and he carried it away
> with him when he died.[21]

Conspired against with increasing deliberation by Agnes,
less deliberately by Herbert who can always furnish himself with
the loftiest of motives, Rickie must also contend with the refined

[20] *L.J.*, p. 188.   [21] *L.J.*, p. 224.

malice of a third opponent, his aunt, Emily Failing. Eventually, in sinister alliance with Agnes, she is to subject his integrity to a greater strain than any contrived at Sawston. Widow of a remarkable man, Anthony Failing, a socialist who wrote brilliant books and believed in putting his theories into practice, she lives at Cadover, her large country house in Wiltshire, and looks on at the world and people with sardonic contempt. She too is afflicted with the hereditary lameness of the Elliots:

> Her age was between elderly and old, and her forehead was wrinkled with an expression of slight but perpetual pain. But the lines round her mouth indicated that she had laughed a great deal during her life, just as the clean tight skin round her eyes perhaps indicated that she had not often cried.[22]

Bored by her isolation at Cadover, she amuses herself at other people's expense, specialises in the contriving of situations that will humiliate and embarrass. When we meet her she is diverting herself over some clumsy attempts at self-education by her enigmatic protégé, Stephen Wonham. Hearing of her nephew's engagement, she summons him and Agnes to Cadover and sets to work to make their visit as memorably disconcerting as possible.

To begin with she is content to play with her victim-guests, inflicting the uncouth Stephen on Agnes, separating the lovers by sending Rickie off on horseback for a pointless ride to Salisbury. But malice gains upon her, intensified by her dislike for Rickie—whose lameness reflects and mocks her own—and by her envy of his happiness with Agnes. She longs to shatter him, to use a thunderbolt—her secret knowledge of Stephen's parentage—to that end. An unfortunate quarrel over religion tips the scale of her determination, and in the course of an afternoon's excursion, she casually lets slip upon the luckless Rickie the truth of his relationship to Stephen, that they are half brothers.

The violence of Rickie's reaction—he faints with horror—disturbs Mrs Failing and induces second thoughts. By indulging her malice she has imperilled her own peace, threatened her social position at Cadover with scandal. She decides to cover

[22] *L.J.*, p. 99f.

up, retrace her steps, make sure that the truth, so recklessly
imparted, shall go no further, least of all to Stephen, who knows
and suspects nothing, and is now got rid of, sent away from
Cadover for the time being. So the situation is saved and Agnes
hurrying off to inform Rickie, makes short work of his horrifying
and quixotic suggestion that Stephen should be told and
acknowledged, that anything so "real" must not be kept from
him. The departing Stephen calls up from the drive, but she
holds Rickie back and he surrenders, does not reply. He had
been writing to Ansell for advice in his dilemma, but now tears
the letter up.

Mrs Failing, though retreating before the disquieting consequences of her thunderbolt, has hardly changed her nature.
She could have followed one thunderbolt with another by
informing Rickie that Stephen was not, as he had assumed, the
son of his father whom he hated, but of his adored mother.
However, she refrains. The "comedy", already threatening to
get out of hand, has gone far enough. That she will not refrain
indefinitely is almost certain, and rendered more so by Rickie
himself. Revolted by her flippancy, he experiences a sudden
insight, and speaks his mind:

> "You used to puzzle me, Aunt Emily, but I understand you at
> last. You have forgotten what other people are like. Continual
> selfishness leads to that. I am sure of it. I see now how you
> look at the world."[23]

For this, for the words in particular "You have forgotten what
other people are like", he knows he will never be forgiven.
Agnes, hoping otherwise, continues to ingratiate herself, to do
what she can to keep Rickie in line. For she plans to make use
of Mrs Failing's literary influence to secure the publication of
the little stories. Moreover there is the money represented by
Cadover, and which will have to be disposed of when Mrs
Failing dies. To secure it, or part of it, Agnes will not hesitate to
connive in due course at the disinheriting of Stephen.

Over against the unholy triumvirate, Agnes, Herbert, Mrs
Failing, dedicated with varying degrees of deliberation to the
spiritual destruction of Rickie, must now be set those who, by

precept or example, would save him from his deteriorating self. The tentative alternative offered him at Sawston School by the Jacksons and eventually repudiated, has been touched on already. But there are other potential allies, in particular Stewart Ansell and, from now on, Stephen Wonham, both possessed of a certain integrity, a spiritual self-sufficiency at least more adequate than Rickie's to the immediate demands of life.

Ansell, that uncompromising intellectual, ruthlessly dedicated to the pursuit of truth, is somewhat in the line of descent from another uncompromising character, Jack Ford of "Other Kingdom". He is a philosopher, in quest of a definition of reality, of the distinction between the real and the unreal. Unsuccessful by ordinary standards—his dissertation for a Cambridge fellowship fails twice—it never occurs to him that he is in consequence a failure. His spiritual home is the reading-room of the British Museum, in whose book-encircled space he can always find peace:

> There he knew that his life was not ignoble. It was worth while to grow old and dusty seeking for truth though truth is unattainable, restating questions that have been stated at the beginning of the world. Failure would await him, but not disillusionment. It was worth while reading books, and writing a book or two which few would read, and no one, perhaps, endorse.[24]

Thus oriented, he can with an unerring eye detect the least element of falsity in human character and behaviour, can perceive the truth about Agnes Pembroke at a glance. She is untruthful and therefore non-existent, and Rickie in succumbing to her also ceases to be real. Ruthlessly and eccentrically he abandons him, ignores his letters. As he explains to his friend Widdrington: "I had two letters from Ilfracombe last April, and I very much doubt that the man who wrote them can exist."[25] The eccentricity, indeed the absurdity of so extreme an attitude, is evident. Ansell, for all his single-minded devotion to the truth as he sees it is also young and, as he himself recognises, inexperienced. Even Rickie, though greatly his inferior

intellectually, is aware of his friend's limitations, of certain
aspects of reality he has still to take into account. Ansell, who
can theorise brilliantly about love and death, knows nothing
yet of lovers or a dying man. Also on the debit side is the
curious fact of his indifference to beauty. Rickie visiting him
in the bosom of his plebeian and affectionate family, is charmed
and envious, but wonders whether one of the bonds that kept
the Ansells so harmoniously united might not be a complete
absence of taste. In the presence of Greek sculpture at the
British Museum Ansell is also at a loss:

> The comfort of books deserted him among those marble
> goddesses and gods. The eye of an artist finds pleasure in
> texture and poise, but he could only think of the vanished
> incense and deserted temples beside an unfurrowed sea.
> "Let us go," he said. "I do not like carved stones."[26]

In the same way the frieze of the Parthenon only moves him to a
sense of its pathos.

Yet Ansell is all the time learning, all the time extending
recognition to new factors of human experience hitherto over-
looked—factors that tend to lead him, almost despite himself,
towards an acknowledgement of the unseen. In the course of a
long conversation with Widdrington at the British Museum he
defends his inaction on Rickie's behalf by insisting that he is
waiting for the right moment and watching out meanwhile for
the "Spirit of Life". Widdrington is surprised. The phrase is
unknown to their mutual philosophy, and they have trespassed
into poetry. Ansell goes on:

> "You can't fight Medusa with anything else. If you ask me
> what the Spirit of Life is, or to what it is attached, I can't tell
> you. I only tell you, watch for it. Myself I've found it in books.
> Some people find it out of doors or in each other. Never mind.
> It's the same spirit, and I trust myself to know it anywhere,
> and to use it rightly."[27]

Almost immediately afterwards, standing among the Greek
statuary, he hears the news that Mrs Elliot is expecting a child,
and is at once at a loss, bewildered. But at least he will admit
his bewilderment, honestly acknowledge that here again are

[26] *L.J.*, p. 205.   [27] *Ibid.*

factors, powers, that he cannot cope with or, as yet, understand.

The decisive moment, when the Spirit of Life declares itself to him and prompts him to action, arrives for Ansell through his encounter with a total stranger, Stephen Wonham, in the garden of Dunwood House. The meeting is anything but auspicious: in fact the two get into a physical fight. But gradually, as they converse, it begins to dawn upon Ansell that there is something remarkable about this uncouth countryman, an essential forthrightness and honesty, an instinctive correctness in his attitude to life. He wonders at himself:

> Was it only a pose to like this man, or was he really wonderful? He was not romantic, for Romance is a figure with outstretched hands, yearning for the unattainable. Certain figures of the Greeks, to whom we continually return, suggested him a little. One expected nothing of him—no purity of phrase nor swift-edged thought. Yet the conviction grew that he had been back somewhere—back to some table of the gods, spread in a field where there is no noise, and that he belonged for ever to the guests with whom he had eaten.[28]

Almost before he can realise it, the Spirit of Life, the impact of something mysterious and unseen, communicates itself to him from Wonham, and only a few minutes later we find him, a prophet inspired, proclaiming the truth, just learned, of Stephen's parentage, hitting out against Agnes and all the falsity of Dunwood House "like any ploughboy". Ansell's moment of spiritual recognition has come with extraordinary force and suddenness, but immediacy of insight is what we expect from him, and hereafter it will not falter. His conviction of the spiritual rightness in Stephen Wonham is such that, at the end of the book we find him installed, an ever welcome guest, in Stephen's home.

Stephen Wonham who, simply by being himself, will do more than anyone to arrest the deterioration of Rickie, has, up to the time of his appearance at Dunwood House, managed only to repel and antagonise him. The disconcerting elements in the man, his loutish animality, drunkenness and vulgarity, fully account for Rickie's horror at the discovery of his relationship

[28] *L.J.*, p. 240f.

to him. However, even the animality has been extenuated for
us, represented as redeemed in part by its spontaneity, its almost
child-like directness. Stephen, who knows nothing whatever
about himself, is incapable of calculation. He does what he has
to do for better or worse, with forthright directness and honesty.
The source of his strength, his integrity, is within himself, and
is shown to derive from the contact, the communion of his
essential being with his environment, with Nature. Were
anyone to inform him of his own spiritual identity with Nature,
he would of course be incredulous. When he gets hold of
Rickie's story of a girl changing into a tree, and gathers from an
annotation by Agnes Pembroke that the girl represents "getting
into touch with Nature", he is simply amused:

> In touch with Nature! The girl was a tree! He lit his pipe and
> gazed at the radiant earth. The foreground was hidden, but
> there was the village with its elms, and the Roman Road, and
> Cadbury Rings. There, too, were those woods, and little beech
> copses, crowning a waste of down. Not to mention the air, or
> the sun, or water. Good, oh Good!
> In touch with Nature! What cant would the books think
> of next? His eyes closed. He was sleepy. Good, oh good!
> Sighing into his pipe, he fell asleep.[27]

Ignorant of himself, motivated purely by instinct, Stephen
yet belongs to the soil, and especially to the soil of Wiltshire.
Occasionally he seems to sense as much as when, in conversation with Ansell, Wiltshire is mentioned and there comes into
his face "the shadow of a sentiment, the passing tribute to some
mystery". Or again there is the curious instinctive affinity
between himself and the goddess Demeter whose picture hangs
from the roof of his attic at Cadover. A child of Nature,
precisely because he is so unaware of the fact, Stephen is also
presented as one who derives, again instinctively, a spiritual
sustenance from the past—a sustenance rendered all the more
compelling because this is Wiltshire, the heart of England, and
from here his ancestors came. For generations they have come
down from their villages to the ancient centre of Salisbury to
buy or to worship, and even before Salisbury, a mere Gothic

upstart, they were there, clinging to the Wiltshire soil, renewing it with sheep and dogs and men, and finding the crisis of their lives upon Stonehenge:

> The blood of these men ran in Stephen; the vigour they had won for him was as yet untarnished; out on those downs they had united with rough women to make the thing he spoke of as 'himself'.[30]

Thus identified with the ancient essence of England itself, Stephen is also revealed to us as the son of a man also spiritually linked with the earth and deriving from it the same directness of heart and mind. The truth of Stephen's parentage, publicly disclosed by Ansell at Dunwood House, is a second and severer thunderbolt for the luckless Rickie. Hitherto he had protected himself against his half brother by supposing him the son of his detested father. Now he must accept that he is the son of the mother he idealises and of a Wiltshire farmer. This man, Robert, introduced into Cadover in the enlightened days of Anthony Failing to demonstrate his theoretical belief in human brotherhood and equality, there met and fell in love with Mrs Elliot. With the same "appalling straightness" inherited by his son, he declares his love and is promptly turned out of Cadover by Mr Failing. Anyone who behaves like that obviously must stay on the farm. Robert, however, patiently pursues his love, discovers Mrs Elliot's unhappiness with her husband, and eventually persuades her to go with him to Stockholm. There he is drowned at sea. No more able than his son to explain himself, to perceive the source of his own integrity, Robert is nevertheless drawn at least into a conscious acknowledgement of the earth, knows when she is hungry or ill, can speak of her tantrums—"the strange unscientific element in her that will baffle the scientist to the end of time". " 'Study away Mrs. Elliot,' " he advises her in the Cadover drawing-room,

> "read all the books you can get hold of; but when it comes to the point, stroll out with a pipe in your mouth and do a bit of guessing." As he talked, the earth became a living being—or rather a being with a living skin—and manure no longer dirty

---

[30] *L.J.*, p. 275.

stuff, but a symbol of regeneration and of the birth of life from life.[31]

Rooted in Nature, and in the past through Nature, Robert and his son after him are presented to us as in some measure spiritually self-sufficient, sustained without ever realising it by communion with the unseen. At the book's end Stephen, sleeping with his child on the hillside, is endowed with transcendent significance, with the belief, though he could not phrase it, that he guided the future of the race, and that "century after century, his thoughts and his passions would triumph in England".[32] Under his influence Rickie has come as close as could be to spiritual redemption, has made the break with Agnes that even Ansell could not effect. True there have been reverses and disappointments, Stephen's inability to forego his animal appetites, but Rickie surrendering his own life at the level crossing to save Stephen's is clearly not intended to have died in vain—despite the bitterness of his final insistence to Mrs Failing that she had been right.

The tragedy of Rickie, momentarily arrested through the interventions of Stephen and Ansell, aggravated by the unholy trio Agnes, Herbert and Mrs Failing, works itself out. It has been a spiritual tragedy, a record of deterioration, a gradually intensifying betrayal of the unseen. Once again in relation to their sensitivity to the unseen, all the characters involved in the central conflict have been assessed and ultimately judged; and always the assessment has been fair, recognition in whatever degree accorded. Herbert, whose allegiance to his Church is no matter of form, has been allowed his share of redeeming qualities. And even Agnes, though unimaginative and deprived finally of an inner life, has had her single extenuating moment of transfiguration through love. In the same scrupulous fashion the deficiencies of the elect, those dedicated in varying degrees of awareness to the unseen, have been faithfully recorded: the inexperience of Ansell and his insensitivity to beauty, the animality of Stephen, the intellectual weakness and impracticality of Rickie. Alone among the leading figures, Mrs Failing, who greets all life with mirthless laughter and has forgotten what people are like, has been presented to us with unqualified

[31] *L.J.*, p. 258.   [32] *L.J.*, p. 320.

disapproval. She and her brother, Rickie's brutal and malicious father, whom she essentially resembles, are once again products of that particular kind of cleverness, of barren intellectualism that the author has already singled out for special condemnation. Cultured and intelligent, they yet derive from what they conceive to be culture nothing eventually but a false sense of superiority and its counterpart, a total and malicious incapacity for people and for life. They and their kind are those for whom culture has become an end in itself, a dead end. Mrs Failing's malice, the brutality of Mr Elliot towards his wife and son, are the product of a spiritual incapacity, in particular of an inability, or perhaps a refusal, to come through culture to an acknowledgement of the unseen. Distrust for the intellectual, the unfeeling manipulator of theories and ideas, already evident in the stories and the first novel, thus becomes more explicit in *The Longest Journey*. Even the well-intentioned intellectual, imaginative and sensitive, is to be allowed no more than a partial capacity for people and for life. Anthony Failing, trying to put into effect at Cadover his idealistic theories of social equality, only partially succeeds. For all his tact and benevolence, he was one who would often,

> stretch out the hand of brotherhood too soon, or withhold it when it would have been accepted. Most people misunderstood him, or only understood him when he was dead. In after years his reign became a golden age; but he counted a few disciples in his lifetime, a few young labourers and tenant farmers, who swore tempestuously that he was not really a fool. This, he told himself, was as much as he deserved.[33]

Perhaps the most explicit denunciation of cultured people playing around with "advanced" ideas comes to us through Robert, who meets them at Cadover and later in Mr Elliot's London drawing-room. They try to shock him with a display of vicious worldliness and sophistication, and though he finds them less vicious than they claim to be he cannot pardon their triviality:

> There grew up in him a cold, steady anger against these silly people who thought it advanced to be shocking, and who

---

[33] *L.J.*, p. 114.

described, as something particularly choice and educational, things that he had understood and fought against for years.[34]

This same cold anger, and for the same reason, the author himself undoubtedly feels. Dilettantism, a deliberate sidetracking of the deeper spiritual implications of a genuine culture, is once again being recognised for what it is, an antispiritual force. Also the especially baneful influence of city life, of London, in generating that force is being demonstrated. Mr Elliot is a Londoner, and Mrs Failing invites her guests to Cadover from London drawing-rooms. Sawston also is a suburb of London and so infected by it. When Stephen is finally expelled from Cadover he takes work in London and encounters with loathing and contempt a particular foreman who typifies the pertness and shallowness of the Cockney. Between this man, the author points out, and that other example of urban degradation, Mr Elliot, the gulf is social rather than spiritual. Both had spent their lives trying to be clever. On the subject of London and its influence, Anthony Failing is allowed the final word:

> "There's no such thing as a Londoner. He's only a country man on the road to sterility."[35]

The author's condemnation of intellectual cleverness in *The Longest Journey* would thus seem to be total. However, we must be careful not to assume from this that the intellect itself is being rejected. Herbert Pembroke, it must be remembered, has already been classed among the goats precisely because of his contempt for the intellect. Obviously what is at issue is not the intellect as such, but the use to which people put it. Herbert himself has a good business-like brain and is anything but opposed to intelligent and practical activity. His contempt in other words is directed against those who, in his view, misuse the intellect in pursuit of the impractical. The philosophical efforts of Ansell and his Cambridge friends, efforts in Ansell's case not even endorsed by academic recognition, move him only to sarcasm. These are young men, however, and his sarcasm is tempered by a patronising commiseration. On the other hand nothing modifies his contempt for the same kind of intellectual

[34] *L.J.*, p. 261.   [35] *L.J.*, p. 274.

perversity in his colleague Jackson. Herbert Pembroke is not possessed of the fashionable intellectuality of the London drawing-room, but he shares with that intellectuality a fundamental indifference to the spiritually ideal.

Judged then, in strict accordance with their sensitivity to the unseen, and by the extent of their acknowledgement of it, consciously or from instinct, the characters now stand before us. It remains to consider and to summarise the nature of the unseen in relation to which their success or failure as individuals has been assessed. Once again the presence of the unseen has been inferred rather than stated, hinted at rather than described; but now the setting is exclusively English and it is with the nature and influence of the English unseen that we are being confronted. This influence, undefined but strongly present, is shown as manifesting itself through Nature, in particular through the medium of the Wiltshire soil, at the geographic heart of England. The special significance of Wiltshire as a geographical focal point, a centre of radiating hills and rivers, has been called to our attention by Rickie. From the Rings above Cadover, he has perceived the whole system of the country spreading before him, with Salisbury, Old Sarum, the Avon valley, the land above Stonehenge. Here, he concludes,

> is the heart of our island: the Chilterns, the North Downs, the South Downs radiate hence. The fibres of England unite in Wiltshire, and did we condescend to worship her, here we should erect our national shrine.[36]

The influence, thus emanating from the Wiltshire soil, is seen above all as an ancient influence, more ancient than the surviving monuments, Salisbury, Old Sarum, even Stonehenge, that bear witness to it. At decisive moments in the story, this brooding presence of the ancient past is indicated. When the truth about Stephen is first launched against Rickie, he is inside the Cadover Rings, those ancient haunted entrenchments, Roman, Saxon or Danish, with their buried dead, and he knows that he is about to faint among them. And where the ancient Roman road to *Londinium* crosses the railway, he performs his final act of sacrifice, saving the life of Stephen at the

[36] *L.J.*, p. 145f.

price of his own. The spirit of the past, forbidding and yet
benevolent, resides in the eternal soil, extending its strength, it
sustaining influence down the generations. Robert, for whom
the earth is still a living being, a symbol of regeneration, and
Stephen who senses as much but cannot phrase it, preserve in
consequence an essential spiritual integrity; while even the best
of those, Rickie, Ansell, Anthony Failing, who have lost their
connexion with the soil, are shown in varying degrees to have
deteriorated. To begin with, idealistically, Rickie attempts to
restore the severed spiritual connexion, to get in touch with
Nature once again by peopling it imaginatively in the classical
manner with divine beings. Initially, as he tries to explain to
Agnes, the process was serious:

> "You see, a year or two ago I had a great idea of getting into
> touch with Nature, just as the Greeks were in touch; and seeing
> England so beautiful, I used to pretend that her trees and
> coppices and summer fields of parsley were alive. It's funny
> enough now, but it wasn't funny then, for I got in such a state
> that I believed, actually believed, that Fauns lived in a certain
> double hedgerow near the Gog Magogs, and one evening I
> walked round a mile sooner than go through it alone."[37]

These fancies receive artistic expression in the little stories, but
soon enough under the influence of Agnes he is reacting against
them, finding them ridiculous, and they and the spirituality to
which they witness prove quite unable to avert impending
tragedy or sustain him through it. After the death of his child
the battle is over:

> Henceforward he deteriorates. Let those who censure him
> suggest what he should do. He has lost the work that he loved,
> his friends, and his child. He remained conscientious and
> decent, but the spiritual part of him proceeded towards ruin.[38]

The ruin is slightly mitigated, temporarily arrested through
the intervention of Stephen. At least from Stephen Rickie
derives the spiritual strength to break away from Agnes and
Sawston. Further mitigation may perhaps be seen in the
sacrificial manner of his death. Again, over against the

absoluteness of failure and deterioration may be set the eventual posthumous publication of the little stories and their success with the discerning. Although that success must be qualified by recognition of the inadequacy of the spirit informing them, as witnessed in their author's life. Obviously more is needed to sustain the shocks and betrayals of everyday life than vague intuitions of the divine in nature, whimsically presented in terms of Greek myth. At Sawston Rickie encounters in Jackson a kindred enthusiast, a believer (up to a point) in gods and fairies, one who also

> "tries to express all modern life in the terms of Greek mythology, because the Greeks looked very straight at things, and Demeter or Aphrodite are thinner veils than 'The survival of the fittest', or 'A marriage has been arranged', and other draperies of modern journalese."[39]

Yet Jackson, though fully cognisant of all the evil in Sawston School, is hardly more effective than Rickie in opposing it. Instead he withdraws, preserves his integrity through disdainful isolation.

So we are brought back in the end to Stephen Wonham, in whose integrity and spiritual strength *The Longest Journey* is brought to rest. Secure, cradled, so long as he does not realise it, within the unseen in Nature, he sleeps on the hillside with his child. In him resides, or so we are invited to believe, the future of the race. Century after century the thoughts and passions that animate him, will triumph in England. From the first he has been presented to us as exceptional, spiritually superior to Rickie and even to Ansell, whose immediate recognition of his greatness has never wavered, and by implication has demanded our own. With all his resources as a writer, the author has sought to reconcile us to Stephen, to engage our sympathies on his behalf. And we must concede that his youthful directness and simplicity, his forthright opposition to injustice, his incapacity to bear a grudge, are all admirable traits. We may even accept his animality, his honest bouts of drunkenness and violence with less fuss and more understanding than the fastidious Rickie. And yet, finally, whether we like Stephen or

[39] *L.J.*, p. 197.

E

have our reservations about him as a man is less important than what we make of the spiritual theory in terms of which he is assessed and judged.

This theory is certainly an extreme one, nothing less than an insistence that self-knowledge, any advance into self-awareness, is not in fact an advance but a retreat. In contrast to almost all the other characters in *The Longest Journey*, Stephen is presented to us as in essence unaware, an unself-conscious creature of instinct who knows nothing about himself.[40] This, we are required to assume, is his special virtue, the source of his strength. For so long as he does not know himself, does not see himself as apart from and so in relation to Nature, Nature will continue to guide and sustain him spiritu-ally, provide his every need. All those on the other hand who have advanced into self-consciousness, substituting for Nature's benign guidance the fallible intellectuality of man, are shown in varying degrees to have deteriorated, to have taken the road of Mr Failing's Londoners towards sterility. Over against the England of intellectual self-consciousness, of Sawston and London and even Cambridge, has been set the England of instinct, of Wiltshire. Stephen alone, sustained like his father before him by the mystic emanations of the ancient soil, has the power of survival. Century after century, the spiritual essence of England will live on in the thoughts and passions that animate him. To him and to his kind, those other self-defeating Englands, after long wanderings in the intellectual waste lands of their own creating, must ultimately return.

Such is the extreme and uncompromising theory informing *The Longest Journey*, and in terms of which Rickie Elliot, for all his spiritual aspirations, has been allowed to go down to defeat. On the other hand, though England has failed him, or he England, the possibility that he could have been saved by other stronger forces coming in from outside, specifically from Italy, has been somewhat pointedly implied. Again and again in the early decisive years of his marriage he has been shown to us as on the point of going to Italy, only to be deflected at the last moment by Sawstonian trivialities. At least we are being invited to speculate that, had he gone there, he too like Philip

[40] *L.J.*, p. 127.

Herriton might well have undergone a process of spiritual stimulation powerful enough to rescue him from himself.

Whether or not *The Longest Journey* presents us with the author's final word on England, on the strengths and limitations of the English unseen, need not yet be decided. In the next novel but one, *Howards End*, the theme of England, of those rejecting or submitting to her invisible agencies, returns for deeper, more explicit consideration. Meanwhile in the next novel, *A Room With a View*, the redemptive power of the Italian unseen, so tantalisingly withheld from Rickie, is allowed to prove itself again.

V

A Room With a View

THE impact of Italy, this time upon a handful of English tourists fortuitously assembled at the Pension Bertolini in Florence, is to be rather less explicitly indicated than before. In fact *A Room With a View* contains rather fewer direct intimations of spiritual forces at work than either of the first two novels. Yet we never cease to be made aware of the Italian "presence" and of the issues, hardly guessed at by the personages involved, to which it gives rise. Lucy Honeychurch, whose salvation through Italy and love is to be the book's central theme, continues almost to the end in ignorance of the impulses at work within herself; yet her final sense of "deities reconciled", her feeling that in gaining the man she loved she had also gained something "for the whole world", will come as no surprise to the reader.

Almost from the moment of our first introduction to her at the Bertolini, Lucy is being revealed as rather less commonplace than appearances might imply. Mr Beebe, for example, the genial, sensible, socially resourceful clergyman, also holidaying in Florence and a guest at the Bertolini, has already made her acquaintance at a parish in Tunbridge Wells and has there had occasion to observe and ponder an "illogical element" in her composition. For Lucy is a musician. No great technician perhaps, and at the piano she strikes no more right notes than are "suitable for one of her age and situation". Through music however she enters a world no longer chaotic and plays on the side of Victory:

> Victory of what and over what—that is more than the words of daily life can tell us. But that some sonatas of Beethoven are written tragic no one can gainsay; yet they can triumph or

despair as the player decides, and Lucy had decided that they should triumph.[1]

Mr Beebe, at the parish concert in Tunbridge Wells is enabled to observe Miss Honeychurch at work. Expecting the commonplace, he finds his composure disturbed by the opening bars of Opus 111:

> He was in suspense all through the introduction, for not until the pace quickens does one know what the performer intends. With the roar of the opening theme he knew that things were going extraordinarily; in the chords that herald the conclusion he heard the hammer strokes of victory.[2]

The applause is respectful, and it is Mr Beebe who starts the stamping and later asks the Vicar of the parish to introduce him. Lucy, he is informed, is full of praises for his sermon, and he wonders why she ever bothered to listen to it. He meets her however and understands. Disjoined from her music stool, Miss Honeychurch,

> was only a young lady with a quantity of dark hair and a very pretty, pale, undeveloped face. She loved going to concerts, she loved stopping with her cousin [Miss Bartlett], she loved iced coffee and meringues. He did not doubt that she loved his sermon also.[3]

However, in the light of the music she had played, or rather of her manner of playing it, Mr Beebe is moved to prophesy:

> "If Miss Honeychurch ever takes to live as she plays, it will be very exciting—both for us and for her."[4]

The challenge to Miss Honeychurch, to live as she plays, is soon upon her. It takes the form of the Emersons, father and son, presentable but insufficiently genteel, whom she encounters that first evening across the dining table at the Bertolini. Overhearing Miss Bartlett's complaints that the Signora of the pension has given them rooms without a view, old Mr Emerson, till then a total stranger, leans across with a suggestion. Since he and his son George have rooms with a

---

[1] *A Room With a View*, p. 40, Pocket Edition. Hereafter cited as *R.V.*
[2] *R.V.*, p. 41. [3] *R.V.*, p. 42. [4] *Ibid.*

view, and since women like looking at a view and men don't, why not exchange? Miss Bartlett icily declines, only to find herself almost violently attacked. Why should she not change? What possible objection could there be? "Quite a scene" ensues, but Lucy has the odd feeling,

> that whenever these ill-bred tourists spoke the contest widened and deepened till it dealt, not with rooms and views, but with— well, with something quite different, whose existence she had not realized before.[5]

The Emersons, it is obvious, will not do socially—especially the father. He has no tact, no gentility and will not keep his opinions to himself. Moreover it does not ever seem to occur to him to speak anything but the truth. Less talkative than his father, indeed somewhat morose, George also and obviously will not do. Equally obviously he is possessed of the same disconcerting directness. Some undefined job on the railway— a porter perhaps—is ascribed to him, and to both father and son the genteel guests at the pension are applying the "Socialist" label. Even so, Lucy finds herself attracted to the young man and is secretly delighted when, through the tactful intervention of Mr Beebe, the offer to exchange rooms is repeated and Miss Bartlett, however ungraciously, is forced to accept.

The Emersons henceforth are unavoidable—Lucy meets them next day in Santa Croce—and she does her best to adjust, to weather each shock to her primness and conventionality as they administer it. George, it turns out, and much to his father's concern, is unhappy, worried about life and the fact that "things won't fit". Even to Lucy he conveys a feeling "of greyness, of tragedy that might only find solution in the night".[6] In his usual direct manner old Mr Emerson appeals to her to lend a hand, not necessarily to fall in love with his boy but to try and understand him. At the same time, disconcertingly, he begs her to let herself go:

> "You are inclined to get muddled, if I may judge from last night. Let yourself go. Pull out from the depths those thoughts that you do not understand, and spread them out in the

sunlight and know the meaning of them. By understanding
George you may learn to understand yourself. It will be good
for both of you.''[7]

To this perceptive, imaginative appeal Lucy is unable to
respond. She laughs, suggests that George needs a hobby like
stamp collecting, and presently rejoins her cousin, Miss Bartlett.
Mr Emerson is saddened, rebuffed, but not finally; and
meanwhile there is "Italy", inevitably at work upon the
unsuspecting Lucy, and already beginning to have an effect.
Awakening that morning and flinging wide the bedroom
shutters on the Arno and all the trivial yet absorbing animation
in the street below, Lucy has come dangerously close to
forgetting the high purpose of her visit:

> Over such trivialities as these many a valuable hour may slip
> away, and the traveller who has gone to Italy to study the
> tactile values of Giotto, or the corruption of the Papacy, may
> return remembering nothing but the blue sky and the men and
> women who live under it.[8]

In the same way a few hours later, in Santa Croce, when she
can forget about acquiring culture for the moment and observe
the life about her, "the pernicious charm of Italy" promptly
exerts itself and she becomes natural and happy.

Then, with startling suddenness, the Italian impact assumes
a more palpable form. Alone and unchaperoned in the Piazza
Signoria Lucy becomes the witness to a murder. Two Italians
by the Loggia had been bickering over a five lire debt. They
spar, and one is hit lightly on the chest:

> He frowned; he bent towards Lucy with a look of interest, as
> if he had an important message for her. He opened his lips to
> deliver it, and a stream of red came out between them and
> trickled down his unshaven chin.[9]

The man is borne away to the fountain, and across the spot
where he had been she sees George Emerson looking at her.
"How very odd! Across something." She faints and when she
recovers on some steps in the Uffizi Arcade it is to the distressing
awareness that this strange young man has held her in his arms.

[7] *R.V.*, p. 37.   [8] *R.V.*, p. 24.   [9] *R.V.*, p. 54.

But more than this, far more, has happened. While they talk,
and George awkwardly and surreptitiously throws into the
Arno some photographs of Lucy's, bought at Alinari's and now
stained with blood, an awareness keeps breaking through to
both of them, a realisation that some decisive spiritual boundary
has been crossed. George is the more explicit, and the boy
verges into the man when he proclaims, "Something tremendous has happened; I must face it without getting muddled. It
isn't exactly that a man has died."[10] For the moment at least
the bafflement over life, the greyness of impending tragedy is
overcome within him and he puzzles and disturbs Lucy with a
sudden declaration: "I shall want to live". Lucy, muddled,
still ridiculously preoccupied with the fact that George has held
her in his arms and that this, if known, may lead to gossip at the
Bertolini, cannot respond so emphatically, does not perceive
with the author that this is the point where childhood has begun
to enter upon the branching paths of youth. Even so, the roar of
the Arno is already suggesting some unexpected melody to her
ears.

After the murder—a characteristically Italian affair: the
murderer had tried to kiss his victim, given himself up to the
police—nothing is ever again to be the same. The very next
day Lucy already assessing her elders with new and critical
insight, surprises herself and everyone by the firmness of her
indignation when the egregious chaplain, Mr Eager, retailing
some dubious and malicious gossip, accuses old Mr Emerson
of having "murdered his wife in the sight of God".

Italy had sounded its imperious summons, and questions
riot within her:

> The well-known world had broken up, and there emerged
> Florence, a magic city where people thought and did the most
> extraordinary things. Murder, accusations of murder, a lady
> clinging to one man and being rude to another—were these the
> daily incidents of her streets? Was there more in her frank
> beauty than met the eye—the power perhaps, to evoke passions,
> good and bad, and to bring them speedily to a fulfilment?[11]

Yet she remains essentially herself, muddled, still unable or
unwilling to spread out her inmost thoughts in the sunlight of

[10] *R.V.*, p. 57.   [11] *R.V.*, p. 71.

understanding: still too frightened by some quality she senses in George Emerson to be able to perceive, let alone admit, her incipient love for him. Once again it is necessary for Italy, through the medium of a simple cab driver, to bring what is latent to a dramatic head.

Mr Eager's intention for the drive to Fiesole had been decorous enough—a discreet *partie carrée* for himself, Mr Beebe, Lucy and Miss Bartlett. Then without consulting anyone Mr Beebe has ruined everything by good naturedly extending the invitation to the Emersons and the clever English lady novelist at the Bertolini, Miss Lavish. Lucy perceives the hand of "Fate", for up to this point she had succeeded in avoiding further contact with George, although each avoidance had made it imperative to avoid him again; but now "celestial irony, working through her cousin and two clergymen"[12] is not permitting her to leave Florence till she has made this expedition with him into the hills.

Fate, or celestial irony, also does not hesitate to make full use of the Italian drivers of the two carriages, one of whom is soon in trouble with Mr Eager for embracing the beautiful girl beside him on the box whom he has claimed to be his sister. Quite a scene ensues, and Lucy to her amazement finds herself appealed to by the lovers, who point to the other carriage which contains George. Why? In the end, and much to the eloquent disgust of old Mr Emerson, the girl is compelled to descend from the box and the expedition continues. At their destination in the hills the party splits up into groups and Lucy, excluded by Miss Bartlett and Miss Lavish who wish to gossip, sets off alone to find the two clergymen. They have disappeared and she approaches the Italian drivers to ask where they have gone. The miscreant of the drive up, a bony young man scorched black by the sun, rises to greet her "with the courtesy of a host and the assurance of a relative". Unable to recall the Italian for "clergyman", she asks for the whereabouts of the "good men", and at once the driver divines her wishes. Confidently he conducts her over the hillside, pausing to pick her some blue violets, and then as she stumbles out onto a little terrace leaves her with the exhortation, "Courage. . . . Courage and love."

[12] *R.V.*, p. 76.

For here standing on the brink of the tremendous view like a swimmer, is a good man certainly, but not the one she had expected:

> George had turned at the sound of her arrival. For a moment he contemplated her, as one who had fallen out of heaven. He saw radiant joy in her face, he saw the flowers beat against her dress in blue waves. The bushes above them closed. He stepped quickly forward and kissed her.[13]

However there is to be no sequel. The silence of life is almost immediately broken by Miss Bartlett, who stands "brown against the view".

Italy, through the medium of a simple Italian cab driver, has achieved its purpose and can for the moment withdraw. The complicated game that had been playing up and down the hill-side all the afternoon is over. Only the cab driver has played it skilfully, using the whole of his instinct rather than the "scraps of intelligence" displayed by the others:

> He alone had divined what things were, and what he wished them to be. He alone had interpreted the message Lucy had received five days before from the lips of a dying man.[14]

Italy in a single instant of life and truth has triumphed, although it might well appear from the immediately ensuing events on the drive down and back in the Bertolini, that for Lucy triumph has been but the fleeting prelude to surrender. For Miss Bartlett, the withered chaperone, already emerging as a life-denying portent, has taken charge. It is Miss Bartlett who bribes the cab driver to keep silence, persuades Lucy to interpret her sublime moment on the hillside as a typical male "exploit", dissuades her from speaking to George again personally, and makes the curt and final dismissal of the young man herself. In the end there is presented to the girl, shocked with emotion and craving for understanding, the picture of a cheerless, loveless world,

> in which the young rush to destruction until they learn better— a shame-faced world of precautions and barriers which may avert evil, but which do not seem to bring good, if we may judge from those who have used them.[15]

---

[13] *R.V.*, p. 86.   [14] *R.V.*, p. 87f.   [15] *R.V.*, p. 98.

Into such a world Lucy is now to be conducted. Diplomatic advantage has been taken of her sincerity, her craving for sympathy, and never again will she expose herself frankly without precaution against rebuff—an attitude that may "react disastrously upon the soul".[16] All the same what has happened, has happened, and the eternal moment will echo on into the future. Perhaps Miss Bartlett perceives as much from Lucy's unsatisfactory answer to her leading question—what would have happened had there been no interruption at that particular moment on the hillside?

"I can't think," said Lucy gravely.

Something in her voice made Miss Bartlett repeat her question, intoning it more vigorously.

"What would have happened if I hadn't arrived?"

"I can't think," said Lucy again.

"When he insulted you, how would you have replied?"

"I hadn't time to think. You came."

"Yes, but won't you tell me now what you would have done?"

"I should have—" She checked herself, and broke the sentence off. She went up to the dripping window and strained her eyes into the darkness. She could not think what she would have done.[17]

Early next morning she leaves with her cousin for Rome, where the company of the cultured Mrs Vyse and her no less cultured son, Cecil, awaits her.

The Italian episode closes. Lucy, accompanied by Cecil Vyse, to whom she will presently announce her engagement, returns to Windy Corner, the Honeychurch home in the Surrey hills near Dorking, with its tremendous view over the Sussex Weald. She has changed, matured, and Cecil observing her in Rome and later among the flower-clad Alps has watched the process, and attributed it, accurately enough, to Italy. Italy, he insists, has worked some marvel in her:

It gave her light and—which he held more precious—it gave her shadow. Soon he detected in her a wonderful reticence. She was like a woman of Leonardo da Vinci's, whom we love not so much for herself as for the things she will not tell us.[18]

[16] *R.V.*, p. 99.   [17] *R.V.*, p. 94.   [18] *R.V.*, p. 108f.

The reticence, the fact that Lucy consents to marry him only at the third time of asking, does not unduly disturb Cecil, as it might a more passionate lover. Some doubts and reservations certainly cloud the rapture of his final acceptance, but these, he has no doubt, will resolve themselves when he transfers Lucy from the bosom of her dull, though worthy family to the more congenial London circles in which he himself moves. Cecil appearing late in the story, is formally described for us. He is medieval, like a Gothic statue:

> Tall and refined, with shoulders that seemed braced square by a effort of the will, and a head that was tilted a little higher than the usual level of vision, he resembled those fastidious saints who guard the portals of a French cathedral. Well educated, well endowed, and not deficient physically, he remained in the grip of a certain devil whom the modern world knows as self-consciousness, and whom the medieval, with dimmer vision, worshipped as asceticism.[19]

Such is the man of Lucy's choice: a choice that her family and friends must now persuade themselves to approve. They do so with reservations—especially Mr Beebe, now installed as rector of the parish to which the Honeychurches belong, and who becomes conscious of "some bitter disappointment"[20] when he hears the news. However, Cecil is eminently eligible, and an engagement, as the author indicates, is so potent a thing that sooner or later it reduces all who speak of it to a state of cheerful awe:

> Away from it, in the solitude of their rooms, Mr. Beebe, and even Freddy, might again be critical. But in its presence and in the presence of each other they were sincerely hilarious. It has a strange power, for it compels not only the lips, but the very heart. The chief parallel—to compare one great thing with another—is the power over us of a temple of some alien creed.[21]

So the engagement establishes itself, and despite some bad moments—Cecil does not submit gracefully to his inspection by the neighbourhood—moves towards its inexorable end. Most disconcerting perhaps is the absence in Cecil's case of any

[19] *R.V.*, p. 106f.   [20] *R.V.*, p. 114.   [21] *R.V.*, p. 116.

evidence of passion. Passion, which should "never ask for leave where there is a right of way",[22] is beyond him, and the one kiss he asks for and receives is an absurd and conspicuous failure. But its effect on Lucy is more disastrous than she can know or admit. It has reminded her of George. She rejects the reminder, takes it in her stride, but presently more than the passing inconvenience of a recollection is to confront her, for George himself, however improbably, is to reappear.

The events and coincidences culminating in this far-fetched result will be the work of Cecil Vyse, or, if the reader should prefer it, of Cecil as instrument of the "Comic Muse", or "celestial irony" or "fate". The whole complex process begins with the introduction of two distressing villas named "Albert" and "Cissie", which have arisen to disfigure the rural beauty of Summer Street, thanks to the negligence of the local landowner, Sir Harry Otway. "Albert" is occupied: "Cissie" still to let. Sir Harry, in quest of a genteel and suitable tenant, appeals to the Honeychurches, and Lucy, coming to his rescue, suggests the two refined and elderly ladies, the Miss Alans, whose acquaintance she had made at the Pension Bertolini. Cecil however, without consulting her, undoes her work, and, mischievously humorous, finds two tenants of his own, a father and son, by name Emerson. He has met them in the National Gallery, in the Umbrian Room, admiring the work of Luca Signorelli, "of course quite stupidly". In the course of conversation he learns of their search for a country cottage, the father to live, the son to come down to at weekends, and promptly he offers "Cissie". Sir Harry with his snobbish request for refinement and gentility had offended him, and now through the Emersons, who evidently possess neither, he means to read him a lesson. References are taken up, the negotiations carried through without a hitch, and here are the Emersons about to be installed. Lucy is indignant, and Cecil, attributing her temper to snobbishness, perceives that the new tenants will be of value educationally. "He would tolerate the father and draw out the son, who was silent. In the interest of the Comic Muse and of Truth, he would bring them to Windy Corner."[23]

Steadily, inexorably, the outer events impinge, close in upon

[22] *R.V.*, p. 132.   [23] *R.V.*, p. 144.

the luckless Lucy. She meets George again, but in unimaginable circumstances, bathing in the woods with Freddy and Mr Beebe: a figure world-weary no longer, but "barefoot, barechested, radiant", calling to her cheerfully. Often she had rehearsed the moment, imagining

> a young Mr. Emerson, who might be shy or morbid or indifferent or furtively impudent. She was prepared for all of these. But she had never imagined one who would be happy and greet her with the shout of the morning star.[24]

And now, with Cecil becoming ever more disagreeable and antagonising Mrs Honeychurch, what must the Comic Muse next contrive but a visit to Windy Corner by Miss Bartlett, whose boiler is being cleaned out and who cannot, Mrs Honeychurch insists, be left with the water turned off and plumbers. Miss Bartlett accepts, and George invited to tennis by Freddy will be coming too. Lucy, declining to gaze inwards, faces the external situation bravely enough, although with a tendency to "nerves". She has met George again and been moved deeply, by his voice, by her own desire to remain near him. "How dreadful if she really wished to remain near him!" The situation, the true nature of her love, is of course obvious enough by now to the reader, but, as the author points out,

> A reader in Lucy's place would not find it obvious. Life is easy to chronicle, but bewildering to practice, and we welcome "nerves" or any other shibboleth that will cloak our personal desire. She loved Cecil; George made her nervous; will the reader explain to her that the phrases should have been reversed?[25]

Miss Bartlett arrives and with her first question "Have you told him about him yet?" confirms poor Lucy's most pessimistic apprehensions. However, she remains bravely optimistic. George will not behave like a cad, he will not tell. Miss Bartlett is not so certain.

George comes to tennis and the stage is set, the personages assembled. Also as a final contribution from the Comic Muse, a novel has been casually introduced which Cecil, that indefatigable humorist, will duly read. It is a very bad novel,

[24] *R.V.*, p. 164.   [25] *R.V.*, p. 174f.

Under a Loggia by Joseph Emery Prank, and Cecil finds its badness so amusing that he must read from it aloud, to the great annoyance of the tennis players. The game ends, he continues to read, and Lucy, with George seated at her feet, makes a happy discovery. Joseph Emery Prank must be none other than the clever novelist at the Bertolini, Miss Lavish. She takes the book herself and her happiness vanishes. One glance is enough to tell that the book's lovers are herself and George, that somehow or other Miss Lavish must have known. Cecil recovers the book and with unerring perversity reads the revealing passage aloud:

> " 'Afar off the towers of Florence, while the bank on which she sat was carpeted with violets. All unobserved, Antonio stole up behind her. . . . There came from his lips no wordy protestation such as formal lovers use. No eloquence was his, nor did he suffer from the lack of it. He simply enfolded her in his manly arms.' "[26]

Disaster could still have been avoided, but on the way to the house, the book, as if it had not worked mischief enough, has been forgotten and Cecil must go back for it, leaving her alone with George, who now blunders against her on the narrow path and again kisses her.

The second great climax of her life has come, and this time she must face it alone. Miss Bartlett, unnerved by exposure— she it was who, in the strictest confidence, had told Miss Lavish—must remain in the background, leaving the initiative, the final confrontation to Lucy. She manages admirably, orders George from the house; but his answer is as usual unexpected and disconcerting. Surely, he insists, surely it is not her intention to marry Cecil Vyse. She tells him not to be ridiculous, but his grave and moving denunciation goes on. Cecil is for an acquaintance, he insists, for society and cultivated talk. He should know no one imtimately:

> "He is the sort who are all right so long as they keep to things— books, pictures—but kill when they come to people. . . . I saw him first in the National Gallery, when he winced because my father mispronounced the names of great painters. Then he brings us here, and we find it is to play some silly trick on a

---

[26] *R.V.*, p. 196.

kind neighbour. That is the man all over—playing tricks on people, on the most sacred form of life that he can find. Next, I meet you together, and find him protecting and teaching you and your mother to be shocked, when it was for *you* to settle whether you were shocked or no. Cecil all over again. He daren't let a woman decide. He's the type who's kept Europe back for a thousand years."[27]

Lucy, commendably calm, hears him out, unmoved even by his declaration that he had loved her ever since the moment in Florence when the man had died. "It is being young," he concludes:

"It is being certain that Lucy cares for me really. It is that love and youth matter intellectually."[28]

With this nonsensical remark, he goes, and Miss Bartlett joins Lucy in stealthy rejoicings. George has gone, perhaps finally, but there is still to be an unexpected sequel. Lucy overhears Cecil selfishly and sarcastically refusing to make up a four at tennis, and the scales fall from her eyes. How has she stood him for a moment? He is absolutely intolerable. And that evening she breaks off her engagement.

George, who had stood on the brink of darkness once before, may now re-enter it; and Lucy, despite the great gain of her renunciation of Cecil, may enter it too. For still she cannot bring herself to recognise, let alone admit that George Emerson is the man she loves. She renounces Cecil, and when he asks for her reasons, finds herself, to her own shame and embarrassment, making use of the very words and criticisms she had just heard from the lips of George. It was as though George had been thinking through her, gaining her an honourable release. Yet she must forget him and his love for her, which is passionate and therefore frightening, must pretend to Cecil that she loves no one at all. Surrendering, ceasing even to try to understand herself, she joins the vast armies of the spiritually benighted, those "who follow neither the heart nor the brain, and march to their destiny by catch-words":

The armies are full of pleasant and pious folk. But they have yielded to the only enemy that matters—the enemy within.

They have sinned against passion and truth, and vain will be their strife after virtue. As the years pass, they are censured. Their pleasantry and their piety show cracks, their wit becomes cynicism, their unselfishness hypocrisy; they feel and produce discomfort wherever they go. They have sinned against Eros and against Pallas Athene, and not by any heavenly intervention, but by the ordinary course of nature, those allied deities will be avenged.[29]

Thus Lucy, pretending to George that she does not love him and to Cecil that she loves no one, advances into darkness, the darkness of withered spinsterhood that had received Miss Bartlett thirty years before.

Immediately, the signs and portents, the downward steps and stages of spiritual deterioration begin to appear. Lying to herself and to Cecil, Lucy now finds out that she must lie to others as well, to her mother and Freddy, to Mr Beebe, even to the servants. To face the truth is to face George, and this she dare not do. So it becomes necessary to conceal the news of her broken engagement, lest George should hear of it and try to see her; and lest she see him by chance in the neighbourhood she must get away. And, since the true reasons for all this cannot be stated or admitted even to herself, she must lie. Providentially she hears that the Miss Alans are planning a trip to Greece, and demands to be allowed to join them. Mr Beebe, influenced by the enigmatic insistence of Miss Bartlett, unexpectedly helps to persuade Mrs Honeychurch, but her permission is given reluctantly with bewilderment. In the days that follow, days of preparation for departure, mother and daughter move inexorably apart. Only once are Lucy's defences penetrated, when Mrs Honeychurch, exasperated beyond endurance, flashes out with,

"Oh, goodness! . . . How you do remind me of Charlotte Bartlett!"

"*Charlotte?*" flashed Lucy in her turn, pierced at last by a vivid pain.

"More every moment."

"I don't know what you mean, mother; Charlotte and I are not the very least alike."

---

[29] *R.V.*, p. 214.

"Well, I see the likeness. The same eternal worrying, the same taking back of words. You and Charlotte trying to divide two apples among three people last night might be sisters".[30]

But the moment of insight passes, dies off into a pointless wrangle. Later that same day, a day of shopping in London, mother and daughter return to Summer Street, and there for Lucy a culmination comes. The Emersons, she learns, have left their cottage and gone. All the secrecy, all the bother about Greece and getting away from Windy Corner has been unnecessary, a waste:

> Waste! That word seemed to sum up the whole of life. Wasted plans, wasted money, wasted love, and she had wounded her mother. Was it possible that she had muddled things away?[31]

But in fact nothing after all is to be wasted, nothing done wrong. The medium of salvation, the one person able to confer it, is still providentially at hand. A series of apparent chances—they call for Miss Bartlett at the rectory, Miss Bartlett and Mrs Honeychurch go to evening service, Lucy decides to wait for them in the rectory—and the climactic encounter is arranged. The maid shows her into Mr Beebe's study and there is some one there already, old Mr Emerson. She is unable to speak. George she had faced, and could face again, but she had entirely forgotten how to treat his father. Although she does not yet realise it, all her defences are down.

To begin with, for Mr Emerson with all his usual directness speaks to her at once of George, she resumes her old manner, continues by implication to lie, to permit the assumption that she and Cecil are still engaged. But now she must hear what has happened to George, that her rejection has broken him up, that once again as in Florence he has lost faith in living. Even against this, however, she continues to close her mind. Then Greece is mentioned, and again she must lie, allowing the implication that Cecil is going with her, only to have the truth, that she is going with the Miss Alans, casually revealed a moment later by Mr Beebe. She would have lied again, but

[30] *R.V.*, p. 237.   [31] *R.V.*, p. 239.

suddenly cannot. Somehow it is no longer possible to cheat so old a man:

> He seemed so near the end of things, so dignified in his approach to the gulf. . . . so mild to the rough paths that he had traversed, that the true chivalry—not the worn-out chivalry of sex, but the true chivalry that all the young may show to all the old— awoke in her, and, at whatever risk, she told him that Cecil was not her companion to Greece. And she spoke so seriously that the risk became a certainty and he, lifting his eyes, said: "You are leaving him? You are leaving the man you love?"[32]

For the last time terror overcomes her and she lies again, makes the long convincing speech that will prove to the world, when the breaking of her engagement is announced, that she loves no one. But Mr Emerson, hearing her out in silence, can say only that he is worried about her, worried at the muddle she may be making of her life:

> "Do trust me, Miss Honeychurch. Though life is very glorious, it is difficult. . . . 'Life', wrote a friend of mine, 'is a public performance on the violin, in which you must learn the instrument as you go along.' I think he puts it well. Man has to pick up the use of his functions as he goes along—especially the function of Love."[33]

And then, in a gust of excitement revelation comes:

> "That's it; that's what I mean. You love George!" And after his long preamble, the three words burst against Lucy like waves from the open sea.[34]

For a moment or two she fights on, but the truth, out in the open at last, can be resisted no longer. She loves George, the old man insists, body and soul, plainly and directly, as he loves her, and if she does not go to him her life will be wasted:

> "He is already part of you. Though you fly to Greece, and never see him again, or forget his very name, George will work in your thoughts till you die. It isn't possible to love and to part. You will wish that it was. You can transmute love, ignore it, muddle it, but you can never pull it out of you. I know by experience that the poets are right: love is eternal."[35]

---

[32] *R.V.*, p. 245f.　　[33] *R.V.*, p. 246.　　[34] *R.V.*, p. 247.　　[35] *Ibid.*

Sobbing, Lucy must capitulate, while the darkness, veil after veil, withdraws, confronting her with her own soul. But the tangle of lies she has woven for herself is still there, and it is too late to undeceive those who have trusted her. She must suffer and grow old away from George. With ruthless kindness however, old Mr Emerson will not permit this and when Mr Beebe re-enters blurts out the truth. In despair, contemptuously rejected by Mr Beebe, Lucy turns to the old man and his face, that of a saint who understands, revives her:

> He gave her a sense of deities reconciled, a feeling that, in gaining the man she loved, she would gain something for the whole world. Throughout the squalor of her homeward drive— she spoke at once—his salutation remained. He had robbed the body of its taint, the world's taunts of their sting; he had shown her the holiness of direct desire. She "never exactly understood," she would say in after years, "how he managed to strengthen her. It was as if he had made her see the whole of everything at once."[36]

Salvation is assured, snatched from defeat, and we return with George and Lucy to the point of first beginning, the Pension Bertolini. Content, absolute for George, is marred for Lucy by the recollection of intransigeance: her mother and Freddy, Cecil and Mr Beebe have not forgiven her, and Mr Beebe perhaps never will. But meanwhile there is passion requited, love attained, and George impelled to reckon up the forces that have swept them to contentment. Some of those forces, seen and unseen, and the mode of their operation, have been indicated already, but must now be subjected to closer examination.

Much has been done, as George points out, by the protagonists: by himself in acting the truth, by his father, by those who had not meant to help—Miss Lavish, Cecil, Mr Beebe: and even, as he and Lucy come with incredulity to realise, by Miss Bartlett. But all those personages, with all the reasons they give themselves for what they do and say, have clearly been presented to us as in part at least instrumental, subservient to unseen forces in themselves and in their environment which some of them can sometimes guess at, but which more often

[36] R.V., p. 250.

than not they do not perceive or understand. Already we have taken note of the decisive role of Italy in awakening the lovers to an awareness of their deeper selves and to the truth of their love for each other. Prior to the intervention of Italy, George was a prematurely disillusioned young man tinged with the greyness of incipient tragedy: Lucy, except in her moments of musical inspiration, a timid, conventional, girl with the shades of Miss Bartlett already hovering about her. Summoned, through love, to the fullness of life, to fulfilment, Lucy falters, surrenders to Miss Bartlett. But the setback is not final, and at Rome and in the Alps Italy continues its sway, working "some marvel" in the girl, as even Cecil comes to realise. Nor, when the scene shifts to England and Windy Corner, does Italy altogether withdraw. The Emersons are brought to Summer Street by Cecil, who must first meet them: this he does in the Umbrian Room at the National Gallery. Italy, or at all events a mutual interest in Italian art—as Mr Beebe later points out—is what has drawn them together. Nor is it perhaps too much to claim that Italy, reappearing in the pages of Miss Lavish's egregious novel, precipitates Lucy and George into the second great crisis of their love, and is thus partly responsible for the dismissal of Cecil Vyse. No spectacular Italian intervention compels the final reversal of Lucy's spiritual deterioration, her response to Mr Emerson's appeal; and yet even here, in the old man's pathetic reminders and recollections of George in Florence, Italy is made immanent, an influence not finally to be denied. And it is of course to Italy, the fountain head of their salvation, that George and Lucy, as their story closes, triumphantly return.

Italy, as an unseen and seemingly irresistible spiritual impulse, has once again demonstrated its power. Other invisible forces however, some of them antagonistic, have also been at work, and amongst these special note must be taken of the hostile influence which the author has characterised as "medieval". The chapter of the book, for example, in which Lucy becomes engaged to Cecil Vyse is entitled "Medieval", and Cecil it will be remembered is described to us as being in essence medieval, like a Gothic statue:

> Well educated, well endowed, and not deficient physically, he remained in the grip of a certain devil whom the modern world

knows as self-consciousness, and whom the medieval, with dimmer vision, worshipped as asceticism.[37]

Side-stepping for the moment that reference to self-consciousness, we note as characteristic of "medievalism", the force that is bidding for the soul of Lucy Honeychurch, an ascetic, life-denying quality, which reveals itself as increasingly at enmity, not only with the fullness of life, but also with truth. And its exponents and familiars, in addition to Cecil Vyse, are Miss Bartlett and, as becomes finally apparent, Mr Beebe. Charlotte Bartlett, already engulfed for thirty years in spiritual darkness, is shown from the first unequivocally at work, falsifying Lucy's first experience of love, presenting her with a cheerless, loveless view of life, inviting her by implication to accept it as her own. Mr Beebe on the other hand, with his geniality, social resource and great kindliness, his inspired recognition of the victorious implications in Lucy's piano playing, is slow to reveal himself. Yet he too is medieval, a life rejector, a religious ascetic. Maiden ladies, we come eventually to learn, are his speciality, indeed his preference. When he hears of Lucy's engagement to Cecil he is conscious of a bitter disappointment only partly to be accounted for by his personal antipathy to the man. And when he hears eventually that the engagement is broken, he exults. Soon after, his medieval belief in celibacy, so reticent, so carefully concealed beneath his social blandness, is exposed:

"They that marry do well, but they that refrain do better." So ran his belief, and he never heard that an engagement was broken off but with a slight feeling of pleasure. In the case of Lucy, the feeling was intensified through dislike of Cecil; and he was willing to go further—to place her out of danger until she could confirm her resolution of virginity. The feeling was very subtle and quite undogmatic, and he never imparted it to any other of the characters in this entanglement. Yet it existed, and it alone explains his action subsequently, and his influence on the action of others. The compact that he made with Miss Bartlett . . . was to help not only Lucy, but religion also.[38]

---

[37] *R.V.*, p. 107.   [38] *R.V.*, p. 229.

In due course, when confronted with Lucy's admission of her
love for George, Mr Beebe stands at last fully revealed:

> Mr. Beebe looked at the sobbing girl. He was very quiet, and
> his white face, with its ruddy whiskers, seemed suddenly
> inhuman. A long black column, he stood and awaited her
> reply.[39]

From this point on he is an open enemy, no longer in the least
interested in Lucy and George, a sinister influence against them
at Windy Corner.

Most vigorous and consistent of those in opposition to the
spiritual darkness of medievalism is old Mr Emerson, whose
chief battle has been against the very stronghold of that
darkness, the Church. Clergymen, with their superstitions—as
he sees them—their denial of the life of the senses, he will resist
to the death. And in fact a death—the death of his wife—had
been involved in his resistance, by his refusal, on principle, to
have his son baptised. When George at the age of twelve
contracted typhoid, a clergyman—the deplorable Mr Eager—
had proclaimed it a judgement. "Oh, horrible," says the old
man in his last fateful talk with Lucy,

> "When we had given up that sort of thing and broken away
> from her parents. Oh, horrible—worst of all—worse than death,
> when you have made a little clearing in the wilderness, planted
> your little garden, let in your sunlight, and then the weeds
> creep in again! A judgement! And our boy had typhoid
> because no clergyman had dropped water on him in church!"[40]

Even so, Mr Eager had triumphed, and Mrs Emerson,
contracting the fever in her turn, had gone under defeated,
thinking of sin. And thus in Florence, Mr Eager was able to
launch his accusation that Mr Emerson had murdered his wife
in the sight of God.

Mr Emerson, a profoundly religious man, and differing
from the clergymen he opposes chiefly by his acknowledgement
of passion, is clearly not advocating licentiousness, not setting up
the senses in opposition to the soul. It is in terms of harmony,
of completeness, that he makes his last appeal to Lucy:

> "I only wish poets would say this, too: that love is of the body;

[39] R.V., p. 249.   [40] R.V., p. 242.

not the body, but of the body. Ah! the misery that would be
saved if we confessed that! Ah for a little directness to liberate
the soul!"[41]

To deny the body, to sin against Eros, is also in Mr Emerson's
uncompromising view (and in that of the author), to sin
against Pallas Athene, the representative of truth. And so it is
that Lucy, frightened into denying the physical aspect of her
love for George, finds herself, as we have seen, forced into the
realms of muddle and untruthfulness, into an intensifying vortex
of lies.

Nevertheless, through the last minute intervention of Mr
Emerson, Lucy is enabled to find and save herself, to conquer
the medieval darkness within her, to snatch victory from defeat.
And so the book's final chapter, in which she returns with
George to Italy, is called "The End of the Middle Ages". Once
again, as in *Where Angels Fear to Tread*, the Italian unseen has
been made to triumph, not so much this time against materialism, Sawstonian forces that ignored or repudiated the unseen in
any shape or form, as against a more insidious adversary. In
A Room With a View the enemy within and without is also
spiritual, an unseen of darkness in opposition to an unseen of
light. To this extent, and despite the comparative simplicity of
the superficial story, the love of a boy and a girl, it can be said
that the fundamental issue, the involvement with human
salvation has deepened.

In one other respect also, the unseen within *A Room With a
View* may be said to have extended its range, reached out in a
new direction. Though tentatively, and with many whimsical
reservations, we are now being invited at all events to consider
the possibility of the workings of Fate. The author does not
personally use the word, preferring such whimsical synonyms as
Celestial Irony or the Comic Muse. According to the author it
is "celestial irony, working through her cousin and two clergymen" that has not permitted Lucy to leave Florence before
making the decisive expedition with George into the hills;
and only Lucy is allowed to speak of Fate. In the same way,
the Comic Muse is made responsible for Cecil's meeting with the
Emersons and his scheme to transfer them to Summer Street,

[41] *R.V.*, p. 247.

and only George, with youth and inexperience against him, may attribute the intervention to Fate. For this he is humorously taken to task by Mr Beebe, who insists on the term "coincidence". In fact he has always been meaning to write a "History of Coincidence". But George will have none of this:

> "I have reflected. It is Fate. Everything is Fate. We are flung together by Fate, drawn apart by Fate—flung together, drawn apart. The twelve winds blow us—we settle nothing—"[42]

Mr Beebe retorts by pointing out that the meeting with Cecil took place at the National Gallery, where he and the Emersons were looking at Italian art. "There you are," he insists,

> "and yet you talk of coincidence and Fate! You naturally seek out things Italian, and so do we and our friends. This narrows the field immeasurably, and we meet again in it."[43]

But George is unrepentant:

> "It is Fate that I am here. . . . But you can call it Italy if it makes you less unhappy."[44]

George, later described as one "ever prone to magnify Fate", is clearly not being given the last word on the matter. But the coincidence of the meeting in the National Gallery is only one of many in the book: too many for us to attribute them all without reservation to the workings of chance. The coincidence of Cecil's meeting with the Emersons would have led nowhere without the further coincidences of the empty villa at Summer Street and Cecil's own resentment at the snobbery of Sir Harry Otway. Coincidence again has revealed the presence of the Emersons at Summer Street to Miss Bartlett. She hears of it from Miss Lavish who happened to be on a bicycling tour, sustained a puncture in the neighbourhood of Summer Street, and, while waiting in the churchyard for it to be mended, sees George Emerson emerge from the villa across the way. Coincidence once more—her boiler is being cleaned out—actually brings Miss Bartlett to Windy Corner, there to continue her enigmatic role of bringing George and Lucy together by seeking to drive them apart. The long arm of coincidence, stretched to its fullest, next introduces into Windy Corner Miss Lavish's

[42] *R.V.*, p. 157.   [43] *Ibid.*   [44] *Ibid.*

Italian novel, so that Cecil may read aloud from it and George and Lucy hear. Coincidence finally, at exactly the right moment, brings first old Mr Emerson and then Lucy to Mr Beebe's rectory, so that, with some assistance, as it transpires later, from Miss Bartlett, the ultimate meeting can take place.

Coincidence on such a scale, a sequence of events depending at every turn on far-fetched chances, partakes unavoidably of the unbelievable. Why, we feel impelled to ask, did the author have to go so far? Certainly it was necessary, for the purposes of the story, that Lucy and George should meet again after their return from Italy. But to contrive that meeting through means so devious, to reassemble on English soil through one coincidence after another almost the entire contingent of the Pension Bertolini, was surely to invite from the reader scepticism, if not actual disbelief. Yet we cannot accept the explanation that the author has been simply careless or unskilful, that so accomplished a novelist has not been able to arrange things more plausibly. For example any number of devices less far-fetched than the intervention of Cecil could have been invented to bring Lucy and George together. But still the author, here and elsewhere, prefers "coincidence", seems indeed to go out of his way to introduce it again and again. George Emerson may certainly be prone to magnify Fate, but as we look back on the sequence of apparent chances, great and small, that have swept him into contentment, we can hardly blame him. The implication of some unseen power contriving and controlling events, is inescapable, and those whimsical references to the Comic Muse and Celestial Irony do no more really than direct our attention to it. What that power may be, whether Fate or Italy or both, is left ambiguous; yet it is unmistakably there. That love and truth, Eros and Pallas Athene, are a part of it is not stated in so many words, but George had certainly helped himself by his devotion to truth, and Lucy by betraying it had come close to defeat. Also the strange, indeed mystical power of love has been brought to our attention particularly in reference to Lucy's engagement to Cecil, a power that compelled not only the lips but the heart also:

> The chief parallel—to compare one great thing with another—
> is the power over us of a temple of some alien creed. Standing

outside, we deride or oppose it, or at the most feel sentimental. Inside, though the saints and gods are not ours, we become true believers, in case any true believer should be present.[45]

Love as an unseen power, for whom an engagement is a means to a further end, is also hinted at in Cecil's encounter with the old women of the neighbourhood at a garden-party. He is disgusted by their smirking approval, but the author is careful to remind us that, racially at all events, they were justified:

> The spirit of the generations had smiled through them, rejoicing in the engagement of Cecil and Lucy because it promised the continuance of life on earth.[46]

Many and various, then, are the unseen forces concerning themselves, at least by implication, in the salvation of a boy and a girl—Italy, Fate, Love and Truth. Or if you prefer it, in the case of the last two, Eros and Pallas Athene. At no point in *A Room With a View* are the unseen and its emissaries being imposed on us explicitly; on the other hand the implications of their workings, especially in the matter of Fate, are too frequent and unmistakable to be lightly set aside. We cannot ignore them, any more than we can ignore, write off as sentimental rhetoric, Lucy's intuition after her last encounter with old Mr Emerson, of "deities reconciled", her conviction that "in gaining the man she loved, she would gain something for the whole world".

The characters of *A Room With a View*, some of them already substantially delineated, now confront us for final analysis, in terms once again of their sensitivity to the unseen—an unseen however rather more complex in its workings than any encountered so far. In the first two novels a comparatively simple distinction was drawn between the saved, who acknowledged the unseen, and the lost, who rejected it: with the important reservation in *Where Angels Fear to Tread*, especially in the case of Gino Carella, that a sensitivity to the unseen may not be invariably beneficial, that it can in fact prove a source of darkness as well as light. In *A Room With a View* this concept of both good and evil spiritual influences emanating from the unseen is taken a stage further, providing in the process a more

[45] *R.V.*, p. 116.   [46] *R.V.*, p. 119.

subtle basis for the judgement of character. Thus Mr Beebe, whose position on the side of medieval darkness has been noted, is no simple offender, no straightforward denier of the existence of the unseen. He is, the author reminds us again and again, a deeply religious, deeply spiritual man. In his make up there is none of the materialism, the opportunistic worldliness of a Herbert Pembroke: and yet he stands before us finally as a man not less and possibly more severely condemned. The simple, unimaginative materialist, indifferent to or unaware of the unseen, may do much harm to himself and to others, but perhaps he is less spiritually lethal than those who are found, despite themselves, on the side of unseen forces active against the light. The antagonisms therefore in *A Room With a View* are at all times spiritual, and in terms of their allegiance, whether to spiritual darkness or spiritual light, the characters must be assessed and judged. Medieval, life-denying darkness is the enemy, and over against it all that can make for human completeness, for fullness of life.

Mr Beebe's exact position in this warfare of conflicting unseens, a position that becomes clear only in belated retrospect, has been already defined. In the surprise of discovering his true nature and motives, the reader may find him inconsistent. What of that earlier insight, for example, into the spiritual potentiality of Lucy, that enthusiasm over her interpretation of Beethoven? What of his prophecy, so ironic in retrospect, that if Miss Honeychurch ever took to live as she played, it would be very exciting for herself and for others? Perhaps Mr Beebe, himself at the time under the influence of Italy, *was* being inconsistent; certainly he could not have believed that Lucy, playing her music on the side of victory, had the triumph of medieval spinsterhood in mind. And what are we to think of his conversation with Cecil at Windy Corner when again he insists on the wonders that Lucy may display when her music and her life are mingled? On this occasion he mentions a picture he had drawn in his Italian diary:

> "Miss Honeychurch as a kite, Miss Bartlett holding the string. Picture number two: the string breaks."[47]

---

[47] *R.V.*, p. 114.

And then he must even admit inwardly that in Florence he had given surreptitious tugs to the string himself.

Inconsistent he would seem to have been up to this point, engaged despite himself on the side of light. But just at this point Cecil reveals his engagement to Lucy, and at once the clerical, the essential Mr Beebe is conscious of a bitter disappointment he cannot conceal, and which his antipathy for Cecil as a man (as we have noted) does not fully account for. From this point on Mr Beebe knows himself and where he stands. When the engagement is broken off he rejoices, and will enter into a compact with Miss Bartlett so that Lucy may confirm her resolution of virginity and be saved for the religion he serves. When he learns of her love for George he is disgusted, suddenly revealed as inhuman, an enemy coldly vindictive in defeat.

Of all the characters in *A Room With a View* Mr Beebe is perhaps the one who receives finally the severest condemnation. For all his blandness, geniality, social resourcefulness, and even kindliness, we are required to classify him unhesitatingly among the "vast armies of the benighted", those whose pleasantry and piety and wit will crack with the passing years, whose very unselfishness will become hypocritical, and who will tend to create discomfort wherever they go. Already despite himself, and all unknowingly, Mr Beebe has this latter tendency, as in his occasional attempts to save a social situation by "diverting the conversation", only to hit on some luckless topic which leaves his hearers more deeply embarrassed than before.[48] Clergymen, those professional mediators of the unseen, have fared somewhat roughly already in the stories and in *The Longest Journey*; now in Mr Beebe, and more scathingly in his sketch of the Rev. Cuthbert Eager, the author's antipathy achieves a climax extending beyond the individual to the Church itself, that latter-day stronghold of medieval darkness, in which, however devotedly, he serves.

In contrast with Mr Beebe, the deplorable Miss Bartlett, whose engagement on the side of medieval darkness has been explicitly stated, ends up by inviting our sympathy and even our admiration. Nothing could have appeared more resolute and

[48] Other instances of this tendency will be found on pp. 140, 225f., and 229.

consistent on the surface than her determination to thwart and frustrate the love that she could but recognise between Lucy and George; nothing could have been more infamous than her success after the episode on the hillside in persuading Lucy to falsify her emotions, in presenting to her her own cheerless picture of a loveless world in which the young rush to destruction until they learn better. Perhaps more than anything this moment of sinister indoctrination prepared the way for Lucy's subsequent behaviour, her panic-stricken resort to lies, the closeness of her involvement in spiritual disaster. Yet in retrospect, in the light of what George and Lucy come to realise in the hour of their contentment back at the Bertolini, it appears that we must think again, re-investigate and re-assess almost every item of Miss Bartlett's behaviour and motivation. Realisation comes to George and Lucy as they reflect on the event that has saved them—her encounter with Mr Emerson at the Rectory in Mr Beebe's study. If only Charlotte had known, says Lucy, that the old man was there she would have prevented the meeting. But she did know, George surprisingly insists:

> "My father . . . saw her, and I prefer his word. He was dozing by the study fire, and he opened his eyes, and there was Miss Bartlett. A few minutes before you came in. She was turning to go as he woke up. He didn't speak to her."[49]

Miss Bartlett knew, yet risked the meeting by herself going to the service in the adjacent church. Why? Lucy's eventual explanation "How like Charlotte to undo her work by a feeble muddle at the last moment", does not satisfy herself or George:

> something in the dying evening, in the roar of the river, in their very embrace, warned them that her words fell short of life.[50]

And so it is for George, in the book's closing moment, to come through with the ultimate realisation, to define the marvel that has taken place:

> "I'll put a marvel to you. That your cousin has always hoped. That from the very first moment we met, she hoped, far down in her mind, that we should be like this—of course, very far down. That she fought us on the surface, and yet she hoped.

---

[49] *R.V.*, p. 254f.   [50] *R.V.*, p. 255.

I can't explain her any other way. Can you? Look how she kept me alive in you all the summer; how she gave you no peace; how month after month she became more eccentric and unreliable. The sight of us haunted her—or she couldn't have described us as she did to her friend. There are details—it burnt. I read the book afterwards. She is not frozen, Lucy, she is not withered up all through. She tore us apart twice, but in the Rectory that evening she was given one more chance to make us happy. We can never make friends with her or thank her. But I do believe that, far down in her heart, far below all speech and behaviour, she is glad.''[51]

Lucy, remembering the experiences of her own heart, is compelled to overcome her immediate instinctive incredulity and to agree.

Miss Bartlett, perceived now in retrospect to have done as much as anyone to encompass the salvation of Lucy and George, will presumably not partake of it herself. Presumably she will continue as before, maddeningly unselfish, causing discomfort and exasperation wherever she goes. But can we be sure of this? Will there not now forever accompany her, far below thought itself, the influence of a secret radiance, the emanation of a task accomplished, with whatever reluctance, in the service of the light? Almost certainly it will be too late for Miss Bartlett to reverse herself, to repudiate the medieval darkness in which for thirty years she has lived and moved and had her being. But even of this we cannot be certain. In respect of Miss Bartlett the author will not commit himself, presenting, even beyond the final insight of George Emerson, an ultimate reticence. It is impossible, he insists disarmingly, "to penetrate into the minds of elderly people!"[52] The heart of the mystery that is Miss Bartlett, her "depths of strangeness, if not of meaning"[53] remain for us, as for Mr Beebe, unfathomable. We must leave her with her frayed gloves, her cheerless world, her infinite capacity to repel affection, remembering nevertheless that she is not frozen, not withered up all through, and that the family saying "you never knew which way Charlotte Bartlett would turn",[54] has not been disproved by events. Remembering finally that upon her also the benediction of the

[51] *R.V.*, p. 255f.   [52] *R.V.*, p. 181.   [53] *R.V.*, p. 225.   [54] *R.V.*, p. 60.

Italian unseen may have fallen; already in Florence Mr Beebe had had occasion to wonder whether Italy might not be deflecting her from the chaperone's prim path. Perhaps we need go no further than Italy to account for all her subsequent inconsistency of behaviour, her eccentricity, her inability to leave George and Lucy alone. And if Italy has been responsible, can we suppose that an influence so powerful will suddenly cease to operate, that Miss Bartlett will not continue to be subject to it, and so spiritually unpredictable, to the end of her days?

And yet Italy is not always triumphant, and must certainly number among her failures the likes of Cecil Vyse. Cecil, as the author explains and as we have noted, is medieval in the sense of his incapacity for life and people, his intrinsic asceticism. But it is important to note further that he and his mother, as well as the lady novelist of the Bertolini, Miss Lavish, are also intellectuals, possessed of that unfeeling and pretentious cleverness so characteristic of the London drawing-room, and which the author, especially in *The Longest Journey*, has been at such pains already to denounce. Cecil is certainly cultured, a brilliant conversationalist, well informed on all the arts, and not without taste; yet we have only to observe him wincing when the Emersons mispronounce the names of Italian painters to know that his brilliance is hollow, his appreciation of the arts essentially unfeeling and superficial, a product not of the heart but the head. In this respect Cecil is his mother's son, and our premonition of what Lucy may be incurring by exchanging Windy Corner for Cecil's London environment is more than confirmed on her short visit to Mrs Vyse's well-appointed flat. A dinner-party consisting entirely of the grandchildren of famous people is arranged and Lucy, to a certain extent, is taken in by it:

> The food was poor, but the talk had a witty weariness that impressed the girl. One was tired of everything, it seemed. One launched into enthusiasms only to collapse gracefully, and pick oneself up amid sympathetic laughter. In this atmosphere the Pension Bertolini and Windy Corner appeared equally crude. . . .[55]

---

[55] *R.V.*, p. 149.

Nevertheless, at the piano afterwards, when invited by Cecil to play Beethoven, she declines, prefers Schumann, whose music, unprofitably magical, does not march once from the cradle to the grave:

> The sadness of the incomplete—the sadness that is often Life, but should never be Art—throbbed in its disjected phrases. . . . Not thus had she played on the little draped piano at the Bertolini.[56]

For her choice of Schumann she is subsequently praised by Cecil to his mother. Schumann was right for the evening, Schumann was "the thing", whereas he idiotically had suggested Beethoven. Lucy is improving, he insists, purging off the Honeychurch taint, not always quoting servants and asking how the pudding was made. And Italy of course has done it. Mrs Vyse, though remembering "the museum that represented Italy to her", agrees, and recommends an early marriage. "Make her one of us", she proclaims before processing to bed.

Though in some ways a nice woman, Mrs Vyse has allowed herself to be swamped by London and its too many people:

> The too vast orb of her fate had crushed her; she had seen too many seasons, too many cities, too many men for her abilities, and even with Cecil she was mechanical, and behaved as if he was not one son, but so to speak, a filial crowd.[57]

The same fate, the same incapacity for human relationships, already characterises Cecil, and will become more marked with the years. For him also Italy has been but a museum, powerless against his medievalism, his alienation from life. Yet Cecil is no materialist, and the rejection of the race of intellectuals to which he belongs (for example in *The Longest Journey*) on the grounds of an insensitivity to the unseen, cannot be applied to him. His tragedy, the intellectual tragedy, is now perceived to go deeper than this. Allegiance to the unseen, to anything unseen, is no longer found to be in itself sufficient; for out of the unseen come forces hostile as well as favourable to life. Cecil, and those intellectuals like him, who "kill when they come to people", are clearly more dangerous because of their wrongly directed spirituality than they would have been without it.

[56] *Ibid.*   [57] *Ibid.*

G

In the same intellectual category as Cecil Vyse, and in her own estimation a most cultured and original person, is the lady novelist of the Bertolini, Miss Lavish. Unlike Cecil however, who can on occasions set aside his pretentiousness and become sincere and dignified, Miss Lavish is pretentious all the time. In his revelation of the true, as opposed to the self-proclaimed, Miss Lavish, the author is unrelenting. Humorously and insidiously, her aggressive insistence on herself as original, unconventional, intellectually superior, is brought to the test of reality—the test in particular of the Emersons. A radical, a believer in "true democracy", one who has flown in the face of convention all her life, she can loudly insist, on the subject of the murder in the Piazza Signoria, that such an event was none the less tragic in her view because it happened in humble life. And yet it is clear that her enthusiasm for humble life depends on its remaining so, on its knowing and keeping its place. The Emersons, however, whose social position if not exactly humble, is also not exactly high, will not keep their place. They aspire to culture, they are visiting Italy, trespassing on the preserve of their educated betters, and for this they must be derided. With what snobbish glee Miss Lavish hears from Miss Bartlett that George Emerson is employed on "the railway"! The railway, she gasps:

> "Oh, but I shall die! Of course it was the railway!" She could not control her mirth. "He is the image of a porter—on, on the South-Eastern."[58]

For Miss Lavish the Emersons are unendurable, the worst kind of Britishers who should be turned back at Dover to save their country's reputation abroad. "They walk through my Italy", she announces, "like a pair of crows." And she plans a merciless revenge upon such as they in her forthcoming novel. Nor do we perceive the shallowness, the pretentious falsity of Miss Lavish only in relation to the Emersons. It is revealed to us at every turn. Proclaiming her unconventionality at the Bertolini, she dares to enter the smoking-room reserved for men—only to emerge a few minutes later, unobtrusively, with a green baize board on which she proceeds to play patience.

[58] *R.V.*, p. 82.

Pretentious in her knowledge of Florence she sets out through the back streets with Lucy for Santa Croce, and promptly loses her way. Pretentious again, she bristles with indignation when Mr Emerson asks her if she has heard of Lorenzo de Medici:

> "Most certainly I have. Do you refer to Lorenzo il Magnifico, or to Lorenzo, Duke of Urbino, or to Lorenzo surnamed Lorenzino on account of his diminutive stature?"[59]

Finally there are her literary pretensions; on the one hand her concept of herself as a gifted novelist, on the other our glimpse of her accomplishment—the "draggled prose" of *Under a Loggia* by Joseph Emery Prank.

Here perhaps, with a shrug and a smile, we could dismiss Miss Lavish, classify her as just one more clever intellectual, whose very cleverness stands as a barrier between herself and the attainment of a genuine spirituality, a communion with the unseen. Miss Lavish however, though humorously presented, a pretentious figure of fun, is also being revealed to us in the final analysis as anything but amusing. She too, like Cecil Vyse, belongs in the category of those who, if given the chance, will kill when they come to people. In *A Room With a View* she does not get that chance, but her zest for gossip and malice, her unscrupulous betrayal of Miss Bartlett's confidences by including them in her novel, are evidence enough of her lethal capabilities. How right George Emerson was when she turned up on her cycling tour in Summer Street not to offer her a cup of tea!

Of Lucy Honeychurch, brought to completeness despite herself, to that harmony between head and heart in which salvation consists, enough has been said already. However, care must be taken to do her justice, to recall the extent to which that final bestowal of salvation has been deserved and earned. Certainly she comes within a hair's breadth of failure, of the fate she prophesies for herself in her singing of the song given her by Cecil:

> Look not thou on beauty's charming,
> Sit thou still when kings are arming,
> Taste not when the wine-cup glistens,

Speak not when the people listens,
Stop thine ear against the singer,
From the red gold keep thy finger;
Vacant heart and hand and eye,
Easy live and quiet die.[60]

And from this, the world of Miss Bartlett, of the gossiping little old Miss Alans, in whose company she plans to escape to Greece, she herself, without the intervention of events and people and spiritual forces beyond her comprehension, could never have won free. Even so those forces, disposing with set purpose of events and people, knew very well what they were up to, what there was in Lucy Honeychurch that had at all costs to be saved. Had it not been there, or not in sufficient strength, doubtless even their best efforts would have failed. But the Lucy confronting old Mr Emerson at the moment of her spiritual crisis, is still the same Lucy who has played Beethoven on the side of victory, of "Heroes—gods—the nonsense of schoolgirls",[61] and it is her own intrinsic spiritual strength that must respond to the climactic summons from out of the unseen and carry her through.

In contrast to the wavering, near-defeated Lucy, George Emerson appears to display an unassailable consistency and strength. The appearance however is deceptive, for we must remember that George too right from the start is threatened spiritually, marked with the greyness of an impending tragedy that may only find solution in the night. Old Mr Emerson knows very well his son's condition, his inability to say "Yes" to life, but cannot help him; and Lucy, appealed to, has nothing to suggest but a hobby, collecting postage stamps. Even so, the absurd and pitiable George, trailing his clouds of unreality, is in Italy, and in Italy the real, with all its transfiguring potential, is never far away. The overwhelming realities of death and love—a man is murdered, Lucy faints in his arms—explode about him and a "spiritual boundary" is promptly crossed, a profound metamorphosis effected. "I will want to live", he proclaims, almost on a note of astonishment. The transfiguration however is still precarious. Lucy betrays him and herself, flees with Miss Bartlett to Rome, and though

[60] *R.V.*, p. 230f.   [61] *R.V.*, p. 91.

Fate—or Italy if you prefer it—confronts her at Windy Corner with a second chance; she persists in her betrayal. The effect of the rebuff on George, received this time from the lips of Lucy herself, is final. As we learn eventually from old Mr Emerson, he has "gone under":

> ". . . he will not think it worth while to live. It was always touch and go. He will live; but he will not think it worth while to live. He will never think anything worth while."[62]

This irresoluteness in the face of life distinguishes George from such partial predecessors as Ford, in "Other Kingdom" and Stewart Ansell, with whom he has in common a devastating capacity for truth. Absolute truthfulness, towards events and people, is the source of his strength and of his insight, but not the whole source; for George, in rather marked contrast to Ansell, is also imaginative, open, as it were, to the unseen. In the presence of Giotto's frescoes of the Ascension in Santa Croce, old Mr Emerson, who has been turned against the spiritual through his experience of the Church, remains obstinately material:

> "I see no truth in them. Look at that fat man in blue! He must weigh as much as I do, and he is shooting into the sky like an air-balloon."[63]

A less sceptical reaction, however, comes from George:

> "It happened like this, if it happened at all. I would rather go up to heaven by myself than be pushed up by cherubs; and if I got there I should like my friends to lean out of it, just as they do here. . . . Some of the people can only see the empty grave, not the saint, whoever he is, going up. It did happen like that, if it happened at all."[64]

Even more strangely indicative of an openness, a sensitivity towards the unseen, has been the strength and literalness of his belief in Fate. We can call it "Italy" if it will make us any less unhappy, but nevertheless according to George it is there, an invisible power contriving events, manipulating people, sweeping him on to final victory. Acting the truth as he saw it had been enough for George, the medium of his own and Lucy's

[62] *R.V.*, p. 242f.   [63] *R.V.*, p. 33.   [64] *R.V.*, p. 34.

salvation, but the truth in question had been an inclusive one, incorporating the unseen, a truth productive of special insight into events and people. George's insight into Cecil Vyse, an insight that was to compel Lucy despite herself to break off her engagement and carry conviction even to Cecil himself, was no theoretical denunciation. It was a spiritually inspired utterance, instinct with prophetic power.

The same spiritual force and integrity informing and sustaining the son, is obviously and no less positively at work within the father. Old Mr Emerson because of his unlucky experiences with the established Church, appears to have turned against the unseen, to have identified it with ignorance and superstition and all that is at enmity with life. His son's inability to be satisfied with the world as he finds it, bewilders him:

> "We know that we come from the winds, and that we shall
> return to them; that all life is perhaps a knot, a tangle, a blemish
> in the eternal smoothness. But why should this make us un-
> happy? Let us rather love one another, and work and rejoice.
> I don't believe in this world sorrow."[65]

The emphasis here is all on this world, this life, asserting themselves against obscurantism, against the life-denying medieval darkness of the unseen. And yet that reference to an "eternal smoothness" does seem to go a little further, to imply the recognition of a different spirituality from that conceived of by the Cecil Vyses, the Mr Beebes, the Reverend Cuthbert Eagers. Mr Emerson, with his childlike courage and directness, his capacity for love, his assured and unerring insight into events and people, is clearly intuitively as well as rationally inspired. Concerning his origins, we are told by the Reverend Cuthbert Eager, that they were humble, that though himself a mechanic he was the son of a labourer, presumably agricultural. From this comparative proximity to the soil would derive undoubtedly his simplicity and honesty, his "appalling straightness" of manner—qualities that connect him unmistak-ably with those other sons of the soil in *The Longest Journey*, Robert and Stephen. And just as these two could be sustained

[65] *R.V.*, p. 38.

spiritually by the soil and by Nature without being conscious
of the fact, so Mr Emerson can remain unaware of his own
involvement with the unseen, can even consciously repudiate it.
Thus once again in *A Room With a View*, through the medium of
old Mr Emerson, unself-consciousness is being recommended to
us, demonstrated as a source of spiritual strength and integrity.
Its opposite, that "certain devil whom the modern world
knows as self-consciousness", is the attribute, as we have
already noted in passing, of Cecil Vyse, the origin of his
medievalism. George Emerson, one generation closer than his
father to self-consciousness, one generation further from the
soil, must appear to us as to that extent threatened, deprived of
the ultimate power to save himself. Only the higher unself-
conscious wisdom of his father, fatefully intervening, rescues
him at the last moment from the dark.

Two lesser, though scarcely unimportant characters remain
for brief assessment; the delightful Mrs Honeychurch and her
son Freddy. Both are attractive, straightforward in thought and
action, concerned with the unseen only through the medium of
Sunday church-going. Perhaps the saving grace of unself-
consciousness is also to some extent theirs, enabling them to
think directly, to see through pretentiousness, to stand by the
truth. Freddy, precisely because he is unaware of his own
profundity, can see right through Cecil Vyse:

> Cecil praised one too much for being athletic. Was that it?
> Cecil made one talk in his way, instead of letting one talk in
> one's own way. This tired one. Was that it? And Cecil was
> the kind of fellow who would never wear another fellow's cap.[66]

Similarly Mrs Honeychurch, portly, amusing and uncomplicated, is under no illusions about Cecil's mother:

> "She goes in for lectures and improving her mind, and all the
> time a thick layer of flue under the beds, and the maids' dirty
> thumb-marks where you turn on the electric light. She keeps
> that flat abominably—"[67]

Insights of this kind, uncontaminated by the wrong sort of
intellectuality, come naturally and spontaneously to Mrs
Honeychurch, often with disconcerting results. Nothing in the

[66] *R.V.*, p. 105.   [67] *Ibid.*

last dark days of her spiritual dishonesty, had so pierced, so pained Lucy as her mother's prophetic outburst: "Oh, goodness! . . . How you do remind me of Charlotte Bartlett!" The final, the spiritual challenge to both Freddy and Mrs Honeychurch comes with their discovery of the love between Lucy and George, and initially at least they are unequal to it, deficient in understanding. Mrs Honeychurch refuses consent to the marriage, and Freddy calls it an elopement. Windy Corner, strongly under the unforgiving influence of Mr Beebe, may perhaps have been alienated for ever. No more than the distant hope is formulated, that, if we act the truth, the people who really love us are sure to come back to us in the long run. Even so, mother and son end up, for all their redeeming qualities, temporarily at least in alliance with Mr Beebe.

In passion requited, love attained, to the sound of the river Arno bearing down the snows of winter to the Mediterranean, *A Room With a View* is brought to its appointed end—with the unseen still in faithful attendance, suggesting to the lovers as we take leave of them the existence of a love more mysterious than their own. In essence perhaps, *A Room With a View* has been after all no more than a second demonstration after *Where Angels Fear to Tread* of the redemptive power of the Italian unseen in impact upon the English character. Once again, moreover, the impact and intervention of the unseen have been presented to us only by implication. Yet, in *A Room With a View*, as we have had occasion to observe, a more extended range for the unseen has been suggested, a more precise indication of its workings implied. The concept of the unseen as a source of spiritual malevolence was present already in *Where Angels Fear To Tread*, but now with greater definiteness and precision we are confronted with individuals in league with that malevolence, and deriving from it an essential hostility to the fullness of life. In the same way the power of the unseen to affect and contrive events which was hinted at in the first novel, has now been taken a decisive step further, to the point where, at least in the estimation of George Emerson, Fate and Italy become synonymous terms.

Even so, in respect of its central redemptive theme, it

cannot be said that *A Room with a View* represents an advance in the author's thinking. Still with us, and still unsolved is the problem of the self-conscious English character, its inability to achieve completeness through its own intrinsic spiritual strength. Once again salvation has had to come from outside, through the intervention of Italy, of the Italian mysticism of the heart. Old Mr Emerson, like Stephen Wonham before him, may be among those in whom the ancient virtue of the soil is still operative, who have kept their souls through unselfconscious simplicity. But for the self-conscious, for George Emerson and Lucy Honeychurch and those like them, obviously the longest journey into self-awareness, into an ever-intensifying intellectuality, can only go on.[68] The crisis of that journey, led up to rather than resolved in the first three novels, is still before us. In *Howards End* we meet it again head on.

[68] In the article, "A View Without a Room", in *The Observer*, 27 July 1958, Forster speculates somewhat ironically and deflatingly on what could have happened to George and Lucy in the four decades following their marriage.

VI

Howards End

In *Howards End* the author's reticence on the subject of the unseen, his reluctance at all events to name it, comes to an end. The term itself, and such phrases as "the impact of the unseen", are to be used from now on openly and frequently. Margaret Schlegel, for example, while speculating on the vulgar manifestations of Christmas in London, feels "the grotesque impact of the unseen upon the seen"; and later, when the request of the dead Mrs Wilcox that Margaret should inherit Howards End is revealed to the Wilcox family, it is noted that "the unseen had impacted on the seen" and they had failed to respond to it. Throughout the book the conflict between the seen, the outer world of the Wilcoxes, and the unseen, the inner world of the Schlegels is basic, and Margaret's mission is to connect, to reconcile the two. "Only connect", is the whole of Margaret's sermon, and the author's too, for he uses the words as the book's motto. Thus when writing to her sister Helen, who can perceive nothing in the Wilcox world but panic and emptiness, Margaret warns her,

> Don't brood too much . . . on the superiority of the unseen to the seen. It's true, but to brood on it is medieval. Our business is not to contrast the two, but to reconcile them.[1]

Of those reflecting in their lives and actions the impact of the unseen, none is more continuously impressive in *Howards End* than Mrs Wilcox. Although she appears but briefly, in fact dies almost as the story opens, her presence whether visible or invisible is constant, influencing events and people, subjecting them at least by implication to a kind of control. With her in

[1] *Howards End*, p. 109, Pocket Edition. Hereafter cited as *H.E.*

consequence and with the house, Howards End, that is an essential part of her, it is appropriate to begin.

An elderly, ailing woman, far from great intellectually, but yet of an undefinable spiritual rarity, she is presented as living in intuitive communication with the past—a past symbolised for her by her house, and by the ancient wych-elm tree that over-shadows it:

> One knew that she worshipped the past, and that the instinctive wisdom the past can alone bestow had descended upon her— that wisdom to which we give the clumsy name of aristocracy. High-born she might not be. But assuredly she cared about her ancestors, and let them help her.[2]

And so, in the first clash at the beginning of the book between Schlegels and Wilcoxes, between Helen and Paul at Howards End, she knows what is happening and what to do:

> When she saw Charles angry, Paul frightened, and Mrs. Munt in tears, she heard her ancestors say, "Separate those human beings who will hurt each other most. The rest can wait."[3]

The Schlegel sisters and the Wilcoxes, husband and wife, had met first as tourists in Germany, and it was perhaps to Margaret that Mrs Wilcox had felt herself especially drawn, detecting in the older and less charming of the sisters a deeper sympathy and a sounder judgement. And in inviting the sisters to Howards End, perhaps it had been Margarets' presence she particularly desired. Margaret however, detained in London by the illness of her brother Tibby, had been unable to go. Now presumably, after Helen's disastrous encounter with Paul Wilcox, the tenuous contact between the two incompatible families has been severed for good. But no—time passes, and the Wilcoxes reappear, instal themselves temporarily by an extreme coincidence in a block of flats across from the Schlegels' town house in Wickham Place. Margaret, for Helen's sake, decides to ignore them, but Mrs Wilcox calls, and the two are presently drawn together in a brief, inconclusive friendship. Margaret, young and vivacious, busily caught up in cultural activities, is as yet only intermittently aware of unusual

[2] *H.E.*, p. 23.   [3] *Ibid.*

qualities in the older woman, even slightly resentful when the suggestion is gently made to her that she lacks experience. Yet she is sufficiently attracted to pursue the friendship and to give a little luncheon-party in Mrs Wilcox's honour. The occasion is not a success. Margaret's delightful young friends, zig-zagging conversationally over thought and Art, bewilder and alarm Mrs Wilcox, wither her delicate imaginings. She leaves early, and Margaret who has taken a full share in the excluding talk, goes with her to the door and experiences an impulse of shame and revulsion, suddenly characterising herself and her friends as "gibbering monkeys":

> "Don't pretend you enjoyed lunch, for you loathed it, but forgive me by coming again, alone, or by asking me to you."[4]

Then she returns to the clever young people who have been discussing her new-found friend and have dismissed her as uninteresting.

Mrs Wilcox, who is not to be hurried into friendship, does not respond again for a time, then invites Margaret to assist her with some Christmas shopping. In the course of it she learns by chance that the Schlegels will soon have to leave their lifelong home in Wickham Place, that it is to be torn down to make way for flats. The information precipitates a disproportionately vehement protest:

> "It is monstrous, Miss Schlegel; it isn't right. I had no idea that this was hanging over you. I do pity you from the bottom of my heart. To be parted from your house, your father's house—it oughtn't to be allowed. It is worse than dying. I would rather die than—Oh, poor girls! Can what they call civilization be right, if people mayn't die in the room where they were born? My dear, I am so sorry—"[5]

Margaret is speechless, persuaded that Mrs Wilcox, over-tired by shopping, has given way to hysteria. But the old lady, thinking in terms of her own beloved home, is not to be deterred. Howards End, she insists, was once almost pulled down, and it would have killed her. Impulsively she begs Margaret to come down immediately to see it with her, but Margaret, shrinking from the effort and the weather, suggests another day. Later,

4 *H.E.*, p. 82.   5 *H.E.*, p. 87.

however, with her mind "focused on the invisible", she perceives her mistake:

> She discerned that Mrs. Wilcox, though a loving wife and mother, had only one passion in her life—her house—and that the moment was solemn when she invited a friend to share this passion with her. To answer "another day" was to answer as a fool. "Another day" will do for brick and mortar, but not for the Holy of Holies into which Howards End had been transfigured.[6]

Imagination triumphs and she decides to accept the invitation, steps across to the flats, only to learn that Mrs Wilcox has gone away for the night. Still inexplicably impelled, she hurries to King's Cross, and is in time to be warmly greeted by Mrs Wilcox on the platform. However, her encounter with Howards End is after all to be for another day. On the way to the train they are met unexpectedly by Mr Wilcox and his daughter Evie, returned from a motoring tour in Yorkshire, and the little, imaginative outing has to be called off.

In fact Margaret's visit to Howards End is not to take place at all, at least in the lifetime of Ruth Wilcox, who, almost immediately, is taken ill and, after great suffering, dies. Margaret visits her once or twice in the nursing-home, and eventually attends the funeral in Hilton churchyard; and there in all conscience the tenuous connexion with the Wilcox family would seem to have come to an end. However, Mrs Wilcox has decided otherwise. By means of a note from the nursing home, she has made the request to her husband that Miss Schlegel (Margaret) should be given Howards End. The Wilcoxes—and the author declines to blame them—are horrified, totally uncomprehending:

> The appeal was too flimsy. It was not legal; it had been written in illness and under the spell of a sudden friendship; it was contrary to . . . her very nature, so far as that nature was understood by them. To them Howards End was a house: they could not know that to her it had been a spirit, for which she sought a spiritual heir.[7]

After due debate they place their mother's note on the dining-room fire.

[6] *H.E.*, p. 90.   [7] *H.E.*, p. 104.

Margaret, despite the suspicions of Charles Wilcox, knows nothing of Mrs Wilcox's strange legacy, is to hear of it only at the end of the book when, by an incredibly devious and tragic route, the spiritual heritage so summarily denied her, has in fact become hers, been willed to her by Henry Wilcox. Then, and only then, confronted with the knowledge of Mrs Wilcox's intention, can she look back, assess correctly the events and people that have led her on, and perceive the continuous impact there has been upon them from out of the unseen. Realisation slips into place "like the headstone of the corner", and she feels her life shaken in its inmost recesses.[8]

The influence of the unseen, specifically of the spirit of Mrs Wilcox from out of the unseen, is the essential theme of *Howards End*. The manifestations of that influence through events and people and the intuitions that come to them must now be indicated, beginning from the moment in the Hilton churchyard when it would seem, for all practical purposes, that the impact of Ruth Wilcox upon events and people would have come to an end.

And for a while certainly, all seems to have ended, with Schlegels and Wilcoxes moving apart in incompatible directions. Then for the second time extreme "coincidence" supervenes. Helen and Margaret, after an evening meeting of a discussion club to which they belong, sit for a while on the Chelsea Embankment and happen to mention Mrs Wilcox and the special significance in her life of Howards End:

> One's own name will carry immense distances. Mr. Wilcox, who was sitting with friends many seats away, heard his, rose to his feet, and strolled along towards the speakers.[9]

Conversation ensues, and presently turns on the subject of houses. Margaret learns that Howards End has been let unfurnished to a desirable tenant, that the Charles Wilcoxes live nearby in Hilton, and that Mr Wilcox, now being looked after by his daughter Evie, has a London house in Ducie Street, and a country house at Oniton in Shropshire. Mr Wilcox expresses concern at the "unprotected" life the sisters lead in London, and the chance encounter, seemingly pointless, ends.

[8] *H.E.*, p. 362.   [9] *H.E.*, p. 138.

Helen, still disillusioned about the Wilcoxes, can only say: "What a prosperous vulgarian Mr. Wilcox has grown!"

For Mr Wilcox, however, the meeting has been anything but insignificant. He is attracted to Margaret and, through Evie, arranges to meet her again. He calls at Wickham Place, invites her to lunch at Simpsons in the Strand. At Wickham Place he arrives as Helen and Margaret are entertaining their new-found protégé, Leonard Bast, and are in fact involved in a quarrel with him. After he has gone, Margaret defends him and her relationship to Mr Wilcox is suddenly sharpened by her detection of his jealousy. From this point, and with astonishing rapidity they are drawn together. Once again houses become a mutual theme. Time and leases are running out, and the Schlegels' eviction from Wickham Place, the prospect of which had once so deeply shocked Mrs Wilcox, is imminent. But a London house to replace it, one acceptable to the sisters as well as to their *difficile* brother Tibby, simply will not materialise. Margaret appeals to Mr Wilcox, the practical man of affairs, to help them in their search, and while they are out of London staying with their aunt, Mrs Munt, at Swanage, he does come through with a suggestion. Evie is getting married and he has decided to give up his house in Ducie Street. If the Schlegels are interested in renting it, Margaret is to come up to London immediately and complete the deal.

Margaret comes, only to find as she had half suspected, that Ducie Street is in part at least a pretext. As they look over the house together, and just as the thought enters her brain, "Had Mrs Wilcox's drawing-room looked thus at Howards End?", Mr Wilcox asks her to marry him. The proposal is not to rank among the world's great love scenes, and Margaret is to be surprised only by her own lack of surprise and by the immensity of joy that comes over her:

> It was indescribable. It had nothing to do with humanity, and most resembled the all-pervading happiness of fine weather.[10]

Aware of a central radiance and identifying it with love, she is also made aware of a presiding influence, of Mrs Wilcox

[10] *H.E.*, p. 174.

straying in and out, an ever-welcome ghost, and "surveying the scene . . . without one hint of bitterness".[11]

Wilcoxes and Schlegels are now indeed and inextricably entangled, much to the distress of Helen who bursts into tears on hearing of the engagement. Nothing could have seemed less likely to have happened. In fact the importunity of the Wilcoxes, their obstinate and incongruous refusal to drop out of sight, had already come home to Tibby. "Who *are* the Wilcoxes?" he had demanded at Swanage. "I don't *manage* the Wilcoxes; I don't see where they come *in*." And Helen agrees with him:

> "No more do I. . . . It's funny that we just don't lose sight of them. Out of all our hotel acquaintants, Mr. Wilcox is the only one who has stuck. It is now over three years, and we have drifted away from far more interesting people in that time."[12]

And now, through impending marriage, the involvement is to become total, with Margaret committed, heroically and willingly, to the difficult task of reconciliation.

Her first public duty as Henry Wilcox's future wife, is to preside over Evie's wedding at Oniton. Before it, however, there is to be an unexpected diversion—her first visit to Howards End. Mr Bryce, the ideal tenant, has turned out to be anything but ideal after all. An invalid, and unable to sleep while in the house, he has decamped abroad, attempting to sublet by putting up notice-boards which Charles Wilcox has indignantly thrown down. Henry determines to hold the tenant to his three-year lease, but meanwhile the house has been left in a disgraceful mess, and a visit of inspection is decided upon. Margaret and Henry motor down and she shelters in the porch from the rain while he goes to the nearby farm for the key. Surveying the garden she is immediately struck by its beauty and by the extreme fertility of the soil. The house is unlocked after all and she enters upon a scene of desolation. Wandering from room to room, she perceives the garden at the back, full of flowering cherries and plums, and beyond it, edged with pines, the beauty of the meadow. She paces back into the hall and suddenly the house reverberates:

[11] *H.E.*, p. 176.   [12] *H.E.*, p. 167.

"Is that you, Henry?" she called.

There was no answer, but the house reverberated again.

"Henry, have you got in?"

But it was the heart of the house beating, faintly at first then loudly, martially. It dominated the rain.

It is the starved imagination, not the well-nourished, that is afraid. Margaret flung open the door to the stairs. A noise as of drums seemed to deafen her. A woman, an old woman, was descending, with figure erect, with face impassive, with lips that parted and said dryly:

"Oh! Well, I took you for Ruth Wilcox."

Margaret stammered: "I—Mrs. Wilcox—I?"

"In fancy, of course—in fancy. You had her way of walking. Good day." And the old woman passed out into the rain.[13]

Exactly what Margaret makes of the incident, we are not told. Henry assumes that she was frightened, and Dolly, Charles' wife, with whom they have tea, asks if she had taken the old woman for a spook—Dolly, for whom "spooks" and "going to church" summarised the unseen. The old woman turns out to have been the eccentric Miss Avery, one of the "crew at the farm" and, as Margaret learns, a long-standing former friend of Ruth Wilcox. That evening, alone at Wickham Place, Margaret allows her mind to rest on Howards End, and starting from there finds herself trying to realise England. The vision does not come, but an unexpected love of the island awakens in her:

It had certainly come through the house and old Miss Avery. Through them: the notion of "through" persisted; her mind trembled towards a conclusion which only the unwise have put into words. Then, veering back into warmth, it dwelt on ruddy bricks, flowering plum-trees, and all the tangible joys of spring.[14]

Howards End, with its tremendous attendant wych-elm tree, bending over it like a comrade, has manifested itself, but at once withdraws, for Margaret's attention is now deflected to Oniton in Shropshire where Evie's wedding is to take place. Assuming that here will be her future home, she determines to do her best, to start out right with the local gentry, to adjust to the demands that will be made on her as eventual hostess.

[13] *H.E.*, p. 213. [14] *H.E.*, p. 216.

H

Oniton however, though she is deeply attracted to it, is to prove only another false start. The house is damp, in the wrong part of Shropshire and too far from London. Without even letting her know, Henry disposes of it, as she learns much to her annoyance on their honeymoon. Wickham Place meanwhile has been torn down and the Schlegel furniture and possessions, with Henry's kind permission, sent down for storage to the still untenanted Howards End. All along it would have been possible for Henry himself to live there; on her visit however, Margaret had discovered, to her amusement, the real as opposed to his many professed reasons for not doing so: namely the immediate and uncongenial proximity of the Charles Wilcoxes. Eventually a firm decision is taken: to camp at Ducie Street for the coming winter and to go down into Sussex in the spring and build. Then for the second time, and no less unexpectedly, there comes news from Howards End. The packing-cases containing the Schlegel books and possessions are being unpacked by the eccentric Miss Avery.

Again an inspection is imperative and Margaret goes down, this time alone, is pleasantly and calmly welcomed by Miss Avery. Then she makes an appalling discovery. The old woman has unpacked everything, fitted up the whole house with the contents from Wickham Place. Wandering dazedly through her own fantastically re-created home, Margaret cannot help laughing, but must insist nevertheless that a mistake has been made, very likely her mistake. Yes, Miss Avery agrees,

> ". . . it has been mistake upon mistake for fifty years. The house is Mrs. Wilcox's, and she would not desire it to stand empty any longer."[15]

A mistake, Margaret insists, a misunderstanding. She and Mr Wilcox are not going to live at Howards End. Intently she examines Miss Avery, trying to understand the kink in her brain, but must admit that here is no maundering old woman:

> Her wrinkles were shrewd and humorous. She looked capable of scathing wit and also of high but unostentatious nobility.[16]

Even so, Margaret can only insist that everything must be

[15] *H.E.*, p. 286.   [16] *H.E.*, p. 287.

repacked, other arrangements for storage made. Yet she takes no immediate decision, decides to consult Henry, who will advise her later to store in London. But Miss Avery is quite unperturbed:

> "A better time is coming now, though you've kept me long enough waiting. In a couple of weeks I'll see your lights shining through the hedge of an evening. Have you ordered in coals?"[17]

Then, before anything can be done about the furniture in Howards End, trouble from another direction intervenes. For months now, alienated by her sister's marriage and by Henry Wilcox's treatment of her protégé, Leonard Bast, Helen has been isolating herself, even to the extent of going abroad. Then when Aunt Juley in Swanage falls seriously ill and Helen, though back in England, refuses to visit her, Margaret decides that her sister is mentally ill and must at all costs be contacted. She consults Henry, who plans an ingenious trap. Helen has asked for some books and since these are at Howards End she should be sent down to fetch them and there taken by surprise. Margaret, with agonised misgivings, consents to the deception. When the time comes, however, she manages to evade Henry, and the doctor accompanying him, and enters the garden alone. One glance at Helen who is waiting in the porch provides a complete explanation of her behaviour. She is with child. The keys of Howards End are in Margaret's hand and she unlocks the door, thrusts Helen inside.

Up to this point, the significance of Howards End, of its connexion with the dead Mrs Wilcox has been to Margaret of only incidental concern. Even the prophetic ministrations of the prescient Miss Avery, had touched her mind rather than her imagination. But now in the one magical night with Helen under the roof of Howards End, within the aegis of its circumambient powers, the intuitions of that gracious overseeing presence begin at last to enter her conscious mind, to soothe away her distress over Helen, over their fleeting inability to find the common love that once united them:

> Explanations and appeals had failed; they had tried for a

---

common meeting-ground, and had only made each other unhappy. And all the time their salvation was lying round them—the past sanctifying the present; the present, with wild heart-throb, declaring that there would after all be a future, with laughter and the voices of children. Helen, still smiling, came up to her sister. She said "It is always Meg." They looked into each other's eyes. The inner life had paid.[18]

Despite Henry's obtuse and unyielding opposition, their one night together is to be allowed—one night in a house which, as Helen puts it, they know is theirs because they feel it to be so. And all the time the sense of Mrs Wilcox, at least in the form of an encompassing wisdom, of one who understands "our little movements", deepens. All of them, Margaret begins to feel —herself, Helen, Henry—are a part of the dead woman's mind:

> "She knows everything. She is everything. She is the house, and the tree that leans over it. People have their own deaths as well as their own lives, and even if there is nothing beyond death, we shall differ in our nothingness. I cannot believe that knowledge such as hers will perish with knowledge such as mine. She knew about realities. She knew when people were in love, though she was not in the room. I don't doubt that she knew when Henry deceived her."
> "Good night, Mrs. Wilcox," called a voice.
> "Oh, good night, Miss Avery."
> "Why should Miss Avery work for us?" Helen murmured.
> "Why, indeed?"[19]

Amidst the endless iterations of the great tree enshadowing the house, they fall asleep; but as the moon rises house and tree are disentangled, clear for a few moments at midnight. Margaret awakes and looks into the garden, finds herielf thinking of the father of Helen's child. How incomprehensible, she reflects,

> that Leonard Bast should have won her this night of peace! Was he also part of Mrs. Wilcox's mind?[20]

The house however, begetter of peace, is not yet itself at peace, and this, its final aim, can come only through tragedy. By morning Leonard Bast has found his way there, only to be encountered by Charles Wilcox, thrashed with the sword snatched from the wall, and in the process killed. The dead

[18] *H.E.*, p. 315.   [19] *H.E.*, p. 331f.   [20] *H.E.*, p. 333.

body is laid on the lawn, water uselessly poured over it. Only Miss Avery, whose every word of prophecy and warning has now been fulfilled, knows what has happened:

> "Yes, murder's enough " said Miss Avery, coming out of the house with the sword.[21]

The rest, the trial and imprisonment of Charles, the breaking of the Wilcoxes, father and son, is only sequel:

> Then Henry's fortress gave way. He could bear no one but his wife, he shambled up to Margaret afterwards and asked her to do what she could with him. She did what seemed easiest—she took him down to recruit at Howards End.[22]

A year later, still installed with Henry and Helen, and now with Helen's baby also, Margaret through Dolly's indiscretion hears of Mrs Wilcox's disregarded intention for Howards End. Then, in full retrospective realisation, she feels her life shaken in its inmost recesses; and realisation also brings with it acceptance, the certain knowledge that nothing after all has been done wrong.

To view such a conclusion, the transfer of Howards End to its rightful spiritual heir, as fulfilling the sole aim and purpose of Mrs Wilcox in life and beyond it, would be of course to oversimplify. Clearly that perturbed, all-understanding spirit has had a deeper end in view, the same end to which Margaret's own life has been dedicated, the reconciliation of the outer world of the Wilcoxes with the inner world of the Schlegels, of the seen with the unseen. Now the nature of those two worlds and of those principally representing them, Margaret and Helen on the one hand, Henry Wilcox and those like him on the other, must be more closely established and explored.

Concerning Margaret Schlegel and her sensitivity to the unseen much has already been stated and implied. Was not this the supreme quality immediately detected in her by Mrs Wilcox, and on the basis of which she later designated her the rightful inheritor of Howards End? And is not Margaret herself already aware of her own sensitivity, explicitly referring in thought and speech to the "impact of the unseen on the seen"? This much scarcely needs further demonstration. But the point

[21] *H.E.*, p. 343.   [22] *H.E.*, p. 353.

must also be made that a belief in the unseen, though explicit, can also be in some measure theoretical, subject to confirmation or rejection by the experience of life. Mrs Wilcox, gently but firmly reminding Margaret of her lack of this very experience, also reminds us of the distance that must be travelled between theory and certainty and thus of a distinction between the Margaret of the moment and of the potential future. Most important therefore at the outset is to realise that the Margaret finally established at Howards End in full realisation of the events and interventions that have brought her there, is one who has made the transition from theory to certainty, become aware through the medium of experience that the unseen does indeed have an impact, a decisive and devastating impact on the seen.

So far in the novels most of the leading characters presented to us have managed to achieve salvation in proportion to their success in opposing the unseen to the seen. In *Howards End* and especially through Margaret Schlegel, the absoluteness, the black and whiteness of this opposition is to be subjected to modification. "Only connect" is the whole of Margaret's sermon, and it is through a harmony, a reconciliation of opposites that she would wish herself to be saved. Thus from the beginning her sensitivity to the unseen in all its manifestations is counterbalanced by a firm and honest acknowledgement of the visible and the practical, especially as it is represented to her by the Wilcox world. While her sister Helen reacts violently and one-sidedly against the outer life of "telegrams and anger", the "panic and emptiness" she had detected in her unlucky encounter with Paul, Margaret refuses to go to such extremes. The Wilcoxes were certainly not "her sort",

> They were often suspicious and stupid, and deficient where she excelled; but collision with them stimulated her, and she felt an interest that verged into liking, even for Charles. She desired to protect them, and often felt that they could protect her, excelling where she was deficient. Once past the rocks of emotion, they knew so well what to do, whom to send for; their hands were on all the ropes, they had grit as well as grittiness, and she valued grit enormously. . . . To Margaret this life was to remain a real force. She could not despise it, as Helen and

Tibby affected to do. It fostered such virtues as neatness, decision, and obedience, virtues of the second rank, no doubt, but they have formed our civilization. They form character, too; Margaret could not doubt it: they keep the soul from becoming sloppy. How dare Schlegels despise Wilcoxes, when it takes all sorts to make a world?[23]

In such a mood as this she writes to Helen, advising her not to brood on the superiority of the unseen to the seen, true though it might be. "Our business is not to contrast the two, but to reconcile them."[24]

With equal insight and sincerity she faces up to the problem posed by money, pre-eminently the outward and visible manifestation of the Wilcox world. The Schlegels have inherited money; and while Tibby takes his for granted as though it were somehow his due, neither Helen nor Margaret can do so. Once again Margaret's attitude is essentially practical, realistic and honest. The money is there, with all its advantages, but at least she will admit as much:

> "I'm tired of these rich people who pretend to be poor, and think it shows a nice mind to ignore the piles of money that keep their feet above the waves. I stand each year upon six hundred pounds, and Helen upon the same, and Tibby will stand upon eight, and as fast as our pounds crumble away into the sea they are renewed—from the sea, yes, from the sea. And all our thoughts are the thoughts of six-hundred-pounders, and all our speeches."[25]

That society is divided, scandalously, into rich and poor, and that something should be done about it, is fully recognised by both Margaret and Helen, and is vividly brought home to them by their involvement with the Basts. But while Helen reacts to the problem emotionally and impractically, it is Margaret who sees what can be done, and eventually does it. At the end of the book we find her quietly and unobtrusively preparing to give away one half of her income over a period of ten years.

Such practicality, with its recognition of the seen, of money as the "warp of the world", is very much a part of Margaret's character. On the other hand it enhances rather than detracts

[23] *H.E.*, p. 109.   [24] *Ibid.*   [25] *H.E.*, p. 64.

from her acknowledgement of the unseen and her conviction of its superiority. About the unseen itself she is certainly unspecific, concerned far less with its nature than with its manifestations within the visible world. As in previous novels, the claims and explanations made on behalf of the unseen by orthodox Christianity are somewhat discounted, especially by Margaret herself. Christmas may be a divine event for some but not for her; she is not a "Christian in the accepted sense", and does not believe that "God ever worked among us as a young artisan".[26] On the other hand we do find her concerning herself in tentative fashion with spiritual certainties of another kind, those offered by Theosophy—greatly to the distress of Henry Wilcox. Over lunch with him at Simpsons in the Strand, she refers frivolously to auras and astral planes and provokes him into serious interrogation:

> "Tell me, though, Miss Schlegel, do you really believe in the supernatural and all that?"
> "Too difficult a question. . . . Because, though I don't believe in auras, and think Theosophy's only a halfway-house—"
> "—Yet there may be something in it all the same " he concluded, with a frown.
> "Not even that. It may be halfway in the wrong direction. I can't explain. I don't believe in all these fads, and yet I don't like saying that I don't believe in them."
> He seemed unsatisfied, and said: "So you wouldn't give me your word that you *don't* hold with astral bodies and all the rest of it?"
> "I could," said Margaret, surprised that the point was of any importance to him. "Indeed, I will. When I talked about scrubbing my aura, I was only trying to be funny."[27]

The impression here of equivocation, indeed of a kind of spiritual dilettantism, is inescapable. Later however, when Henry and Margaret are on their honeymoon, we find Margaret still probing:

> "What a practical little woman it is! What's it been reading? Theo—theo—how much?"
> "Theosophy."[28]

---

[26] *H.E.*, p. 85.   [27] *H.E.*, p. 163.   [28] *H.E.*, p. 276.

And later still when, under the impact of tragedy, Margaret is led to speculate on the nature of immortality, the possibility of endless levels beyond the grave taught by the theory that Henry has censured, occurs to her.

Clearly the certitudes of Theosophy, its information in particular on the spiritual nature of man and his spiritual environment, are not being subscribed to more than tentatively by Margaret herself. Indeed they must take their place along with other manifestations of the occult, superstitions and so on, to which she finds herself attracted, but on which she cannot quite make up her mind.[29]

Far from positive about the occult, unable to formulate any definite beliefs on the nature of the unseen, Margaret is on firmer ground in the value she places on culture and personal relationships, in her realisation of their dependence on a spiritually sensitive inner life. In the matter of culture she is revealed at the beginning of the book as exposed to, and even intermittently subject to, the familiar dangers of intellectualism. Busily involved in the London world of Art and Thought, she could very well have succumbed to it altogether and become a sort of female Cecil Vyse. However her intrinsic common sense, her "continual and sincere response to all that she encountered in her path through life" provide the counterbalance she needs. Again and again, especially in her encounter with Mrs Wilcox, she is brought up short, made aware of values and horizons undreamed of by those for whom culture itself has become an end. When Mrs Wilcox takes a day in bed because "there is nothing in London to get up for", and when the tone and range of her voice suggest that "pictures, concerts, and people are all of small and equal value"[30] Margaret is unsympathetic, even shocked on culture's behalf. Then with uncharacteristic tactlessness she arranges the inappropriate little luncheon-party for Mrs Wilcox, and herself gets so carried away by the clever conversation of her friends as to lose sight of her excluded guest

---

[29] When Margaret is told by Mrs Wilcox of the pig's teeth embedded in the bark of the wych elm at Howards End, and of the healing power attributed to them, she declares, "I love folklore and all festering superstitions" (p. 75). She would be equally attracted no doubt to the "wild legend of immortality" associated with the atheist's grave in Tewin churchyard (p. 341).

[30] *H.E.*, p. 74.

altogether. Even here however, she is brought up short, made conscious of a personality in Mrs Wilcox that transcended those of herself and her friends, and "dwarfed their activities". And later, as Mrs Wilcox prepares to leave, and comments on the interesting life "you all lead in London", she experiences a complete revulsion.

Even so, she still remains caught up, committed, and when the moment comes for her to concentrate on house-hunting she finds that she cannot break loose from culture and has her time "wasted by concerts which it would be a sin to miss, and invitations which it would never do to refuse".[31] Through it all, however, persists her over-riding allegiance to life and to people, her recognition that culture must never be an end in itself, a justification—as in the case of her brother Tibby—for selfish withdrawal. Culture as a means to something further, both seen and unseen, has "worked in her case", as she justly claims; but it has worked because, as with books for example, she has been careful to use them rightly, as sign-posts; has not succumbed to the weakness of mistaking the sign-post for the destination. And so, not surprisingly, we find her as time passes, and especially after her marriage, becoming not less cultured, but cultured in a different way:

> As for theatres and discussion societies, they attracted her less and less. She began to "miss" new movements, and to spend her spare time re-reading or thinking, rather to the concern of her Chelsea friends. They attributed the change to her marriage, and perhaps some deep instinct did warn her not to travel further from her husband than was inevitable. Yet the main cause lay deeper still; she had outgrown stimulants, and was passing from words to things. It was doubtless a pity not to keep up with Wedekind or John, but some closing of the gates is inevitable after thirty, if the mind itself is to become a creative power.[32]

As with culture, so also in Margaret's view, with successful personal relationships—both would have to be the product of a spiritually sensitive inner life. From an early age she has recognised the closeness of any human being to the unseen and has sought for it in her approach to people. Many delightful

[31] *H.E.*, p. 159.   [32] *H.E.*, p. 276f.

relationships with individuals culturally oriented like herself duly became possible. As we have seen, however, a certain dissatisfaction with those early friends, a sense of their onesidedness, their commitment to only a part of life, has tended to gain on her. Theirs is a sensitivity to the unseen at the expense of the seen, and only those prepared to connect the two, harmonise them within themselves, are capable of friendship and of its final manifestation, love. As with the cultured, oversensitive to the unseen, so also inevitably with the uncultured, those like Henry Wilcox whose commitment to the seen at the expense of the unseen is virtually total. Engaged to him, Margaret accepts the challenge, does not at the outset anticipate undue difficulty. All she need do is point out to him the salvation latent within his soul, and in the soul of every man, and in due time and under sympathetic guidance he too may build the "rainbow bridge" connecting the prose in him with the passion, the unseen with the seen, and on its highest curve love will alight, "glowing against the grey, sober against the fire".[33] Initially she fails, defeated by Henry's obtuseness, his refusal to be bothered with his own inside, and she goes on failing until tragedy detonates—the tragedy of one who cannot connect until he is broken. Yet Henry's failure, and Margaret's failure with him, serve only to confirm the rightness of her theory: that a capacity for personal relationships belongs only to those capable of harmony. Without the "rainbow bridge" we are meaningless fragments,

> half monks, half beasts, unconnected arches that have never joined into a man. . . . Only connect the prose and the passion, and both will be exalted, and human love will be seen at its height. Live in fragments no longer. Only connect, and the beast and the monk, robbed of the isolation that is life to either, will die.[34]

A process of change then, of spiritual metamorphosis, is to be witnessed in the character of Margaret Schlegel, a change that has revealed itself in the gradual maturing of her attitude towards culture and in the field of personal relationships. Her sensitivity to the unseen and to its manifestations has remained

---

[33] *H.E.*, p. 196.   [34] *H.E.*, p. 196f.

constant, but has itself developed, become with time and experience ever less speculative; until at the book's end, when the headstone of retrospective realisation falls into place, all doubts, all merely speculative intuitions concerning the unseen, would seem to have merged themselves into certainty. With the actual nature of the unseen as conceived by Margaret we will deal later. But now a second representative from the side of culture and spiritual sensitivity, the one closest to Margaret herself, must concern us.

For the excess of her sensitivity to the unseen, her unyielding conviction that the "Invisible lodges against the Visible"[35] and that the former is superior to the latter, Helen Schlegel has already been taken to task by her sister, warned not to brood on the contrast between the two, but to attempt their reconciliation. But it is of the essence of Helen's character that she cannot do so, cannot connect, cannot reconcile, and her obtuse insistence on exalting the unseen at the expense of the seen is no less potentially tragic than the reverse obtuseness we find in Henry Wilcox. And yet so complete is our sympathy with Helen, our recognition of her intrinsic generosity of spirit, that when tragedy does in fact come, it is only with an effort and something of a shock that we find ourselves impelled to recognise the extent to which the destruction of the Basts and the breaking of the Wilcoxes must be laid at her door. With the utmost sympathy, but with ruthless impartiality nevertheless, the author continues to insist with Helen also, that one-sidedness, whether spiritual or material, is fatal. Helen Schlegel, quite literally as it turns out, is one of those who kill when they come to people.

As in the case of Margaret, Helen, though vague and imprecise as to the nature of the unseen and the mode of its operation, is convinced of its existence and of its supreme importance. For her the purely spiritual is the real. Unreality and mystery begin only with the body. Margaret, reflecting on this absoluteness, finds herself dismayed:

> All vistas close in the unseen—no one doubts it—but Helen closed them rather too quickly for her taste. At every turn of

---

[35] *H.E.*, p. 253.

speech one was confronted with reality and the absolute. Perhaps Margaret grew too old for metaphysics . . . but she felt that there was something a little unbalanced in the mind that so readily shreds the visible. The business man who assumes that this life is everything, and the mystic who asserts that it is nothing, fail, on this side and on that, to hit the truth.[36]

An imbalance then, an excessive commitment to the unseen, is to be looked for in Helen. Like Margaret, she too will approach the unseen intuitively, will dabble in the occult, in Theosophy and spiritualism and superstition, will display an excess of interest in the subconscious self.[37] She too will qualify for friendship only those in whom the inner life is oriented in some measure towards the invisible. But whereas Margaret, resolutely determined to give the outer life its due, can check and counterbalance the pull of the unseen, Helen, under the impact of events, will do nothing but surrender to it ever more one-sidedly.

The rejection of the outer life, already inherent in her nature, assumes finality for Helen through her involvement with the Wilcoxes. All the more so because, with characteristic impulsiveness, she had briefly and emotionally surrendered to the Wilcox creed. For one brief moment on her visit to Howards End the Wilcox family had appeared to her haloed with rightness and truth. When Mr Wilcox or Evie or Charles informed her that all the Schlegel fetishes, Equality, Votes for women, Socialism, were nonsense, Art and Literature more often than not nonsense, politeness to servants unnecessary, she had accepted and rejoiced, had felt herself swathed in cant and happy to be rid of it. A fleeting impulse of love for Paul Wilcox had duly resulted. Paul however has second thoughts and is frightened, and immediately the violent, the irreversible reaction sets in:

> "Somehow, when that kind of man looks frightened it is too awful. . . . When I saw all the others so placid, and Paul mad with terror in case I said the wrong thing, I felt for a moment that the whole Wilcox family was a fraud, just a wall of newspapers and motor-cars and golf-clubs, and that if it fell I should find nothing behind it but panic and emptiness."[38]

---

[36] *H.E.*, p. 205f.   [37] *H.E.*, p. 204.   [38] *H.E.*, p. 27.

This initial episode falls into the background, but for Helen the effect is final, not to be modified by time. Over against the outer Wilcox world of "telegrams and anger", is to be set permanently the inner Schlegel world of "personal relations", within which only those committed in some measure to the invisible can belong. Against the Wilcox world in all its manifestations, especially that of money, she is to continue relentlessly unyielding, the focus of her resentment shifting under the impact of events from Paul to his father. After the chance encounter on the Chelsea embankment, she can see no more in Henry Wilcox than a "prosperous vulgarian", and tacitly assumes that Margaret will agree. The same attitude, the same extreme assumption is with her later, on the Downs above Swanage; when Margaret whispers the news of Henry's proposal, she is simply amused:

> "It's just like a widower," she remarked. "They've cheek enough for anything, and invariably select one of their first wife's friends."[39]

And when the truth, of Margaret's seriousness, is brought home to her, she bursts into tears "Panic and emptiness", she sobs, "Don't!"[40]

Almost immediately it is revealed that Leonard Bast, the Schlegels' protégé, who has left his job for one less well paid on Henry Wilcox's casual advice, need not have done so, and her resentment and indignation against him and his world break into the open. From this point forward, the enemy, money and those who live for and by it, is clear in view. Earlier, in conversation with Henry, Margaret had attempted a definition of her sister's uncompromising point of view:

> "Helen daren't slang the rich, being rich herself, but she would like to. There's an odd notion, that I haven't yet got hold of, running about at the back of her brain, that poverty is some-how 'real'. She dislikes all organization, and probably confuses wealth with the technique of wealth. Sovereigns in a stocking wouldn't bother her; cheques do. Helen is too relentless. One can't deal in her high-handed manner with the world."[41]

---

[39] *H.E.*, p. 181.   [40] *H.E.*, p. 182.   [41] *H.E.*, p. 191.

The high-handedness however is to go on and to intensify—to reach its climax when Helen, "in her oldest clothes, and dominated by that tense, wounding excitement that had made her a terror in their nursery days",[42] brings the starving Basts into the middle of Evie's wedding.

After this climactic gesture Helen disappears, withdraws to the Continent. The reason (that she is pregnant) does not emerge until later, but Margaret, confronted with apparent eccentricity, reviews her sister's behaviour over the previous four years and finds it morbid:

> The flight from Oniton; the unbalanced patronage of the Basts; the explosion of grief up on the Downs—all connected with Paul, an insignificant boy whose lips had kissed hers for a fraction of time. . . . Reaction against the Wilcoxes had eaten into her life until she was scarcely sane. At twenty-five she had an idée fixe. What hope was there for her as an old woman?[43]

Inevitably such one-sidedness, such an unbalanced rejection of the world of appearances, has its effect in the area, most sacred to Helen, of personal relations. Indeed it is precisely here that the consequences of her failure to achieve a balance, to connect, are most destructive. Henry Wilcox because of some unlucky financial advice, and because of a world made in his image, is certainly in part to blame for the fate of the Basts. But it is Helen through sheer impracticality, sheer inattention to the details and processes of the visible world, who destroys them finally:

> The expedition to Shropshire crippled the Basts permanently. Helen in her flight forgot to settle the hotel bill, and took their return tickets away with her; they had to pawn Jacky's bangles to get home, and the smash came a few days afterwards.[44]

Even her later attempt to redeem disaster by a gift of five thousand pounds is characteristically unreal, an unbalanced gesture that takes no account of the fact that such a sum to such a man as Leonard Bast is without meaning. The money is politely refused, and Helen compelled to re-invest some shares she has already sold, becomes, thanks to the good advice of her stockbrokers, slightly richer than before.

[42] *H.E.*, p. 236f. [43] *H.E.*, p. 293. [44] *H.E.*, p. 335.

The final blow however, the death of Leonard, has yet to fall, and the extent of Helen's responsibility for this must also be recognised. Leonard is in the last stages of heart disease, but the immediate cause of death is the violence of Charles Wilcox directed against him as Helen's seducer. Leonard also thinks of himself as a seducer, and has come to Howards End to confess as much to Margaret. It becomes clear, however, from what Helen herself says, that the initiative had come from her. The impulsive gesture of atonement on her part at Oniton, of consolation, could have been justified if love had sanctified it, but in fact there had been no love, only the desire to make amends, to offer herself, as later she was to offer money, and have done with Leonard for ever. As she says to Margaret at Howards End:

> "I want never to see him again, though it sounds appalling. I wanted to give him money and feel finished. Oh, Meg, the little that is known about these things."[45]

To conclude, on the other hand, that Helen never, at any time, except within the context of her warfare with the Wilcoxes, cared for Leonard Bast, is certainly excessive. Yet the context, increasingly as time passed, was always there, and Helen's remorse at Oniton, her offer of herself and of money, measured the extent of her recognition that she had used the "Basts" impersonally, that for them as individuals she had had at best an incidental concern. She, in other words, who had always proclaimed the sanctity of personal relations, had in this instance betrayed them, failed to achieve the connexion whose issue is love.

The severity of the judgement on Helen, the penalty exacted for her one-sidedness—a man killed, another in prison, herself the mother of an illegitimate child—may seem disproportionate. And yet in terms of the author's essential theme the rightness, the inevitability of such consequences has to be accepted. Within the vital field of personal relations, no half measures, no allowance for good intentions, are to be expected. Either the unseen must harmonise with the seen and love be generated, or hate, the logical antithesis, with all its destructive potentiality

[45] *H.E.*, p. 330.

will take over. In absolute terms therefore, Helen is correctly judged. On the other hand, though there must be condemnation, the punishment of tragedy once exacted is taken no further than is strictly just. Helen brings down on herself the consequences of her own one-sidedness, but at least one aspect of that one-sidedness, an excessive and impulsive idealism, confers a redemptive, mitigating influence. Helen is one for whom the best is the enemy of the good, but at least an aspiration towards the best together with a genuine devotion to the unseen is at all times unwaveringly within her. Hitherto in the novels no more than an acknowledgement of the unseen in its benevolent aspect has been deemed sufficient for salvation, for the transfiguration of human life. Now however a one-sided and excessive preoccupation even with the right unseen is being recognised as potentially harmful. Dedication to such an unseen ensured for Helen many radiant qualities, not least her sensitivity to the arts. On the other hand it had also a limiting, an alienating effect, cutting her off to an ever-increasing degree from the fullness of life and from people. Impulsive, affectionate, a passionate believer in personal relations, she yet lacks the full capacity, the balance necessary for their achievement. It is Margaret, the less attractive of the two sisters, who meets the challenge of the personal, and so escapes from the world in which Helen remains, "where nothing happened except art and literature, and where no one ever got married or succeeded in remaining engaged".[46] Unable to compete adequately, to recognise all the factors involved in the human situation, Helen fails, involves herself and others in tragedy. Yet tragedy as always brings with it catharsis, and the Helen who has passed through it, precisely because she has come to doubt her ability to love, is clearly now capable of it, has indeed found it in her child. And the capacity has come through reconciliation, of the unseen with the seen, the inner with the outer, as manifested by her final surprised discovery that Henry Wilcox is no longer an enemy, that she likes him.

In defence of the Wilcoxes, their obvious defects and limitations, their single-minded preoccupation with the outer life of appearances, little more can be ventured than Margaret herself

[46] *H.E.*, p. 160.

has already been shown to allow. Indeed the temptation to
dismiss them all out of hand, to write off even Margaret's
attempt to come to terms with them as a conspicuous failure, is
hard to resist. Yet resist it we must. The Wilcox world of motor
cars and money, of efficiency and practicality and grit, is
dangerously inadequate, but on the other hand *Howards End*
itself is nothing less than a demonstration that we cannot do
without it, that somehow or other, through acknowledgement
rather than commitment, we must build it in. A house cannot
stand by bricks and mortar alone, but, as Mrs Wilcox pointed
out to Margaret's intellectual friends, "It cannot stand without
them." Schlegels may be superior to Wilcoxes in numberless
respects, yet the author himself reminds us that a world com-
posed entirely of Schlegels would be a "grey, bloodless place",
even though, "the world being what it is, perhaps they shine
out in it like stars".[47]

The Wilcox world therefore, and its representatives, demand our acknowledgement—an acknowledgement which, as
Margaret and Ruth Wilcox were both to discover, did not
exclude the possibility of personal love. It follows that we must
address ourselves with special care to the assessment of Henry
Wilcox, identifying on the one hand the obvious limitations, on
the other those qualities which in however slight a measure
might hint at the immaterial, and without which neither
Margaret nor Ruth Wilcox could have reacted towards him
with loyalty and love.

In relation to the unseen itself, as Margaret found in the
initial stages of their relationship, Henry Wilcox was resolutely
obtuse, either failing to notice it or ignoring it when he did.
Against Margaret's interest in the occult, in auras and astral
planes, he reacts with uneasy hostility, forcing her to admit, at
least for the time being, that she does not hold with such things.
The same uneasy hostility felt for the unseen itself, is extended
also towards its manifestations. The social and artistic ideals
of the Schlegels, spiritual in origin, are met by the Wilcoxes
with indifference or patronising contempt. With apparently
unassailable confidence they present their private and collective
fortress to a world made in their likeness and subject, as they

[47] *H.E.*, p. 29.

persuade themselves, to their own control. Although it is only the Schlegels who can actually perceive the fortress, and the need for it, who can recognise the spiritual vacuum of panic and emptiness against which it is an instinctive defence.

The blatant materialism of the Wilcoxes manifests itself inevitably in their thoughts and actions, their personal relations, the environment they create for themselves. Indifference to the arts expresses itself in tastelessness, in the tasteless interiors for example at Ducie Street and Hinton, in the outrage of the garage they attach to Howards End. Inability to connect, to weave the rainbow bridge for love between the seen and the unseen, reflects itself in an incapacity for genuine affection and so for friendship. Margaret who can bring herself to love Henry, soon finds out that his set of acquaintances promise to be another matter. He had no knack, she finds, for surroundng himself with nice people, being content to settle "one of the greatest things in life haphazard". Thus, while his investments generally went right, his friends went wrong:

> She would be told, "Oh, So-and-so's a good sort—a thundering good sort", and find, on meeting him, that he was a brute or a bore. If Henry had shown real affection, she would have understood, for affection explains everything. But he seemed without sentiment. The "thundering good sort" might at any moment become "a fellow for whom I never did have much use, and have less now", and be shaken off cheerily into oblivion. Margaret had done the same as a schoolgirl. Now she never forgot anyone for whom she had once cared; she connected, though the connection might be bitter, and she hoped that some day Henry would do the same.[48]

Henry, however, cannot connect, at any level, and his incapacity to do so, to think and act imaginatively at every point of crisis, is to reduce Margaret to eventual despair. She has tolerated, in part supported his rejection of the Basts, dismissed as none of her concern his infidelity to Ruth Wilcox, accepted, though sick at heart, his inhuman devising of a trap for Helen by luring her to Howards End. The sticking point, however, beyond which compromise, the sacrifice of her own integrity cannot be permitted, has to come. Helen who has

[48] *H.E.*, p. 219f.

sinned, just as Henry himself has sinned, requests her one night of refuge at Howards End and is promptly refused permission. With his failure to see the connexion—"You have had a mistress —I forgave you. My sister has a lover—you drive her from the house"—he passes beyond hope, beyond forgiveness, and Margaret's decision is taken, she must leave him. Perhaps if she had known more of his spiritual insensitivity, especially to Ruth Wilcox—his rejection of the dying woman's request for Howards End, his callous thwarting of her desire to die there and not in a nursing-home—she might have left him sooner.

Yet we have still to account for Margaret's indulgence towards Henry Wilcox, her ability to love and marry him. Already we have noted her awareness of redeeming qualities actual or latent within him, her sense of a spiritual potentiality to which she felt she could appeal. Henry, though always formidable, was also likeable, a thoughtful and generous host, possessed for all his deficiencies of an "imperishable charm". His is a nature, moreover, not without nobility. When, for example, the bitterness of the Wilcoxes, assembled to consider their mother's request for the disposal of Howards End, directs itself spitefully against Margaret, Henry Wilcox will have none of it. Margaret, he insists, was not in collusion with the matron of the nursing-home, knew nothing of Ruth Wilcox's bequest, had every right to attend the funeral. The Wilcoxes at their worst, suspicious, grasping, stupid, are exemplified in Charles who can feel for the Schlegels and all that they represent only an uncomprehending and eventually savage hatred. Indeed Henry's finer qualities, his potentiality as a human being, become more apparent to us by our recognition of their very non-existence in his elder son. Even so, it is not easy to make out a case for Henry Wilcox, to rest content with the book's concluding slight indications that tragedy, by breaking him, has effected a significant and salutary change. Certainly he has altered, is not so much ill as "eternally tired", and as Margaret explains:

> "He has worked very hard all his life, and noticed nothing. Those are the people who collapse when they do notice a thing."[49]

---

49 *H.E.*, p. 355.

Perhaps we are to assume that, however late and tragically, Henry has at last "connected", and from now on the spiritual latencies, working their way in some measure to the surface, will lead him in the direction of love. Perhaps there is just enough in this to vindicate Margaret's persistent hopefulness, her recognition of that in Henry Wilcox to which Ruth Wilcox also had been able to respond. That Ruth Wilcox had married Henry at a time of financial crisis, to save her beloved Howards End, is admitted, and that he had saved it for her, without either fine feelings or deep insight, we are also told. But from what we know of Ruth Wilcox, we cannot suppose that hers was a marriage of convenience, a calculated means to a noble end. She too must have sensed in Henry Wilcox at least a potentiality which Margaret in her turn is to recognise and love.

Of the remaining Wilcoxes, Charles, Paul, and Evie, and by marriage, Dolly, it is enough to say that, with fairness and insight, their many defects and few redeeming qualities are subtly and comprehensively made clear. Charles, whose spiritual incapacity expresses itself in hatred, envy and eventual violence, is the Wilcox extremist, unattractive, almost repellent. Two years in prison, we cannot but feel, is no more than he deserves. Yet even Charles, with scrupulous fairness, is accorded his single moment of redeeming insight, his instinctive, fleeting recognition of the significance of Howards End. When Henry Wilcox is about to use the house as a trap for Helen, Charles blunders in with a protest: "Pater, we may as well keep Howards End out of it." He cannot explain himself, and incurs his father's anger; but Margaret feels as if, "over tremendous distance, a salutation had passed between them".[50]

Over against Charles, the Wilcox extremist, must now be set an extremist of a very different kind, Tibby Schlegel. Tibby, though humorously and delightfully presented, is in cold reality anything but a delightful young man. Unlike his sisters, he accepts the privileges of his position, especially that of money, without a qualm. Self-indulgent and *difficile*, he is concerned with the visible world only in so far as it ministers to his private artistic and intellectual interests. Over the years, passing from

[50] *H.E.*, p. 300.

the school that he tolerates to an Oxford which exactly suits
him, he matures slightly, though not to the extent of overcoming
the most serious product of his one-sidedness, his lack of interest
in people. "Just as some people cease to attend when books are
mentioned, so Tibby's attention wandered when 'personal
relations' came under discussion."[51] Even so, as the author
concedes, there are worse lives. Tibby, for all his limitations, is
possessed of a character and a brain, and though selfish and
affected in manner is neither cruel nor insincere. In particular
his interest in the arts, though coldly intellectual and so
uncreative, is genuine. Left to his own impersonal pursuits,
Tibby would have continued to harm no one but himself;
Helen, however, breaking in upon his Oxford isolation and
confiding in him about the Basts, forces him despite himself into
involvement with the personal. The negotiations on behalf of
the Basts he carries out competently enough, but the test that is
to reveal his incapacity is yet to come—significantly enough
through his encounter with the Wilcox extremist, Charles.
The interview between them takes place at Ducie Street where
Tibby's delicate intonations are no match for the bullying
impertinence of Charles. Almost before he can realise it, he has
named Leonard Bast as his sister's seducer:

> Without intending it, he had betrayed [her] confidence; he
> was not enough interested in human life to see where things
> will lead to. He had a strong regard for honesty, and his word,
> once given, had always been kept up to now. He was deeply
> vexed, not only for the harm he had done Helen, but for the
> flaw he had discovered in his own equipment.[52]

And of course his indiscretion is to prove lethal. For Leonard's
arrival at Howards End and the calling out of his name is
Charles's cue to assault him and cause his immediate death.
Also it should be recalled that, even before his interview with
Charles at Ducie Street, Tibby, had he so wished, could have
made contact with Leonard; and had he done so might well
have hesitated to disclose Margaret's whereabouts. Tibby,
however, is asleep, after a good lunch, and when the parlour-

---

[51] *H.E.*, p. 268.   [52] *H.E.*, p. 328.

maid announces an unknown caller and offers to ask who it is, he tells her not to bother. So Leonard, a victim to Tibby's self-indulgent indifference to people, is directed to Howards End.

The flaw in Tibby's character, discovered too late, is the flaw once again of one who has come to conceive of culture as an end in itself, in isolation from its dual relationship to both the unseen and the seen. Unlike Helen, with her excessive devotion to the unseen at the expense of a seen which she identifies with the Wilcoxes, Tibby would insist on committing himself in neither direction. Art itself, divorced from its human significance, is what concerns him—art reduced inevitably to considerations of technique. It is significant at the performance of Beethoven's Fifth Symphony that Tibby, who is profoundly versed in counterpoint, follows the music with the score; and that Margaret finds herself so enraged by his determination to treat music as music, that she dare not even argue with him. Tibby, though intelligent, humorous and decent, a warmer, straighter character than, for example, Cecil Vyse (whom, incidentally, he names and professes to admire) is nevertheless one more in the series of flawed intellectuals, disdainful of the seen and yet uncommitted, except in theory, to the unseen. The recognition of the flaw in his own equipment comes too late to save him from contributing to the tragedy of Leonard Bast, from killing when he comes to people. Even so, and though we are told nothing, it is perhaps legitimate to speculate on the impact of that tragedy on Tibby's later development.

One more important character, poised like Tibby somewhere between the unseen and the seen, though with aspirations in both directions, remains for consideration—Leonard Bast. Leonard, an under-privileged young man, degraded by his marriage, encounters the Schlegels by chance at a concert, where Helen, leaving early, walks off with his umbrella. The umbrella restored, in humiliating fashion, he vanishes into the impersonal greyness of London, presumably never again to re-emerge. Leonard, though pathetic and perhaps deserving of a better fate, is obviously no concern of the Schlegels, is not even of their class. However, the Basts, like the Wilcoxes, do not drop out of sight because they are expected to do so, and, after an interval, first the wife, Jackie, and then Leonard are back at Wickham Place. Jackie, disturbed by Leonard's sudden disappearance, and finding the card which Margaret had given him, comes calling. In due course Leonard too must make his appearance to explain the call. The explanation he gives of his prolonged absence from home—he had tried to "get back to nature" by taking a walk into the country by night—appeals to the imagination of Helen and Margaret, but when it is over and Leonard has vanished for the second time, again it would appear that the Schlegels have seen the last of him. However, the sisters go out to their discussion society, and after it on the Chelsea Embankment are re-united with Henry Wilcox, whose opinion on the Bast problem they proceed to invite. His contribution, on learning the name of the insurance firm for which Leonard works, is that he should clear out of it with all possible speed as it will smash by Christmas. Inevitably, the sisters decide that Leonard must be warned, and at Helen's suggestion invite him to tea. The visit is a failure, in fact ends in a vulgar scene; nevertheless Leonard heeds the warning he has been given and later, in a letter to Helen, writes that he has indeed left his job at the insurance company for another, at a reduced salary, in a bank. Henry is on hand to be informed of this, and promptly drops his casual thunderbolt—that the insurance company in question, having weathered its financial crisis, is no longer a bad concern and Leonard need never have left it. This revelation and Henry's obtuse refusal to admit any kind of responsibility, violently antagonise Helen, for whom, from now on, the Basts are to become an obsession, an integral element in her indictment of the entire Wilcox world. Leonard loses his job at the bank, and Helen swoops to the rescue, snatches up him and his bewildered Jackie to confront Henry at Oniton and force from him an offer of employment. Persuaded by Margaret, Henry agrees, until he recognises in Jackie a woman who had been his mistress ten years before. Defeated, the Basts again vanish, and though Helen must bear Leonard's child, even she cannot but hope and suppose that the whole tragic involvement has at last worked itself out. However, all that has happened so far, from the lost umbrella at the concert to the climax of remorse at Oniton, is but a prelude, a preparation for the tragic fulfilment to come. To understand that fulfilment and the necessity that preceded it, the obstinate involvement despite themselves of Schlegels and Wilcoxes and Basts, it becomes necessary to pass from events to people, in particular to a consideration of Leonard personally, of that force, that inner potentiality which is to lead him, all unaware of what is really happening, to his death at Howards End.

After the concert and the humiliation of the lost umbrella, we follow Leonard into the genteel squalor of his home, and make the discovery that he is anything but commonplace, that his aspirations to culture though pathetic and misguided are genuine, that the deplorable Jackie is a fate he might well have been spared. The impulse underlying the aspirations, the cause of the discontent within him, is not immediately suggested; however, the first hint of an explanation comes with his re-appearance at Wickham Place to clear up the mystery of Jackie's call. Margaret, who has forgotten the umbrella episode and fails to recognise the young man before her, sees him nevertheless, with his mournful eyes and drooping moustache, as a typical Londoner:

> One guessed him as the third generation, grandson to the shepherd or ploughboy whom civilization had sucked into the town; as one of the thousands who have lost the life of the body and failed to reach the life of the spirit. Hints of robustness survived in him, more than a hint of primitive good looks, and Margaret, noting the spine that might have been straight, and the chest that might have broadened, wondered whether it paid to give up the glory of the animal for a tail coat and a couple of ideas.[53]

Leonard, however, combating his own sterility by aspiring to culture, would not have agreed with her. For the primitive natural man, separated from him by no more than a generation, he has now nothing consciously but contempt. Only with shame can he be brought to admit that his grandparents, from around Oniton in Shropshire, were agricultural labourers, or, as he puts it, "just nothing at all".[54] Even so the ancient sustaining past, the instinctive mysticism of the English soil, to which so

---

[53] *H.E.*, p. 121f. [54] *H.E.*, p. 250.

much was attributed in *The Longest Journey*, is not yet quite dead in him, can manifest itself in strange impulses to which, all uncomprehending, he has to respond. The outcome of one such impulse, his walk at night into the country south of London, he describes to Margaret and Helen in a manner alternately affected and movingly direct. The affectation is all cultural, the directness, although he cannot realise it, his own. In terms of books and their authors—Meredith, Stevenson, Jefferies, E. V. Lucas—he seeks affectedly to explain himself, to justify the oddity of his impulse to "get back to the Earth". But Helen asks him if the dawn on his walk was wonderful, and Leonard reaches back despite himself to his own essence and is transformed:

> With unforgettable sincerity he replied, "No." The word flew again like a pebble from the sling. Down toppled all that had seemed ignoble or literary in his talk, down toppled tiresome R. L. S. and the "love of the earth" and his silk top-hat. In the presence of these women Leonard had arrived, and he spoke with a flow, an exultation, that he had seldom known.[55]

Culture, the aspiration to a culture that he is destined never to attain, reasserts itself and Leonard's outburst of sincerity ends in a swamp of books. Fleetingly however, and precisely because he does not realise it, he has found himself:

> He had visited the county of Surrey when darkness covered its amenities, and its cosy villas had re-entered ancient night. Every twelve hours this miracle happens, but he had troubled to go and see for himself. Within his cramped little mind dwelt something that was greater than Jefferies' books—the spirit that led Jefferies to write them; and his dawn, though revealing nothing but monotones, was part of the eternal sunrise that shows George Borrow Stonehenge.[56]

Leonard Bast, driven by the inroads of urban sterility to attempt culture, is destined to fail. The ever-widening gulf between the natural and the philosophic man is to prove, in his case, uncrossable. Adverse events also, the brutal impact of the Wilcox world, are to contribute to his destruction. At Oniton,

[55] *H.E.*, p. 126. [56] *H.E.*, p. 127.

a despairing and remorseful Helen, tries to recall him to his essential self, to an admission at least of life's beauty and significance—music, walking at night—but he, on the brink of destitution, resists her:

> "Walking is well enough when a man's in work," he answered. "Oh, I did talk a lot of nonsense once, but there's nothing like a bailiff in the house to drive it out of you. When I saw him fingering my Ruskins and Stevensons, I seemed to see life straight real, and it isn't a pretty sight. My books are back again, thanks to you, but they'll never be the same to me again, and I shan't ever again think night in the woods is wonderful."[57]

Under the brutal impact of events, Leonard deteriorates, accepting and eventually demanding money from his relatives, losing his desire for work. However, he remains alive and honest with himself in relation to the past, and the horror of his last days is also alleviated by a new-found tenderness for Jackie. To the last, he is never negligible, redeemed by a still faintly continuing core of spiritual integrity, for which, without being able to realise it, he has his ancestors to thank. His final pilgrimage is to Howards End, a place and an environment within which the ancient earthbound communion with the unseen, still survives, however precariously. Leonard dies, destroyed by London and by his own failure to achieve the cultural substitute for the spirituality he has lost; but his death is also a sacrifice. His son by Helen, soon to be born, will become the inheritor after Margaret of Howards End.

With Leonard Bast, this somewhat extended study of the characters in *Howards End*, the assessment of them in relation to the seen and the unseen, is concluded. The seen, perhaps a little one-sidedly, has tended to be identified with the Wilcoxes and with the environment made in their image, London. The unseen on the other hand, apart from its manifestations through culture, has been associated with Howards End. The nature of that unseen, as revealed through the book's characters, and directly by the author himself, must now be more specifically indicated. As has been noted already, Howards End is pre-

[57] *H.E.*, p. 251.

sented to us as a special locality, a kind of mystery centre presided over, in life and after it, by Ruth Wilcox.[58] Though threatened by urban encroachment, it has managed to preserve itself, to retain at least something of its former beauty and spiritual significance. Howards End, it must be remembered, was once a farm. The other farms surrounding it, Avery's and Sishe's, have fallen in and become residential, bought up by a City magnate who made his pile in copper. Only Howards End, unsentimentally saved by Henry Wilcox, has retained its shrunken identity, its link down the generations with the ancient agricultural past of England. This is the past worshipped by Ruth Wilcox, the source of her aristocratic wisdom, the abiding place of her ancestors from whom that wisdom comes. That the author, once again, as in *The Longest Journey*, is identifying himself also with the past, insisting upon it as the one true means to the spiritual salvation of England, is suggested so undogmatically in *Howards End* that we may almost overlook it, even suppose that we are being invited to perceive in some sort of harmony between Schlegels and Wilcoxes the eventual English hope. Unequivocally however, the author states otherwise. When Leonard Bast on his fateful journey to Howards End passes through the countryside, it is noted that here men have been up and working since dawn:

> Their hours were ruled, not by a London office, but by the movements of the crops and the sun. That they were men of the finest type only the sentimentalist can declare. But they kept to the life of daylight. They are England's hope. Clumsily they carry forward the torch of the sun, until such time as the nation sees fit to take it up. Half clodhopper, half board-school prig, they can still throw back to a nobler stock, and breed yeomen.[59]

Meanwhile the best that even the best of the Schlegels are good for, is to hold the line. Howards End and all that it signifies has been saved for the moment and provided with a

---

[58] The exceptional fertility of the soil at Howards End should be noted. It is observed by Margaret on the occasion of her first visit (p. 211). The mystic response of the soil is apparent at the end of the book when Helen exclaims that there will be "such a crop of hay as never!" (p. 362).

[59] *H.E.*, p. 341f.

spiritual heir, but only eight or nine meadows lie between it and a "red rust", the creeping inroad of London. And London, as Helen realises, is only a part of something else, of the melting down of life all over the world. Howards End and such localities as Oniton, the Purbeck Downs, the Oderberge are all survivals, logically unqualified to exist. Only in the weakness of logic can any hope for them and through them for the future be found. They represent the earth itself patiently waiting, beating time:

> "Because a thing is going strong now, it need not go on for ever" [says Margaret]. "This craze for motion has only set in during the last hundred years. It may be followed by a civilization that won't be a movement, because it will rest on the earth. All the signs are against it now, but I can't help hoping, and very early in the morning in the garden I feel that our house is the future as well as the past."[60]

Howards End, survival of an earth-oriented past, is also the future, the destination to which England itself must eventually return. The Wilcoxes, only superficially attached to the place, would certainly sooner or later have abandoned it, allowed the creeping urban rust to sweep it away. From this fate Margaret mediating between Wilcox and Schlegel, between unseen and seen, delivers it, and is to this extent a rightful heir. It is made clear however that the future of Howards End belongs elsewhere, that even Schlegels are no more than stars in the contemporary greyness, spiritual preservers and caretakers until the civilisation of movement shall come to rest.[61] Undoubtedly a truer heir will be Helen's child, separated by only one lost generation from the redeeming soil. That neither Schlegels nor Wilcoxes are fitted to provide an appropriate heir is also stressed by the fact that Margaret and Henry are childless and likely to remain so. Indeed, Margaret admits to Helen that she does not love children, and is "thankful to have none".[62]

[60] *H.E.*, p. 359.

[61] The possibility that, in the author's view at the time (1910), the civilisation of movement and expansion might already be slowing down, is suggested in the casual exchange between Leonard Bast and his neighbour, Mr Cunningham, who has been reading in the paper of a decline in the Manchester birth-rate. If this goes on, he says, "the population of England will be stationary in 1960" (p. 50).

[62] *H.E.*, p. 357.

Howards End then—the conclusion is inescapable—takes us no further spiritually than its predecessor, *The Longest Journey*. Once again the English yeoman imbued with nature's instinctive wisdom, is made the sole representative of hope. He is the competent receiver waiting to resume his interrupted heritage, when the eventual and inevitable bankruptcy of cosmopolitan civilisation has been declared. The interim, the period of greyness, of beating time, will belong for better or worse to the Schlegels and Wilcoxes.   Self-conscious, cut off from the instinctive wisdom of the past, they must proceed consciously, poised between seen and unseen and partaking of both. Caught up in the perpetual flux of which London is but a foretaste, they can depend only on each other, on personal relations which, in consequence, will come under greater stress than ever before. As Margaret realises,

> Under cosmopolitanism . . . we shall receive no help from the earth.   Trees and meadows and mountains will only be a spectacle, and the binding force that they once exercised on character must be entrusted to Love alone. May Love be equal to the task![63]

In Margaret's case Love succeeds, and the destruction worked by the seen and the unseen operating in isolation from each other, though not avoided, is at least finally contained. Here is a victory based on conscious insight and self-awareness, but we may not conclude from this that self-consciousness as such, so often the source of the wrong sort of intellectualism, has ceased to be condemned.   Helen in conversation with Leonard Bast at Oniton brings forth her remarkable theory of the two kinds of people, those who possess and those who lack the capacity to say "I".   The "I" sayers are the enlightened, their opposites those from whose heads "the little thing that says 'I' " is missing.[64]   Among the latter are the Wilcoxes, Pierpoint Morgan, Napoleon—the "wanters" and the destroyers.   The theory is convincing, one of the most interesting and far-reaching to be found in the whole of *Howards End,* and the author would appear to endorse it.   If he does so however, it can be only in passing.   For to say "I" is to become self-

[63] *H.E.,* p. 275.   [64] *H.E.,* p. 247.

conscious, indeed to have achieved a position of self-awareness from which thereafter there can be no retreat. Yet retreat is what Margaret Schlegel and the author through her, come finally to demand, a retreat from self-conscious to instinctive living, from conscious cosmopolitanism back to the pre-conscious earth-bound past. In *Howards End* that past, though unobtrusive, is a continuing presence, conveyed to us through Mrs Wilcox's sensitivity to her ancestors, through passing references to Stonehenge and to such surviving memorials as the ruined castle at Oniton and the Six Hills near Hinton, those tombs of ancient warriors, in whose presence Margaret is to learn from Henry that the Wilcoxes have been broken, that there will be a verdict of manslaughter against Charles.

Spiritually, then, there is no change, no progress beyond the English unseen already suggested to us in *The Longest Journey*, beyond those, like Stephen Wonham, cradled subconsciously within it and constituting in consequence England's only hope. Even Mrs Wilcox, it should be remembered, is a very simple, unintellectual woman, living in instinctive rather than conscious communion with the past. On the other hand in *Howards End* the nature of the unseen itself and the mode of its impact on life and people is rather more specifically indicated. Margaret, for example, is very conscious of the existence of a spiritual world, and, somewhat haphazardly, seeks to inform herself about it through a study of Theosophy. The certitudes of Theosophy, the information it claims to offer on the spiritual nature of man and his spiritual environment, are initially dismissed by Margaret on Henry's insistence; but, as we have noted, she continues to study the subject, and at Howards End, in the turmoil and horror succeeding the death of Leonard Bast, it is to the findings of Theosophy in support of her own concept of immortality that her mind returns:

> Margaret believed in immortality for herself. An eternal future had always seemed natural to her. And Henry believed in it for himself. Yet, would they meet again? Are there not rather endless levels beyond the grave, as the theory he had censured teaches? And his level, whether higher or lower, could it possibly be the same as hers?[65]

---

[65] *H.E.*, p. 351.

Convinced at one moment of the soul's survival after death, and even of a process of communion between the living and the dead: able to conceive of all those involved with the dead Mrs Wilcox as fragments of her mind, Margaret can yet contradict herself, speculate that there may in fact be nothing beyond death, or at most individuals differing in their nothingness. And yet in final retrospect, when the headstone fits into the corner and she hears of Mrs Wilcox's disregarded intention that she should inherit Howards End—then it would seem that all previous doubts and reservations had been silenced. In a single moment of insight and intuition, the impact of the unseen as a literal fact has revealed itself to her.

At no point, in so many words, does the author commit himself, unequivocally stating that the unseen exists and that from out of it the dead continue to manifest, influencing and even intervening in the conduct of human affairs. Yet the implications of such an intervention, at all events by Ruth Wilcox, are clearly there, and attention has been drawn to them. To her had to be attributed, at least in some measure, the persistent involvement despite themselves of Schlegels and Wilcoxes, in particular through the far-fetched "co-incidence" of the meeting on the Chelsea Embankment. In her presence, an ever-welcome ghost surveying the scene without a hint of bitterness, Henry proposes to Margaret. Meanwhile there has also been for both Schlegels and Wilcoxes a perpetually frustrating search for a house to live in, and parallel with it a persistently tenantless Howards End, presided over and eventually prepared for occupancy through the medium of the Schlegels' own furniture by the prophetic Miss Avery. At the same time, and despite all likelihood, the Schlegels have become involved with the Basts, events set in train that are to assume the looming proportions of impending tragedy in a remote village in the marches of Wales. Oniton is nothing to the Wilcoxes, and for Margaret no more than another false start in her quest for a home. On the other hand it does have meaning for Leonard Bast, who meets the crisis of his life in an environment, as he points out to Helen, where his grandparents had lived and worked the land. Nor should we now fail to notice the connexion at this juncture between Ruth Wilcox and the luckless Jackie—Henry's mistress, as it turns out, ten years before. Margaret at all events makes the connexion, and while forgiving Henry herself, sees that Mrs Wilcox, "that unquiet yet kindly ghost",[66] must be left to her own wrong. It is as though at Oniton, Ruth Wilcox and the ancestors of Leonard are drawn together in a wise severity to superintend, if not actually to secure, the catharsis through tragedy that has now to come.

The tragedy happens. Leonard is killed, Charles imprisoned, the Wilcoxes broken—all, so it would seem, that Howards End in its full significance might be saved for the present and preserved at least some way into the future through Leonard's and Helen's child. All this happens; for all of it the spirit of Ruth Wilcox must be held in part at least responsible. Yet the temptation to oversimplify, to conceive of all those caught up in the march of events as puppets, invisibly manipulated, must be resisted. At no point in *Howards End* do any of the characters cease to be themselves, to think and act in terms of their own strengths and weaknesses. From first to last, they are the architects of their own salvation or destruction, free at every vital turning-point to decide and choose. For character itself, as the author demonstrates through Margaret and Helen and even Henry, has nothing fixed or irreversible about it, is always undergoing, through the experience of life itself, a process of change. The change for Helen and Leonard Bast, for Henry and Charles and Tibby comes too slowly to keep pace with events, until tragedy is no longer avoidable. But right to the last an upward turn, a break in the linkage of events, remained possible. If Tibby at Ducie Street had managed to bestir himself, to overcome for a moment his indifference to people, at least to the point of enquiring the name of the visitor at the door, Leonard Bast would certainly not have been directed at his instigation to Howards End. Even so, and when all is said, we are left with a residue of that which cannot be explained in terms of personal character. Nothing in the character of Margaret, for example, accounts for her far-fetched yet essential meeting with Henry Wilcox on the Chelsea Embankment. Nothing sufficiently personal explains the

[66] *H.E.*, p. 257.

chronic inability of Schlegels and Wilcoxes to find themselves a house, or the no less persistent availability of Howards End. The author, had he chosen to do so, might well have left it at that, postulating or implying the blind workings of coincidence or chance. But this he does not do. Much that happens in *Howards End* is initiated and controlled by the individuals concerned, acting as they do because they are what they are. Clearly, however, we are also being required to accept that they are not entirely free, that to some extent and by an invisible agency outside themselves they are indeed being manipulated.

That the intervention of the unseen through the agency of the dead culminates in *Howards End* in tragedy, is perhaps disturbing, sufficient to call in question the benevolence of the forces involved. Tragedy, however, is clearly presented to us, not in terms of vengeance or punishment, but as a means to a further end, a spiritual fulfilment which, even those who must suffer for it, have only to understand to approve. That some of them, the imprisoned Charles for example, may never understand, at least in life, is possible. But for the rest, as the concluding pages of the book make clear, truer relationships and hope, on this side of the grave, have become possible. The Wilcoxes and even the Schlegels to a lesser degree, had been broken, and Leonard Bast had died that the future of Howards End might be assured, but that future is also theirs and England's. In retrospect, as Margaret realises, nothing has been done wrong. The special powers of Ruth Wilcox, operative in death as in life and radiating out from the mystery centre that is Howards End, have done no more than demonstrate that tragedy though a necessary part of life is not its essence, but in fact just one more manifestation of the unshakeable benevolence of the unseen. The author himself, in his observations on the dangerousness of life, implies as much specifically:

> Life is indeed dangerous, but not in the way morality would have us believe. It is indeed unmanageable, but the essence of it is not a battle. It is unmanageable because it is a romance, and its essence is romantic beauty.[67]

---

[67] *H.E.*, p. 113.

The concept of a spiritual world intervening, at all events with ultimate benevolence, in human affairs is thus present in *Howards End*. On the other hand the possibility of the unseen as a source of darkness, of malevolence is also once again, as in the three preceding novels, suggestively introduced; in a new form, however, and more insidiously—in fact with the suggestion, never quite contradicted, that splendour and heroism, indeed all that lends point and purpose to human endeavour, does not exist.

This suggestion, first hinted at in Helen's intuition of the panic and emptiness underlying the Wilcox world, is extended and reinforced for her when she listens to a performance of Beethoven's Fifth Symphony. The significant passage in the music comes at the beginning of the third movement, when, for Helen, the "goblins" appear:

> The music started with a goblin walking quietly over the universe, from end to end. Others followed him. They were not aggressive creatures; it was that that made them so terrible to Helen. They merely observed in passing that there was no such thing as splendour or heroism in the world.[68]

After an interlude they return and make the observation for the second time:

> Helen could not contradict them, for, once at all events, she had felt the same, and had seen the reliable walls of youth collapse. Panic and emptiness! Panic and emptiness! The goblins were right.[69]

The transitional passage to the final movement comes, and Beethoven, as if things were going too far, takes his goblins and makes them do his bidding:

> He appeared in person. He gave them a little push, and they began to walk in major key instead of in a minor, and then—he blew with his mouth and they were scattered! Gusts of splendour, gods and demi-gods contending with vast swords, colour and fragrance broadcast on the field of battle, magnificent victory, magnificent death! Oh, it all burst before the girl, and she even stretched out her gloved hands as if it was tangible.

[68] *H.E.*, p. 34. [69] *H.E.*, p. 34f.

> Any fate was titanic; any contest desirable; conqueror and conquered would alike be applauded by the angels of the utmost stars.[70]

Up to this point Helen Schlegel has been speaking to us, but now, in a series of direct questions to which he supplies answers, the author himself steps into the picture. The goblins, he asks, had they been there at all, or were they but the phantoms of cowardice and unbelief that one healthy human impulse would serve to dispel? And the answer follows. Men like the Wilcoxes or President Roosevelt might say yes, but Beethoven knew better:

> The goblins really had been there. They might return—and they did. It was as if the splendour of life might boil over and waste to steam and froth. In its dissolution one heard the terrible, ominous note, and a goblin, with increased malignity, walked quietly over the universe from end to end. Panic and emptiness! Panic and emptiness! Even the flaming ramparts of the world might fall.[71]

Beethoven, however—and again it is the author addressing us—chooses to make all right in the end:

> He built the ramparts up. He blew with his mouth for the second time, and again the goblins were scattered. He brought back the gusts of splendour, the heroism, the youth, the magnificence of life and of death, and, amid vast roarings of a superhuman joy, he led his Fifth Symphony to its conclusion. But the goblins were there. They could return. He had said so bravely, and that is why one can trust Beethoven when he says other things.[72]

Whether or not, here or anywhere else in his music, Beethoven is really saying as much, proclaiming the paradox attributed to him by the author and Helen Schlegel, is perhaps debatable. That the author himself accepts the paradox, indeed comes to rest within it, cannot be disputed. The goblins, though malignant, are really there, and courage consists in accepting not repudiating them. They are there, and they are

[70] *H.E.*, p. 35.   [71] *Ibid.*   [72] *H.E.*, p. 35f.

right.[73] The universe, according to the author's interpretation of Beethoven, is thus at one and the same time replete with significance and without any significance at all.

The paradox, which is to return in force in the author's final novel, is scarcely tenable; nevertheless, as an insidious note of ultimate qualification, it is allowed to echo on through the whole of *Howards End*. Like Beethoven, Forster chooses to make all right in the end, resolving the Schlegel-Wilcox discord, connecting the seen with the unseen in final harmony, proclaiming the purpose and meaning of life. But still we are to be denied final certainty. The unseen exists and our idealism depends on it. On the other hand the unseen is also conceived of as invalidating that idealism.

A reserve of intractable pessimism thus beclouds the concluding radiance of *Howards End*. The unseen, manifesting through the spirit of Mrs Wilcox, triumphs; on the other hand there may have been no triumph, no more than a pointless gesture in a void. Even so, and pessimism notwithstanding, we have once again been called to witness a process of spiritual salvation and the means by which it has been attained. Once again, as in *The Longest Journey*, those in quest of salvation have been required to dispense with foreign influences, to find or lose themselves solely on English ground. And again the spirit of the past, the ancient mysticism of the English soil has been identified as the finally disposing factor. Ultimately, and in relation to England's hope, *Howards End* is still uncompromising, a repetition of the absolute insistence of *The Longest Journey* that all those divorced from nature and committed to self-consciousness are irreversibly on the road to spiritual sterility. The Schlegels, and especially Margaret, are among the saved finally, but only to the extent that they have been brought to identify themselves with Howards End, to recognise it as the tenuous connecting link between the past and future of England. Involved despite themselves in the urban and the intellectual,

---

[73] The suggestion that the function of the goblins is to keep the splendour of life from boiling over and wasting to steam and froth, is echoed in a later observation that "again and again must the drums tap and the goblins stalk over the universe before joy can be purged of the superficial" (p. 342). But the goblins do more than purge away the excesses of splendour and joy; they state, as a fact with which Forster agrees, that splendour and joy are meaningless, non-existent.

they connect the seen with the unseen, avoid the sterility that waits on those who identify exclusively with one or the other. Their achievement is considerable, but finally inadequate. At best it qualifies them to be drawn into the spiritual orbit of Howards End, to provide it with an appropriate heir, to withstand the continuing threats to its survival.

Even so, and up to a point, the Schlegels, Margaret in particular, must be numbered among the saved. In this connexion, however, a factor of some significance must finally be taken into account, namely that they are not wholly English, that their father and in consequence many of their relatives are German. A foreign, a German influence is thus very much involved as a contributing factor to that all important sensitivity of theirs to the unseen. Their father, a man of unshakeable principle, had naturalised himself in England in protest against and in flight from the imperialism and materialism of his own country. The mild intellectual light, the imagination of the German past has vanished, gone with the little courts of Esterhaz and Weimar that nurtured it, and England, though tending in the same direction, is to be preferred. The enlightened paternal spirit continues to work strongly in the Schlegel sisters and is from time to time explicitly acknowledged. At the luncheon given by Margaret for Mrs Wilcox there is some patronising denigration of the sentimentality in German art and Margaret speaks out defiantly. The continent, she insists, with Germany particularly in mind, is for good or for evil, interested in ideas:

> Its Literature and Art have what one might call the kink of the unseen about them, and this persists even through decadence and affectation. There is more liberty of action in England, but for liberty of thought go to bureaucratic Prussia. People will there discuss with humility vital questions that we here think ourselves too good to touch with tongs.[74]

Or again there is Helen on the Downs above Swanage with her German cousin Frieda, whose sententious observation that one can be certain of nothing but the truth of one's own emotions,

[74] *H.E.* p. 81.

has fallen somewhat damply on the conversation. Yet Helen likes her cousin the better for having made it:

> It was not an original remark, nor had Frieda appropriated it passionately, for she had a patriotic rather than a philosophic mind. Yet it betrayed that interest in the universal which the average Teuton possesses and the average Englishman does not. It was, however illogically, the good, the beautiful, the true, as opposed to the respectable, the pretty, the adequate. It was a landscape of Böcklin's beside a landscape of Leader's, strident and ill-considered, but quivering into supernatural life. It sharpened idealism, stirred the soul.[75]

A German influence, therefore, is clearly and strongly at work in making the Schlegels what they are. It is moreover a far-reaching influence, extending eventually right into the heart of Howards End. It is her father's sword, symbol of yet another ancestral intervention, which Margaret finds suspended by Miss Avery above the Schlegel bookcases, and which Charles later snatches down in anger when confronted with Leonard Bast.[76] Though half German and thus assisted spiritually from an external, non-English source, the Schlegels are also and far more intensely committed to the maternal, the English side of their ancestry, to the point of taking England for granted as their home. Even so, we must always remember that they are not entirely English, not representative of those, like Ruth Wilcox, who can still depend for their salvation upon the unassisted resources of the English unseen. The Schlegels who have advanced into self-consciousness, cut themselves off irrevocably from the ancient mysticism of the soil, may qualify at best for only a limited degree of salvation. But even to this they will not attain unaided. For them, and for those English like them, the salutary impulse from another country, Italy, Germany, will still be required.

[75] *H.E.*, p. 180.
[76] Perhaps another ancestral intervention may be detected in the fact that the Wilcoxes and the Schlegels first met in Germany.

VII

A Passage to India

IN the fifth and final novel, while the setting and events could hardly be more different, the basic concept of the unseen attained to in *Howards End* remains substantially unaltered. Once again an elderly lady of rare and indefinable quality is to die, and then from out of the unseen to exercise a continuing influence on events and people. The unseen itself, in terms of which those people and those events are to be interpreted and assessed, will be perhaps rather less explicitly vouched for than in *Howards End*. The term "unseen", for example, and such phrases as "the impact of the unseen" will not be made use of. Yet the unseen will be present at all times, the more insistently for being taken for granted, and it is to Mrs Moore, true successor in almost every respect of Ruth Wilcox, that we must turn at the outset for the principal indications of its nature and mode of operation.

Like her predecessor, Mrs Moore is unremarkable intellectually, a kindly, pious, rather commonplace old lady whom the uninitiated could easily overlook. She has come to India for no other purpose initially than to accompany Miss Quested, who is to marry her son, Ronny, the resident magistrate at Chandrapore. Something of her quality is conveyed to us on the occasion of her first meeting with Dr Aziz, in the mosque. Assuming her to be just another intruding, insensitive Englishwoman, he is rude and aggressive, demanding whether she has removed her shoes. She has however done so, out of respect, because "God is here", and he is immediately apologetic. From this point on an affinity establishes itself between them, that survives even his disconcerting discovery that she is much older than her voice in the darkness had suggested. They mention their respective families, and Aziz detecting her sympathy, bursts out with an account of the humiliations inflicted upon him that evening by his superior, Major Callendar, and his equally callous wife. "You understand me", he concludes emotionally, "you know what others feel. Oh, if others resembled you!" Mrs Moore is surprised, insists that she does not understand people very well, only knows whether she likes or dislikes them. But this too Aziz emotionally endorses with a final tribute. "Then you are an Oriental", he proclaims.[1]

He escorts her back to the Chandrapore Club and the episode closes, could have ended with itself. In fact it had been for both of them, the Mohammedan and the Englishwoman, an end and a beginning, final in the nature of the relationship it had established, prophetic of an involvement whose imminence neither could foresee.

Mrs Moore returns to the segregated world of British India that has already claimed her son, and into which Miss Quested may or may not marry. She is distressed by it, and on occasions critical of its fantastic inhumanity. But she is still essentially a visitor, one on a passage to and through India, uncommitted to what she sees. She is interested in Indians, and, like Miss Quested, anxious to see "the real India". But when eventually Ronny and Adela announce their engagement, her immediate thought is: "My duties here are evidently finished, I don't want to see India now; now for my passage back."[2] Even so, India itself has begun to affect her personally, through the impact of its alien beauty, and more disturbingly in the recesses of her religious life. Mrs Moore is a devout Christian; for example, in remonstrating with Ronny over his attitude towards Indians, she brings in the Christian argument that God is love and has put us on earth to love our neighbours. Ronny, familiar with a religious strain in his mother, and associating it with bad health, is gloomy and anxious; but it is Mrs Moore herself who is eventually dissatisfied, feeling that she has made a mistake in mentioning God at all, although with advancing age she is finding it increasingly difficult to avoid him:

[1] *A Passage to India*, p. 26, Pocket Edition. Hereafter cited as *P.I.*
[2] *P.I.*, p. 99.

He had been constantly in her thoughts since she entered India,
though oddly enough he satisfied her less. She must needs
pronounce his name frequently, as the greatest she knew, yet
she had never found it less efficacious. Outside the arch there
seemed always an arch, beyond the remotest echo a silence.[3]

Mrs Moore has been, and still continues, a deeply religious
person, gifted with spiritual insight into character and capable
of unusual spiritual intuitions. When, for example, Ronny and
Adela tell her of their mysterious collision on the Marabar road
in the Nawab Bahadur's car, she shivers and murmurs intuitively "A ghost!"[4] And yet, under the impact of India, a
process, apparently insidious and undermining, is clearly at
work within her, associated with failing health but not explained
by it—a process that is to culminate, suddenly and overwhelmingly in the course of her expedition to the Marabar
caves.

Ruth Wilcox, it will be remembered—on the basis of the
little we are told—passed out of life in a state of unaffected
serenity, greeting with an equal eye the deep she was entering
and the shore that she must leave; and for Mrs Moore also
there may well have come before the end a spiritual equipoise
not dissimilar. In the meantime, however, and as the result of
what happens to her in the Marabar cave, she has to pass
through a phase of ultimate doubt and disillusion, has to
experience the nihilism of the "goblin footfall" passing quietly
over the universe from end to end. Physically, the effect of the
cave she enters is alarming enough. Crammed with villagers
and servants, the circular chamber begins to smell and she
comes close to fainting. Swept back from the entrance, she hits
her head and for an instant goes mad, "hitting and gasping like
a fanatic". But more than the crush and the stench is afflicting
her. There is also a terrifying echo. And it is this noise,
"Boum" or "ou-boum", that accompanies her when she
emerges and begins insidiously to undermine her very hold on
existence:

Coming at a moment when she chanced to be fatigued, it had
managed to murmur, "Pathos, piety, courage—they exist, but

[3] *P.I.*, p. 55f.　　　　　　[4] *P.I.*, p. 101.

are identical, and so is filth. Everything exists, nothing has
value."[5]

Seated alone in the open, while the others go back into
another cave, she tries to recover, to go on with a letter to her
children, reminding herself

> that she was only an elderly woman who had got up too early
> in the morning and journeyed too far, that the despair creeping
> over her was merely her despair, her personal weakness, and
> that even if she got a sunstroke and went mad the rest of the
> world would go on. But suddenly, at the edge of her mind,
> Religion appeared, poor little talkative Christianity, and she
> knew that all its divine words from "Let there be light" to "It is
> finished" only amounted to "boum". Then she was terrified
> over an area larger than usual; the universe, never compre-
> hensible to her intellect, offered no repose to her soul, the mood
> of the last two months took definite form at last, and she
> realized that she . . . didn't want to communicate with anyone,
> not even with God.[6]

The mood of resentful despair established at the Marabar
persists, becomes if anything intensified. Mrs Moore withdraws
into herself, allows the ensuing madness in Chandrapore, to
rage about her unheeded. Even the arrest and imprisonment of
Aziz, leaves her apparently indifferent, and she sends him no
message nor tries to see him. Adela Quested, prostrate from
the experience she believes she has had in the cave, stays with
the McBrydes and constantly asks for Mrs Moore to come to
her, but she stays perversely aloof. The time comes for Adela's
return to Ronny's bungalow, where the old lady "puffy, red
and curiously severe", is revealed to her on a sofa. She does
not get up, and "Here you are both back", is her only greeting.
Only when Adela mentions the "echo" in her mind, does Mrs
Moore pay her any attention, and then to comment unhelp-
fully, indeed with malice. If the girl doesn't know what the
echo is, then it is no good telling her. And in any case what is
there to *say*?

> "I have spent my life in saying or in listening to sayings; I have
> listened too much. It is time I was left in peace. Not to die,"

[5] *P.I.*, p. 156.   [6] *P.I.*, p. 156f.

she added sourly. "No doubt you expect me to die, but when I
have seen you and Ronny married, and seen the other two and
whether they want to be married—I'll retire then into a cave
of my own." She smiled, to bring down her remark into
ordinary life and thus add to its bitterness. "Somewhere where
no young people will come asking questions and expecting
answers. Some shelf."[7]

Not surprisingly, poor Adela is reduced to tears. Even on the
subject of marriage and love, the old lady is now embittered and
cynical: "Love in a church, love in a cave, as if there is the
least difference, and I held up from my business by such
trifles."

Only once and then in passing and indifferently does she
mention Aziz, "Of course he is innocent"; but when Ronny
insists that if she thinks so it is her duty to say so in court, the
same resentful petulance returns:

"Oh, why is everything still my duty? when shall I be free
from your fuss? Was he in the cave and were you in the cave
and on and on . . . and Unto us a Son is born, unto us a Child
is given . . . and am I good and is he bad and are we saved?
. . . and ending everything the echo."[8]

And from this to the brutal conclusion that Adela had started
the machinery and it would work to its end. Ronny's decision
that his mother is doing no good to herself or anyone and should
leave India at once is inevitable.

She leaves, still involved, as the author now explains, in the
"twilight of the double vision" to which the elderly are subject,
when the horror of the universe and its smallness have become
manifest at one and the same time:

If this world is not to our taste, well, at all events there is
Heaven, Hell, Annihilation—one or other of those large things,
that huge scenic background of stars, fires, blue or black air.
All heroic endeavour, and all that is known as art, assumes that
there is such a background, just as all practical endeavour,
when the world is to our taste, assumes that the world is all.
But in the twilight of the double vision, a spiritual muddledom
is set up for which no high-sounding words can be found; we

[7] *P.I.*, p. 208f.   [8] *P.I.*, p. 214.

can neither act not refrain from action, we can neither ignore nor respect Infinity.[9]

Perhaps for Mrs Moore, during her last hours on Indian soil, there comes at least a premonition of alleviation. The train bearing her to Bombay passes through a place called Asirgarh, an enormous fortress among wooded hills, which soothes and charms her. She can connect nothing with it but its name, and yet it seems to say to her "I do not vanish". And on the boat itself, when the thousand palm trees around the anchorage climb the hills to wave her farewell, they seem to laugh and say: "So you thought an echo was India; you took the Marabar caves as final? . . . What have we in common with them, or they with Asirgarh? Good-bye!" But Mrs Moore has no time to answer. The sunstroke that had suggested itself to her mind at the Marabar is upon her, and she dies at sea, is committed to the deep while the ship is still on the southward track to round Arabia:

> She was further in the tropics than ever achieved while on shore, when the sun touched her for the last time and her body was lowered into yet another India—the Indian Ocean.[10]

Mrs Moore is dead, but no more at rest and disposed of in the sea than Ruth Wilcox in Hinton churchyard. Despair and disillusion had kept her from intervening in the events now moving to a climax in Chandrapore. However a premonition of impending death—she mentions it twice—may well have been upon her, a recognition, more instinctive than conscious, that intervention to be effective would have to be postponed.

The news of Mrs Moore's death does not reach Chandrapore until the trial of Dr Aziz is over. Even the reader is not informed of it. She is present of course in the memory of those who knew her, but only in retrospect are we to be made aware that more than the superficiality of human memory has been involved. Adela, while waiting for the trial to begin, remembers her, but she also does more than remember—she looks round for her in the court room and has to remind herself that she is far away at sea. However, a more definite indication of what is

---

[9] *P.I.*, p. 216.   [10] *P.I.*, p. 266.

really happening comes with the mention in the course of evidence of Mrs Moore's name. McBryde, whose negligent assumption of the prisoner's guilt has been lashing his Indian listeners to fury, casually makes the accusation that Aziz, in order to get rid of her, had behaved brutally to the other English lady at the scene, crushing her into a cave among his servants. The words produce a storm:

> Suddenly a new name, Mrs. Moore, burst on the court like a whirlwind. Mahmoud Ali had been enraged, his nerves snapped; he shrieked like a maniac, and asked whether his client was charged with murder as well as rape, and who was this second English lady.[11]

The magistrate rules against any further reference to Mrs Moore, and Ronny dryly intervenes to state that his mother should by now have reached Aden; but emotion not rationality has taken charge. After a further impassioned outburst from Mahmoud Ali—"Give us back Mrs. Moore for five minutes only, and she will save my friend"—he hands over his papers and leaves, calling farewell to Aziz from the door with intense passion. Then the tumult increases:

> The invocation of Mrs. Moore continued, and people who did not know what the syllables meant repeated them like a charm. They became Indianized into Esmiss Esmoor, they were taken up in the street outside. In vain the Magistrate threatened and expelled. Until the magic exhausted itself, he was powerless.[12]

The chanting goes on, and Ronny dislikes it more than he is prepared to admit. "It was revolting to hear his mother travestied into Esmiss Esmoor, a Hindu goddess." Adela on the other hand does not at all mind it. Up to this moment she has felt tense and faint, her mind haunted more than ever by the mysterious echo. Now she speaks to her friends more naturally and healthily than usual. They are not to worry about her, she says:

> "I'm much better than I was; I don't feel the least faint; I shall be all right, and thank you all, thank you, thank you for your kindness." She had to shout her gratitude, for the chant, Esmiss Esmoor, went on.[13]

---

[11] *P.I.*, p. 233.   [12] *P.I.*, p. 234.   [13] *P.I.*, p. 235.

Then, suddenly, it stops. "It was as if the prayer had been heard, and the relics exhibited." And it is precisely at this point that Adela goes forward to give her evidence. At the sound of her own voice, all fears and anxieties fall away:

> A new and unknown sensation protected her, like magnificent armour. She didn't think what had happened, or even remember in the ordinary way of memory, but she returned to the Marabar Hills and spoke from them across a sort of darkness to Mr. McBryde. The fatal day recurred, in every detail, but now she was of it and not of it at the same time, and this double relation gave it indescribable splendour.[14]

Smoothly the questioning voice of Mr McBryde leads her along the paths of truth to the crucial, the carefully rehearsed and pre-arranged declaration that Dr Aziz had followed her into the cave. But here she hesitates:

> Her vision was of several caves. She saw herself in one, and she was also outside it, watching its entrance, for Aziz to pass in. She failed to locate him. It was the doubt that had often visited her, but solid and attractive, like the hills "I am not—" Speech was more difficult than vision. "I am not quite sure."[15]

The crisis is past, the intervention consummated; although only Fielding, seated in the body of the court with an Indian child on his knee, knows what is happening, that a "nervous breakdown", as he puts it, is taking place and that his friend is saved; for the others, a final and unequivocal, "Dr. Aziz never followed me into the cave", is necessary. Immediately, through all the shouting and confusion, the Magistrate, shrieking to be heard, demands a withdrawal of the charges, and again Miss Quested must respond:

> Something that she did not understand took hold of the girl and pulled her through. Though the vision was over, and she had returned to the insipidity of the world, she remembered what she had learnt. Atonement and confession—they could wait. It was in hard prosaic tones that she said "I withdraw everything."[16]

Not only Aziz, but Miss Quested also have been saved, and to the spirit of Mrs Moore, though never in so many words, the

[14] *P.I.*, p. 236f. [15] *P.I.*, p. 238. [16] *P.I.*, p. 239.

gift of salvation is certainly being attributed. However, her self-appointed task of reconciliation through love is by no means yet accomplished, for some of the evil set in train by the Marabar is still active, has still to work itself out. The news of her death is received in Chandrapore and immediately the implications of her continuing influence, indeed of her presence become pronounced. As a living person, she had made no particular impression on anyone in Chandrapore. Even Aziz, despite the romance of their first meeting in the mosque and his identification of her as an Oriental, managed subsequently to forget all about her for weeks at a time. And Mrs Moore herself, though always interested and at times emotionally attracted was equally forgetful, fully aware of Aziz as an individual only when he was there. Yet in the aftermath of the trial, and before he is even aware of her death, Aziz begins to invoke her name and her memory in a manner altogether surprising to the more literal-minded Fielding. He will, he says, consult Mrs Moore as to whether or not he should pardon Adela. He goes on,

> "Is it not strange? I keep on forgetting she has left India. During the shouting of her name in court I fancied she was present. I had shut my eyes, I confused myself on purpose to deaden the pain."[17]

Eventually, to save Miss Quested from the appalling damages she may have to pay, Fielding begins to take advantage of his friend's new preoccupation, to appeal deliberately to his memory of Mrs Moore. In the end he succeeds. With a passionate and beautiful outburst Aziz yields, renouncing the whole compensation, because he feels it to be Mrs Moore's wish "that he should spare the woman who was about to marry her son". And meanwhile even the prosaic Adela is not unaffected. Her first reaction on hearing of the death is to realise that Mrs Moore was already dead when her name was called in court, and later, in conversation with Fielding, when they try to reason out what actually did happen in the cave, she insists that one person, Mrs Moore, did know, and when pressed by Fielding falls back on the "pert, meagre word"—telepathy.

[17] *P.I.*, p. 263.

At the same time, in Chandrapore itself, the death, intuitively apprehended at the trial, begins to take on subtler and more lasting forms. A legend springs up that an Englishman had killed his mother for trying to save an Indian's life, and two distinct tombs containing Esmiss Esmoor's remains are reported. McBryde investigates and finds the beginnings of a cult, earthenware saucers and so on.

The spiritual presence of Mrs Moore, benevolently presiding, can achieve much, but evil, with an independent existence of its own, cannot be counteracted fully. It continues to propagate itself, singling out for insidious attack the trust and friendship between Fielding and Aziz. False rumours of an affair between Fielding and Miss Quested begin to circulate, and when Fielding goes on leave Aziz persuades himself that the two are going to marry, and that for this reason Fielding has tricked him into renouncing his compensation. In the last gutterings of the hot weather in Chandrapore he persuades himself that the hideous and treacherous marriage has taken place. But Mrs Moore has been only apparently defeated, has done no more than yield the infected environment of Chandrapore to the enemy. Elsewhere, and by other means she will continue her intercession. In the last days of her life she had spoken disparagingly, even cynically, about marriage, but now a marriage, very different from the one imagined by Aziz and his friends, is to take place. On his return to England, Fielding, introduced by Miss Quested, meets Stella, Mrs Moore's daughter by her first marriage, and falls in love. The courtship is not described, but we can certainly conceive of Mrs Moore, like Ruth Wilcox before her on a parallel occasion, approving and consenting, an ever-welcome ghost. Aziz, informed of the marriage by a letter which he does not read, is deliberately deceived by Mahmoud Ali into believing that the ultimate betrayal has in fact occurred, that Fielding has married Miss Quested. The tragic estrangement between the former friends is now complete, and yet only seemingly final. For Aziz presently leaves Chandrapore and, preceded there by the enigmatic Hindu, Professor Godbole, takes service in the native state of Mau. And this is the state through which Mrs Moore had passed on her way by train out of India; here in

L

fact is Asirgarh, the fortress among wooded hills, that was but a name to her yet seemed to say "I do not vanish". Now its hour has come. To it will be drawn, in a manner we must hesitate to call fortuitous, all those whose presence is required for the purposes of final reconciliation. The presence of Mrs Moore herself is confirmed for us through the medium of Professor Godbole. The tremendous alleviation of the monsoon has come to Mau and with it the great Hindu festival of Gokul Ashtami. At its ecstatic heart stands Professor Godbole, who at the height of his religious involvement remembers Mrs Moore:

> Chance brought her into his mind while it was in this heated state, he did not select her, she happened to occur among the throng of soliciting images, a tiny splinter, and he impelled her by his spiritual force to that place where completeness can be found.[18]

At this point his senses grow thinner, and the image of a wasp presents itself, reminding us that on one occasion in Chandrapore Mrs Moore herself had seen a wasp on the tip of a peg and felt attracted to it, called it a "Pretty dear".[19] As the Hindu ceremony moves to its climax, Mrs Moore again and with increasing vividness presents herself, and "round her faintly clinging forms of trouble".[20] Professor Godbole is a Brahman, she a Christian, but it makes no difference; it makes no difference either that she might be a trick of his memory or a telepathic appeal:

> It was his duty, as it was his desire, to place himself in the position of the God and to love her, and to place himself in her position and to say to the God, "Come, come, come, come." This was all he could do. How inadequate! But each according to his own capacities, and he knew that his own were small. "One old Englishwoman and one little, little wasp " he thought, as he stepped out of the temple into the grey of a pouring wet morning. "It does not seem much, still it is more than I am myself."[21]

Invoked and identified by Professor Godbole, Mrs Moore is certainly there, present within the spiritual circumambience

[18] *P.I.*, p. 298.   [19] *P.I.*, p. 38.
[20] *P.I.*, p. 302.   [21] *P.I.*, p. 303.

of the religious festival, at one with it in love. Before such an assembled might of benevolence the clinging forms of still unresolved trouble must presently give way.[22]

Fielding, now an Inspector of Schools, is drawn to Mau on official business, accompanied by his wife and her brother. Aziz hears of their arrival with embittered resentment. The wife of course, by his reckoning, is Miss Quested, that "treacherous hideous harridan", and he proposes to keep himself sternly aloof. A meeting, however, is scarcely avoidable, and takes place in the rain at the shrine of a saint, oddly enough a Mohammedan. Fielding and his brother-in-law, driven out of the shrine by a swarm of bees, amuse Aziz, out walking with his children, and he decides to greet them after all. Friendliness, however, does not ensue. Fielding is older and sterner, Aziz impertinent and unyielding. Then he refers to Fielding's boy companion, as "Mr. Quested", and the fantastic, long-drawn misunderstanding is at an end. "I'm only Ralph Moore", says the boy blushing. Aziz trembles, turns purplish grey, hating the news, hating to hear the name of Moore, but it is too late to withdraw. Scathing and scornful, Fielding demands an explanation. He had written to Aziz a dozen times mentioning his wife by name. There is no explanation, no excuse, but shame turns to rage in Aziz and brings back his self-respect:

> "Yes, yes, I made a foolish blunder; despise me and feel cold. I thought you married my enemy. I never read your letter. Mahmoud Ali deceived me. I thought you'd stolen my money, but"—he clapped his hands together, and his children gathered round him—"it's as if you stole it. I forgive Mahmoud Ali all things, because he loved me." Then pausing, while the rain exploded like pistols, he said "My heart is for my own people henceforward . . . I wish no Englishman or Englishwoman to be my friend."[23]

However, he returns to his house excited and happy:

---

[22] The third section of *A Passage to India*, "Temple", has appeared to some critics as a superfluous afterthought, adding nothing to the novel as a whole— inevitably so, if the spiritual presence and purpose of Mrs Moore at Mau is not recognised.

[23] *P.I.*, p. 315.

It had been an uneasy, uncanny moment when Mrs. Moore's name was mentioned, stirring memories. "Esmiss Esmoor . . ." —as though she was coming to help him. She had always been so good, and that youth whom he had scarcely looked at was her son. Ralph Moore, Stella and Ralph, whom he had promised to be kind to, and Stella had married Cyril.[24]

Soon after, Aziz rides over to the Guest House to attend to the bee stings suffered by Ralph Moore, and on the way his hardness and cynicism against the English return. He is even prepared to treat the young man harshly, until checked by his disconcerting words, "Your hands are unkind", and by his appearance:

> What a strange-looking youth, tall, prematurely aged, the big blue eyes faded with anxiety, the hair impoverished and tousled! Not a type that is often exported imperially. The doctor in Aziz thought, "Born of too old a mother," the poet found him rather beautiful.[25]

Taking refuge in anger, he resumes his bullying, even mentioning the harm done to him by Miss Quested in Chandrapore. However, when the time comes to go he holds out his hand, quite forgetting that he and the young man are not friends, and indeed ready to apologise for his unkindness. But Ralph Moore already knows that he has ceased to be unkind—the one thing, as he points out, that he always knows. In that case, Aziz tells him, he is an Oriental:

> He unclasped as he spoke, with a little shudder. Those words— he had said them to Mrs. Moore in the mosque in the beginning of the cycle, from which, after so much suffering, he had got free. Never be friends with the English! Mosque, caves, mosque, caves. And here he was starting again.[26]

He gives the young man the ointment he has brought, the one little present, all that he has, for Mrs Moore's son.

Mrs Moore has come back to him, through her son, through the very tones of his voice. She was his best friend in all the world. He is silent, puzzled by his own gratitude:

> What did this eternal goodness of Mrs. Moore amount to? To nothing, if brought to the test of thought. She had not borne

---

[24] *P.I.*, p. 315.   [25] *P.I.*, p. 321.   [26] *P.I.*, p. 324.

witness in his favour, nor visited him in the prison, yet she had stolen to the depths of his heart, and he always adored her.[27]

The torrent of recovered love carries him along, expresses itself in hospitality, in the desire to do one final act of homage to Mrs Moore's son. He takes him out on the lake that they may witness together the climax of the religious festival, the consigning of the god to the water. Across the water comes to them the incessant chanting of the crowd:

> He knew with his heart that this was Mrs. Moore's son, and indeed until his heart was involved he knew nothing. "Radhakrishna Radhakrishna Radhakrishna Radhakrishna Krishnaradha," went the chant, then suddenly changed, and in the interstice he heard, almost certainly, the syllables of salvation that had sounded during his trial at Chandrapore.[28]

The clinging forms of trouble perceived by Professor Godbole are all but dissipated. Friends again, though aware that this must be their last meeting, Aziz and Fielding go for a ride in the Mau jungles. Nonsense and bitterness are past, and they go back laughingly to their old relationship as though nothing had happened. Aziz, determined to do kind actions all round and "wipe out the wretched business of the Marabar for ever", has come at last to a realisation of the courage and integrity of Miss Quested, and has written her a charming letter. From now on his children will be taught to speak of her with affection and respect.

Nor is the Marabar and its aftermath alone at issue, subject to the reconciling effluences of Mau. Fielding's marriage to Stella, as he confides to Aziz, was also in difficulties, and these too have been smoothed away. From her point of view, Mau has been a success. Both she and her brother, who suffer from restlessness, have been calmed, and Stella has "found something soothing, some solution of her queer troubles here".[29] In the language of theology, her union with Fielding has been blessed. Aziz has no wish to concern himself with Fielding's marriage, to meet either Stella or Ralph again, but something —not a sight, but a sound—flits by him, causing him to re-read his letter to Miss Quested and add a final word:

[27] *P.I.*, p. 325.   [28] *P.I.*, p. 327.   [29] *P.I.*, p. 332 .

"For my own part [he writes], I shall henceforth connect you
with the name that is very sacred in my mind, namely, Mrs.
Moore."[30]

Reconciliation, the cancelling out of evil and estrangement,
has been accomplished, the beneficent impact of the unseen,
once again through the medium of a death, triumphantly
exerted. This much, though apparent to the reader, is perhaps
less clear to the protagonists involved. Margaret Schlegel, it
will be remembered, was accorded a flash of retrospective
insight into the workings through Ruth Wilcox of the unseen.
In *A Passage to India* however, such insights, except perhaps in
the rather enigmatic case of Professor Godbole, are absent.
Neither Fielding, nor Miss Quested, nor even Aziz, though they
are all on occasion reminded of Mrs Moore, reveal any awareness of her as a spiritual presence, any realisation of her as the
source of a disposing and controlling power. In this respect, in
its rendering of human character, *A Passage to India* has somewhat less to offer spiritually than *Howards End*. Only in its
closing pages, with the appearance of Ralph and Stella Moore
do we sense ourselves in the presence of individuals complex
and subtle enough to measure up to a Margaret or a Helen
Schlegel. And neither are more than lightly sketched in.
Characters in other words of a comparative simplicity are
being presented to us, characters somewhat or greatly limited
in spiritual range and potentiality and in their understanding
of themselves. Even Mrs Moore herself in her lifetime seems
rather less endowed spiritually than her predecessor, Ruth
Wilcox. Yet to all the same standard of evaluation is being
applied. Once again the unseen is the disposing factor, and in
terms of their sensitivity to it the characters in *A Passage to India*,
now to be assessed, think and speak and act and have their
being.

To begin at the lowest level, paradoxically .enough with
India's rulers, the sun-dried bureaucrats of the British Raj, we
find, with reason and justification, that a degree of collective
assessment has been employed. Compelled by the intrinsic
falsity of their position to impose uniformity upon themselves,
they exist only shadowily as separate individuals. Whether

[30] *P.I.*, p. 333.

Turton or Burton, there is only the difference of a letter.
Newcomers to their inhuman system may resist it briefly, say to
themselves like Adela Quested, "I should never get like that".
But in two years for a man, six months for a woman, the
collective as opposed to the individual personality will of
necessity impose its sway.

Concerning the collective attitude of the ruling British little
need be said. It is in the circumstances both inevitable and
inexcusable. The British having casually and irresponsibly
acquired India can justify their retention of it only in terms of
the formula "England holds India for her good". Something
may be said in defence of the formula, of India's need for
Western efficiency and Western concepts of justice, and even the
enlightened Fielding, it must be remembered, in his final
capacity as an Inspector of Schools hardens himself, comes into
line to some extent with India's "oppressors". But from
moment to moment the formula is wearing thinner, coming to
require for its implementation an assumption of racial
superiority that has no foundation in fact. For the British, who
must rule and persuade themselves of their right to do so, no
alternative to such an assumption and to the mutual hatred
that it must generate is possible. The Indians, disillusioned with
mere justice, may plead for a different attitude, for "kindness,
more kindness, and even after that more kindness", but
kindness with its implication of a common humanity, at least
for those in daily contact with the subject peoples of India, is
out of the question. Only by shutting their minds to their own
humanity, to that which must make them equal, are they able to
carry on.

The cultivation of a collective and intrinsically false
personality does not come easily. For an individual, even so
conventional and limited as Ronny Heaslop, there were initial
difficulties, residues of an imaginative nature to be suppressed
and overcome. He and those he seeks to imitate possess an
instinctive realisation that the imaginative, anything even
remotely suggestive of the unseen, is disruptive. Their ignorance of the Arts, for example, is notable and a matter for pride.
Theirs is the standard Public School attitude, flourishing more
vigorously than in England:

> If Indians were shop, the Arts were bad form, and Ronny had
> repressed his mother when she enquired after his viola; a viola
> was almost a demerit, and certainly not the sort of instrument
> one mentioned in public.[31]

And it is the same with religion, of which only the sterilised
Public School brand, "which never goes bad, even in the
tropics"[32] is permissible. To go beyond this in a country such
as India, where religion is indistinguishable from life itself,
would be fatal. Thus Ronny, whenever he entered mosque,
cave or temple, "retained the spiritual outlook of the Fifth
Form, and condemned as 'weakening' any attempt to understand them".[33] Even in England, the young Resident Magistrate of Chandrapore would hardly have been remarkable
imaginatively. But yet there had once been the viola, and, as
we learn incidentally, a certain feeling for nature, a belief in the
sanctity of personal relationships. It was among the grand
scenery of the English Lakes that he had first met and become
attracted to Miss Quested. This much there had once been,
and an English environment might well have sustained and
developed it. But in India, thousands of miles from any scenery
he can understand, these slight spiritual stirrings are summarily
rejected. They belonged, with Miss Quested herself eventually,
"to the callow academic period of his life which he had out-
grown—Grasmere, serious talks and walks, that sort of thing".[34]

The same systematic rejection of the spiritual characterises
collectively and individually the entire British colony of
Chandrapore, embracing and explaining equally the extreme
and brutal Callendar, the judicious, fair-minded yet ultimately
inhuman Turton, the quietly intelligent McBryde, whose
Bible nevertheless is the Mutiny records rather than the
Bhagavad Gita. Committed to inhumanity, they and their
women-folk can never admit the spiritual which would render
their inhumanity impossible. Mrs Moore may remind Ronny
in Christian terms that "God has put us on earth to love our
neighbours and to show it, and He is omnipresent, even in
India, to see how we are succeeding". But Ronny is compelled
to reject this as mere maundering, to attribute it in self-defence

[31] *P.I.*, p. 43.   [32] *P.I.*, p. 267.
[33] *Ibid.*   [34] *P.I.*, p. 268.

to his mother's age and illness. The unseen, so long as it confines itself to endorsing the National Anthem, is acceptable, but not when it would attempt to influence his life.

Concerning the tragic consequences of the collective British attitude, the events leading up to and from the Marabar, again little need be said. Sooner or later, they or their equivalent, had to happen. As we are made to see, to reject the unseen as a force for good is not to get rid of it, but simply to create a vacuum, swept and garnished, for the unseen as a force for evil to enter in. When the Marabar strikes, Fielding is the first to sense what is happening, that a mass of madness has arisen and must be forced back into its pit before it shall overwhelm them all.[35] Later, in the English club, censured for his refusal to suspend the light of reason, he apprehends not only madness but evil itself, a force propagating in every direction with "an existence of its own, apart from anything that was done or said by individuals".[36] Thus by a final irony, the English in Chandrapore become the unwitting instruments of a force for malevolence that they have conjured up through malevolence and can now neither control nor understand.

In contrast to his baneful compatriots, the casual, instinctively good-natured Fielding is one to whom our hearts go out in corresponding relief. He is admirable at the outset, romping around unselfconsciously at the deplorable "Bridge Party", and becomes more so with his unquestioning loyalty to the arrested Aziz. Yet there is irony here also, for Fielding in theory at all events and by his own admission is a "blank, frank atheist", even less committed to the saving grace of the unseen than his church-attending, conventionally religious fellow countrymen. Yet the contradiction is more apparent than real, and Fielding's atheism is less a fixed dogma than the reflexion of an open mind on spiritual matters. As we shall see, occasional intuitions unaccountable in terms of his professed philosophy do occur to him and are accompanied by a sense of inadequacy, of a something deeper to which he should have attained.

Age, experience and circumstance have made Fielding the man he is, enabled him to resist the insidious pressures of British India. Caught by India comparatively late in life, he takes the

[35] *P.I.*, p. 170.　　　　[36] *P.I.*, p. 195.

country as he finds it, responds to it neither with the callowness
of youth nor with the rigidity of the seasoned Anglo-Indian.
Successful with his pupils in the little Chandrapore college, and
with their parents, he is very soon distressed and puzzled by the
ever-widening gulf between himself and his compatriots:

> Outwardly of the large shaggy type, with sprawling limbs and
> blue eyes, he appeared to inspire confidence until he spoke.
> Then something in his manner puzzled people and failed to
> allay the distrust which his profession naturally inspired. There
> needs must be this evil of brains in India, but woe to him
> through whom they are increased![37]

Rational and cheerful, happiest in the give-and-take of private
conversation, he conceives of the world as a place in which men
are trying to reach one another and can do so best through
good will, culture and intelligence—a creed ill suited to
Chandrapore:

> He had no racial feeling—not because he was superior to his
> brother civilians, but because he had matured in a different
> atmosphere, where the herd-instinct does not flourish. The
> remark that did him most harm at the club was a silly aside to
> the effect that the so-called white races are really pinko-grey.
> ... The pinko-grey male whom he addressed was subtly
> scandalized; his sense of security was awoken, and he com-
> municated it to the rest of the herd.[38]

Distressed, but not unduly, Fielding settles down, establishes the basis for his life in Chandrapore. He makes limited
use of the English club, is tolerated by the men, though not by
the women. He discovers that while it is possible to keep in with
Indians and Englishmen, he who would keep in with English-
women as well, must drop the Indians, and this he is not
prepared to do. Indian friends, Aziz among them, come his
way and he accepts them readily. Independent, a confirmed
bachelor, satisfied that if he loses one job he can get another, he
seems personally uncommitted, one who in his own phrase
"travels light". But the lightness, the casualness, a source of
concern and bewilderment to Aziz and his friends, are deceptive.
When the Marabar strikes and his friend is imprisoned,

[37] *P.I.*, p. 65.   [38] *P.I.*, p. 66.

Fielding, unaccountably in terms of his own rational philosophy, does not waver. An instinct stronger than reason and
self-interest, strong enough to withstand the collective madness
of his own countrymen and the pressure of circumstantial
evidence, informs him that Aziz is innocent, and with an
absoluteness that later surprises him, carries him through.
Characteristically he does not at the time probe into himself or
seek for the disregarded inner source of his suddenly unassailable conviction; but nevertheless, following the crisis at the
English club when he has declared his belief in Aziz and broken
with his countrymen by resigning, a moment of intuition comes.
To recover "mental balance" as he puts it, he goes out onto the
club verandah and is immediately confronted with the astonishing evening beauty of the Marabar Hills. The moment is
exquisite, yet he feels it passing him by. It was as though
someone had told him about it, and he had been obliged to
believe. Suddenly he feels dubious and discontented, wonders
whether

> he was really and truly successful as a human being. After
> forty years' experience, he had learnt to manage his life and
> make the best of it on advanced European lines, had developed
> his personality, explored his limitations, controlled his passions
> —and he had done it all without becoming either pedantic or
> worldly. A creditable achievement, but as the moment passed,
> he felt he ought to have been working at something else the
> whole time,—he didn't know at what, never would know,
> never could know, and that was why he felt sad.[39]

Fielding's sadness, his moments of self-questioning and
doubt, are the measure of his sensitivity to the unseen, to that
within and without himself which, with his conscious intellect,
he can only deny. His, in other words, is a limited sensitivity,
and much that has the stamp of the unseen upon it passes him
by. For example, he is blankly incapable of recognising or even
sensing anything spiritually exceptional in Mrs Moore. For
him she is no more than a commonplace old lady, and he
becomes quite impatient with Aziz for his fantastic and
elaborate chivalry towards her. It is clear, furthermore, that
something of the same exceptional spirituality extends to Mrs

[39] *P.I.*, p. 199.

Moore's daughter, Stella, and here also after their marriage
Fielding finds himself at a loss. He recognises that his wife and
her brother are "after something", whereas he and Aziz and
Miss Quested are, roughly speaking, not after anything. In
consequence there are difficulties in the marriage which only
the beneficent influence abroad at Mau can smooth away.
Fielding's spiritual limitation is also revealed to us, together
with that of Miss Quested, in the conversations he has with her
after the trial. Substantially they are in spiritual agreement;
that there is no heaven for instance, that the dead do not live
again. Although Fielding undermines his own rationalism by
insisting that though heaven does not exist, honesty can get us
there, and by acknowledging that it is difficult as we get on in
life to resist the supernatural:

> "I've felt it coming on me myself. I still jog on without it,
> but what a temptation, at forty-five, to pretend that the dead
> live again; one's own dead; no one else's matter."
> "Because the dead don't live again."
> "I fear not."
> "So do I."
> There was a moment's silence, such as often follows the
> triumph of rationalism.[40]

The news of Mrs Moore's death reaches them, and after it,
in the last of their conversations, her name occurs. They are
discussing the Marabar, what really happened in the cave, and
Miss Quested makes the extraordinary assertion that Mrs
Moore knew, through the medium, she suggests, of telepathy.
But the meagre word falls to the ground, signifies the measure
again of her's and Fielding's spiritual inadequacy:

> She was at the end of her spiritual tether, and so was he. Were
> there worlds beyond which they could never touch, or did all
> that is possible enter their consciousness? They could not tell.
> They only realized that their outlook was more or less similar,
> and found in this a satisfaction. Perhaps life is a mystery, not a
> muddle; they could not tell. Perhaps the hundred Indias
> which fuss and squabble so tiresomely are one, and the universe
> they mirror is one. They had not the apparatus for judging.[41]

---

[40] *P.I.*, p. 250.   [41] *P.I.*, p. 273f.

They part affectionately, with mutual respect, but again on a note of sadness, the sadness of unfulfilment:

> A friendliness, as of dwarfs shaking hands, was in the air. Both man and woman were at the height of their powers—sensible, honest, even subtle. They spoke the same language, and held the same opinions, and the variety of age and sex did not divide them. Yet they were dissatisfied. When they agreed, "I want to go on living a bit," or, "I don't believe in God," the words were followed by a curious backwash as though the universe had displaced itself to fill up a tiny void, or as though they had seen their own gestures from an immense height—dwarfs talking, shaking hands and assuring each other that they stood on the same footing of insight. They did not think they were wrong, because as soon as honest people think they are wrong instability sets up. Not for them was an infinite goal behind the stars, and they never sought it. But wistfulness descended on them now, as on other occasions; the shadow of the shadow of a dream fell over their clear-cut interests, and objects never seen again seemed messages from another world.[42]

Subject to spiritual limitations, Fielding is as a direct consequence somewhat limited in life also and in personal relations. Yet a degree of instinctive spirituality is there, and through it he can achieve much, warmth of heart, integrity, the passion of his identification with Aziz in the crisis of the Marabar. Such achievements are of the spirit, unaccountable in terms of logic and self-interest. However, the level of spiritual power attained in the hour of crisis is not to be maintained, and almost immediately afterwards the identification loosens. The misunderstandings that arise and that culminate in a point of complete alienation, are due almost exclusively to Aziz, who thinks and behaves with culpable irrationality. Yet Aziz and his Indian friends though illogical in their thoughts, were right emotionally, sensing as they did in Fielding the beginning of a process of withdrawal. Even the sensitive Hamidullah is compelled to admit that "of late he no longer addressed us with his former frankness", and Fielding himself, stopping at Venice on his way home on leave and confronted with its beauty is

[42] P.I., p. 274f.

made conscious of himself as a European, and so of disloyalty
within himself to his absent friends:

> The buildings of Venice, like the mountains of Crete and the
> fields of Egypt, stood in the right place, whereas in poor India
> everything was placed wrong. He had forgotten the beauty of
> form among idol temples and lumpy hills; indeed, without
> form, how can there be beauty? . . . Writing picture post-cards
> to his Indian friends, he felt that all of them would miss the joys
> he experienced now, the joys of form, and that this constituted
> a serious barrier. They would see the sumptuousness of Venice,
> not its shape, and though Venice was not Europe, it was part
> of the Mediterranean harmony. The Mediterranean is the
> human norm. When men leave that exquisite lake, whether
> through the Bosphorus or the Pillars of Hercules, they approach
> the monstrous and extraordinary; and the southern exit leads
> to the strangest experience of all.[43]

Fielding marries in England, returns to India, and when we
next encounter him at Mau he is an Inspector of Schools,
already in line to some extent with the "oppressors" of India.
He has hardened, and though he can laugh at the educational
waste and inefficiency he finds in Mau, he no longer travels as
lightly as in the past. Education is a continuous concern with
him, "because his income and the comfort of his family
depended on it". After correcting Aziz on the subject of his
marriage, he is able to go back with him laughingly to their
old relationship, but in fact things are not and can never again
be quite the same:

> He had thrown in his lot with Anglo-India by marrying a
> countrywoman, and he was acquiring some of its limitations,
> and already felt surprise at his own past heroism. Would he
> to-day defy all his own people for the sake of a stray Indian?[44]

The completeness of his reconciliation with Aziz is thus
conditional on their never meeting again, and this in turn is the
measure of a certain deterioration. Each can look back with
pride to the past, but the time of their "glad morning friendship" and the spiritual apotheosis that it represented is over.
Fielding of course will never deteriorate to the level of a Turton,

[43] *P.I.*, p. 293.   [44] *P.I.*, p. 332.

a Ronny Heaslop, or a Callendar; the fundamental warmth of heart, though less impulsive than it used to be, is still manifestly within him. We may even speculate that through the influence of Stella, emissary of Mrs Moore, spiritual apprehensions of which he is not yet capable, may yet come his way. But meanwhile the Fielding we take leave of after the last ride of reconciliation with Aziz, is a man whose sensitivity to the unseen is measured by his own recognised inability to acknowledge it, by his sad and fleeting awareness of a "something else" at which he should have been working the whole time: a man in consequence whose capacity for life and for love remains qualified.

Almost within the same spiritual category as Fielding, and no less limited in life and in love, is the unfortunate, well intentioned Adela Quested. Like Fielding, a thorough-going intellectual, a rationalist, she does not go quite so far as he does in the matter of belief. She is not an atheist, and in the overwhelming days before the trial of Aziz she resumes, "after years of intellectualism", her morning kneel to Christianity:

> There seemed no harm in it, it was the shortest cut to the unseen, and she could tack her troubles on to it. Just as the Hindu clerks asked Lakshmi for an increase in pay, so did she implore Jehovah for a favourable verdict. God who saves the king will surely support the police.[45]

The abberration into prayer, and prayer at so primitive a level, was hardly typical, the product of outrageous circumstance and an abnormal state of mind. But though she might repudiate prayer and, on intellectual grounds, orthodox Christianity, Miss Quested must yet be distinguished from Fielding by the fact of her acknowledging, more or less explicitly, the existence of an unseen. We may assume that her interest in the arts and in nature was in some vague measure linked to it. Intellectualism holds her back from a belief in immortality, yet, in marked contrast to Fielding, she is highly recognisant of Mrs Moore both in life and after death, respects her belief in ghosts and attributes to her the irrational power of telepathy. Such spirituality as Fielding achieves expresses

[45] *P.I.*, p. 220.

itself outwardly in life and in personal relations, an area in which Miss Quested despite her good intentions is conspicuously less successful. Inwardly however she is perhaps the stronger of the two, capable of superior and more far-reaching intuitions.

Miss Quested's somewhat pathetic incapacity for life and people appears initially in the extreme caution of her approach to Ronny, the man she has come out to India to marry. There is something almost ludicrous in her wariness, her careful, purely intellectual weighing up of the pros and cons. Largely incapable of spontaneous feeling, she must regulate her thought and conduct intellectually, remind herself in every situation what honesty and sincerity would require her to think and do. Determined to do the right thing by Ronny and by India, she approaches both impersonally, and the effect, as Fielding later observes, is priggish, depressing. "She goes on and on", he complains to Aziz, "as if she's at a lecture—trying ever so hard to understand India and life, and occasionally taking a note".[46] But he is ashamed a little of his roughness, when Aziz remarks that he found her so nice and sincere. Her sincerity, and at the same time her recognition of her own intrinsic deficiencies, appears very clearly at the Marabar picnic when she puts her Anglo-Indian problem before Aziz:

> "Some women are so—well, ungenerous and snobby about Indians, and I should feel too ashamed for words if I turned like them, but—and here's my difficulty—there's nothing special about me, nothing specially good or strong, which will help me to resist my environment and avoid becoming like them. I've most lamentable defects. That's why I want Akbar's 'universal religion' or the equivalent to keep me decent and sensible."[47]

The honesty and humility, the recognition of her own spiritual insufficiency, are characteristic of the best in Miss Quested and to some extent counterbalance her defects—but to some extent only. Very soon there are slight indications that intellectual honesty and self-knowledge will not be enough and that the Anglo-Indian environment, unopposed by an adequate spirituality, will indeed prove too much for her. For example,

[46] *P.I.*, p. 124.   [47] *P.I.*, p. 152.

after the accident in the Nawab Bahadur's car that leads to her becoming engaged after all to Ronny, she refers to "our old gentleman of the car" in a tone of voice whose patronising negligence is exactly what he desires. He is sure that from now on she will understand India and his position within it from his point of view.

The experience to which she is subjected in the Marabar caves is of course quite beyond the scope of her intelligence and her limited spiritual resources. She is in fact reduced by it, even after the initial shock has subsided, to a condition of inner chaos. Intellectually she can only grasp at the gross physical explanation imposed upon her by her countrymen and try to persuade herself that it must be true. Nevertheless, and despite herself, she cannot make it fit, cannot accommodate within it the echo first heard in the cave and now continuing, "raging up and down like a nerve in the faculty of her hearing" and infecting the whole surface of her life. Intuition, rather than reason directs her at this point emotionally to Mrs Moore, who alone, she feels, has the power of understanding and cure. Only Mrs Moore can drive back the terrible sound to its source, and seal the broken reservoir of evil. For she too, like Fielding, can sense the immanence of evil, can even hear it entering the lives of others.[48]

But Mrs Moore, at this stage, declines to be helpful, and when appealed to directly responds with a bitterness and perversity that reduces poor Adela to tears. Yet the very presence of Mrs Moore has its effect on her. For the first time she is able to mention Aziz by name, and the sound of it rings out "like the first note of a new symphony". An extraordinary expression, half relief, half horror passes over her face and the truth breaks through to her: "Ronny, he's innocent; I made an awful mistake." Then she touches her ear and announces that her echo is better. The moment passes, and Ronny recovering himself from a "shiver like impending death" is able to impose once more the official intellectual explanation. Mrs Moore departs, and Adela, her echo back again in full force, must face defenceless the ordeal of the coming trial.

Yet she is not entirely defenceless. The experience through

[48] *P.I.*, p. 203.

M

which she has been passing, to the very extent that it has
partaken of the logically inexplicable, has been a spiritual one,
the product of a manifestation from out of the unseen. The
impact is an evil one, but its effect has been nevertheless to
awaken her spiritually, to endow her with an intuitional
capacity she had never before possessed. In no other way can
we account for her sudden apprehension of Mrs Moore as the
only person possessed of the necessary spiritual power to
understand and counteract her predicament. Mrs Moore
declines to assist her, and the very perverseness of her refusal
has in it an element of the mysterious, the prophetic. It is as
though in the depth of her being, an instinctive wisdom, already
conscious of impending death, is actively restraining her,
holding her back from Adela, delaying her intervention so that
it may come at the right moment and so with irresistible effect.

That moment comes, as we have noted, at the trial, its
imminence being indicated to us by the mystical nature of the
chant, Esmiss Esmoor. At once there is a significant change in
Adela, an access of confidence, a sensation of health. A certain
anxiety as to what she may have to reveal in public accompanies
her as she goes to give her evidence, but at the sound of her own
voices ceases:

> A new and unknown sensation protected her, like magnificent
> armour. She didn't think what had happened, or even
> remember in the ordinary way of memory, but she returned to
> the Marabar Hills, and spoke from them across a sort of
> darkness to Mr. McBryde.[49]

The past lives again for her and she re-enters it, but it is a
transfigured past, beautiful and significant, possessed of an
indescribable splendour. She is of it and yet not of it, fully
aware of the distinction between the actuality she remembers,
and the heightened version of it passing before her inward eye.
She does not characterise what is happening to her as a
"vision", though she will use the word later, but the visionary,
the spiritual nature of the experience through which she is
passing is self-evident. Vision carries her on to the moment of
climactic realisation and then, its purpose accomplished, at once

[49] *P.I.*, p. 236.

withdraws. In a flat, everyday voice she makes the declaration that Dr Aziz never followed her into the cave. Justice, the impersonal justice of the court, demands a further unequivocal renunciation, and though the vision no longer supports her, a sufficient residue of its power remains:

> Something that she did not understand took hold of the girl and pulled her through. Though the vision was over, and she had returned to the insipidity of the world, she remembered what she had learnt. Atonement and confession—they would wait. It was in hard prosaic tones that she said, "I withdraw everything."[50]

The moment of vision, of spiritual apotheosis, is over and Miss Quested reverts to the insipidity not only of the world but also of her daily self. Yet presently there are indications that the everyday Miss Quested, with the advanced intellectual outlook, is not altogether the same. In conversation with Fielding, who must now rather unwillingly protect her, she tries to explain what happened to her in court and finds the resources of her well-equipped mind already inadequate. The "vision"— significantly the word now occurs to her—disappears whenever she tries to remember and interpret it. "Events presented themselves to me in their logical sequence", she says eventually, but realises that the reality had been quite different. And there is another alteration, noted by Fielding, that compels him to a new-born respect not altogether accountable by her act of courage:

> Although her hard school-mistressy manner remained, she was no longer examining life, but being examined by it; she had become a real person.[51]

She does not know what has happened to her, does not associate the "vision" that has pulled her through in any way with Mrs Moore—indeed she has still to hear of her death—yet when Fielding suggests that she had been exorcised in the court room by a direct question from McBryde, she reacts curiously:

> "Exorcise in that sense. I thought you meant I'd seen a ghost."

[50] *P.I.*, p. 239.   [51] *P.I.*, p. 254.

"I don't go to that length!"

"People I respect very much believe in ghosts," she said rather sharply. "My friend Mrs. Moore does."

"She's an old lady."

"I think you need not be impolite to her, as well as to her son."[52]

Almost immediately afterwards the news of the death is given her, and though her mind does not consciously revert to the notion of a ghost, she does break out with "She was dead when they called her name this morning. She must have been buried at sea."

Indications of a change, a development, spiritually precipitated, are already there, but tentatively, suggesting no more perhaps than a potentiality for the future. In other respects, and though raised somewhat, even ennobled by humility and resignation, she is still her chilly self, still invested with the old inadequacies. Her courage and integrity had been great, but only Fielding could appreciate them. Hamidullah, speaking for India, and with ruthless insight is less impressed:

> If she had shown emotion in court, broke down, beat her breast, and invoked the name of God, she would have summoned forth his imagination and generosity—he had plenty of both. But while relieving the Oriental mind, she had chilled it, with the result that he could scarcely believe she was sincere, and indeed from his standpoint she was not. For her behaviour rested on cold justice and honesty; she had felt, while she recanted, no passion of love for those whom she had wronged. Truth is not truth in that exacting land unless there go with it kindness and more kindness and kindness again, unless the word that was with God also is God. And the girl's sacrifice—so creditable according to Western notions—was rightly rejected, because, though it came from her heart, it did not include her heart.[53]

The same limitation is apparent shortly after when Fielding suggests to her that a letter of personal apology to Aziz might be seemly. At once she is remorseful. Why did she not think of it herself? Why did she not rush up to Aziz after the trial? Even so, she is still at a loss, her instincts will not help her, and she

[52] *P.I.*, p. 250.   [53] *P.I.*, p. 254f.

must appeal to Fielding to dictate what she should say. But the letter they concoct together is a failure, full of moving phrases but not moving as a whole. With characteristic honesty and insight Fielding explains why:

> "Our letter is a failure for a simple reason which we had better face: you have no real affection for Aziz, or Indians generally. . . . The first time I saw you, you were wanting to see India, not Indians, and it occurred to me: Ah, that won't take us far. Indians know whether they are liked or not—they cannot be fooled here. Justice never satisfies them, and that is why the British Empire rests on sand."[54]

In the course of their last conversation together, as we have seen, Fielding and Miss Quested draw together, reach the limits of the spiritual tether beyond which their conscious intellectualism will not permit them to go—yet with a certain wistfulness, while "the shadow of a shadow of a dream" falls over their clear-cut interests, and objects never seen again seem "messages from another world". Miss Quested will return to England, where she fits in, has friends, will make a career for herself and be quite all right. And where she will perform the one act still to be required of her, that of introducing Fielding to Stella Moore. Less successful than Fielding in external life and personal relations, more afflicted by that specially English attribute, the undeveloped heart, she has yet undergone an inner spiritual experience to which the out-going Fielding could not have attained. Unassisted from out of the unseen, un-inspired by the spirit of Mrs Moore, she would have remained herself, a prosaic and intimidated witness, and Aziz would not have been saved. But spirit can communicate only with spirit, and without at least some measure of intrinsic susceptibility to the unseen, the integrity in Miss Quested that proceeded from it would have lacked the power to respond.

For Indians generally, Hindu or Moslem, the English undeveloped heart, sad instrument of all their woe, can be no more than an object of wonder and incomprehension. Afflicted in their turn with an excess rather than a deficiency of feeling, their collective problem is to control the heart, not develop it.

[54] *P.I.*, p. 270.

Such is the case collectively with all the Indians introduced to
us in *A Passage to India*, and with the Moslem Dr Aziz perhaps
most explicitly of all. Soon after we first meet him among his
Indian friends he visits his favourite Mosque and there medi-
tates on a more perfect Mosque that he might himself build one
day with his tomb nearby and on it a Persian inscription:

> Alas, without me for thousands of years
> The Rose will blossom and the Spring will bloom,
> But those who have secretly understood my heart—
> They will approach and visit the grave where I lie.[55]

He regards the quatrain, from the tomb of a Deccan king, as
profound philosophy, for he always holds pathos to be profound, and the phrase in particular, the secret understanding of
the heart, moves him to tears. Living in and through the
feelings, knowing nothing except through the medium of the
heart, he and his Indian friends inevitably suggest an emotional
parallel between India and Italy. Indeed such a parallel
explicitly occurs to Fielding:

> To regard an Indian as if he were an Italian is not, for instance,
> a common error, nor perhaps a fatal one, and Fielding often
> attempted analogies between this peninsula and that other,
> smaller and more exquisitely shaped, that stretches into the
> classic waters of the Mediterranean.[56]

Of course there are differences, especially in a land as saturated
as India in religious tradition, but it is more than permissible
to place Aziz, for better and for worse, in the line of descent
from such as Gino Carella, to perceive a similarity in the
"mysticism of the heart" at work in both of them.

Aziz, though scarcely a mystic at all in his own estimation, is
nevertheless one deeply committed by tradition and instinct to
the unseen. Yet his conscious beliefs are tempered, if not with
scepticism, at least with an intermittent uncertainty. For
example, his wife has died and he can at one and the same time
conceive of her in Paradise, and ask himself whether such a
place of survival exists beyond the tomb:

> Though orthodox, he did not know. God's unity was indubit-
> able and indubitably announced, but on all other points he

---

[55] *P.I.*, p. 22.   [56] *P.I.*, p. 65.

wavered like the average Christian; his belief in the life to come would pale to a hope, vanish, reappear, all in a single sentence or a dozen heart-beats, so that the corpuscles of his blood rather than he seemed to decide which opinion he should hold, and for how long. It was so with all his opinions.[57]

God as the Friend, who never comes but is not disproved, indubitably exists; to this extent at least the secret understanding of Aziz's heart does not waver. But for the rest there is fluidity, a kind of opportunistic equivocation. A belief in ghosts runs in his blood, but on occasion he can also deny them. When the Nawab Bahadur tells the story of the ghost on the Marabar Road that caused the accident to his car, Aziz chooses to hold aloof, admonishing the Nawab's grandson to do likewise:

> "You know, my dear fellow, we Moslems simply must get rid of these superstitions, or India will never advance. How long must I hear of the savage pig upon the Marabar Road? . . . Your grandfather belongs to another generation, and I respect and love the old gentleman, as you know. I say nothing against him, only that it is wrong for us, because we are young. I want you to promise me—Nureddin, are you listening?—not to believe in Evil Spirits, and if I die . . . to bring up my three children to disbelieve in them too."[58]

Believing and disbelieving, according to the heart-beat of the moment, Aziz is still fundamentally religious, and, when confronted with the blank, frank atheism of Fielding, he is instinctively scandalised. Yet, like Fielding, he remains essentially incurious about the unseen, content to accept and leave unexplained his own intermittent emotional intuitions. The spiritual simplicity and incuriosity of his mind becomes especially evident in relation to Hinduism, a religion he does not and does not want to understand. Yet he can recognise its greatness of depth and subtlety, and may even on occasion attempt to sound it out. One such attempt is made when, in the presence of Miss Quested, he asks Professor Godbole to explain the special nature of the Marabar Caves and realises that something, perhaps incommunicable, is being held back. Yet he continues obstinately to probe:

[57] *P.I.*, p. 59.   [58] *P.I.*, p. 104

The dialogue remained light and friendly, and Adela had no conception of its underdrift. She did not know that the comparatively simple mind of the Mohammedan was encountering Ancient Night. Aziz played a thrilling game. He was handling a human toy that refused to work—he knew that much. If it worked, neither he nor Professor Godbole would be the least advantaged, but the attempt enthralled him and was akin to abstract thought. On he chattered, defeated at every move by an opponent who would not even admit that a move had been made, and further than ever from discovering what, if anything, was extraordinary about the Marabar Caves.[59]

In comparison with Hinduism, the Mohammedan religion is clearly being presented to us as limited, at least according to Fielding. The shallow arcades of the mosque, in his view, provide but a limited asylum:

"There is no God but God" doesn't carry us far through the complexities of matter and spirit; it is only a game with words, really, a religious pun, not a religious truth.[60]

Yet the Mosque and all that it signifies does carry Aziz, if not far enough, at least some of the way into the unseen, further in fact, as again Fielding realises, than he himself can penetrate. When he goes for his last ride in the jungles of Mau with Aziz, and establishes his order of spiritual priorities, Aziz is pushed at least a little ahead:

"My wife's after something. You and I and Miss Quested are, roughly speaking, not after anything. We jog on as decently as we can, you a little in front—a laudable little party. But my wife is not with us."[61]

Aziz, we may therefore conclude, is what he is by reason of a spiritual sensitivity genuine yet one-sided. Equally one-sided, unsubjected to the necessary discipline of thought, are the expressions of that sensitivity in his life and also, to the extent that he is a poet, in his art. One-sidedness, however, as in the case of Gino Carella, a mysticism of the heart to the exclusion of the head, possesses, along with its potential for goodness, a parallel potential of a very different kind. Personal relations in particular, that depend for their origin and continuation on

[59] *P.I.*, p. 80.   [60] *P.I.*, p. 287.   [61] *P.I.*, p. 331.

spontaneity of feeling and nothing else, are intrinsically
precarious, prone to extremes both of love and hate. And such
are the relationships achieved by an Aziz, living unpredictably
from heart-beat to heart-beat, capable of sustaining almost
simultaneously an absoluteness of devotion, an absoluteness of
distrust.

The paradox and its tragic consequences are of course most
evident in his relationship to Fielding. Conducted by the
secret understanding of the heart into immediate friendship,
he gives of himself unreservedly, taking even the barrier of race
in his stride. The final compact, the unreasoning union of
hearts, is ratified, at least on his side, when he shows to Fielding
the portrait of his dead wife, although Fielding is saddened by
his own inability to respond quite so emotionally. The relationship develops, perhaps reaches its zenith at the Marabar picnic,
when Aziz returning from his visit to the caves finds that his
friend, thanks to a lift from Miss Derek, has unexpectedly
arrived:

> "Fielding! Oh, I have so wanted you!" he cried, dropping
> the "Mr." for the first time.
> And his friend ran to meet him all so pleasant and jolly,
> no dignity, shouting explanations and apologies about the
> train.[62]

For Aziz the moment is enough, its own justification, and he
has no desire, no impulse to look beyond it, whereas Fielding
knows that the next time they meet, Aziz, incapable of intellectual continuity, may be cautious and distant. In this instance
their next meeting will take place in the Chandrapore jail,
where, unapproachable through misery, and in return for all
that Fielding has done and will be doing to save him, Aziz has
nothing coherent to offer but "You deserted me".

In the aftermath of the trial, at the Victory Banquet and
beyond it, affection extravagantly returns, with Fielding,
"Cyril" now, re-established in unassailable friendship, but still
from heart-beat to heart-beat only and as the impulse of the
moment shall decide. The intellectual continuity of retrospect
and anticipation correctly assumed by Fielding as essential to

[62] *P.I.*, p. 162f.

any enduring relationship, is simply unavailable to Aziz. He has no sense of fact or evidence and when suspicions presently arise, especially over Fielding's chivalry towards Miss Quested, the intellectual explanations that would dispose of them carry no weight. Instead he allows them to riot emotionally:

> Aziz did not believe his own suspicions—better if he had, for then he would have denounced and cleared the situation up. Suspicion and belief could in his mind exist side by side. They sprang from different sources, and need never intermingle. Suspicion in the Oriental is a sort of malignant tumour, a mental malady, that makes him self-conscious and unfriendly suddenly; he trusts and mistrusts at the same time in a way the Westerner cannot comprehend. It is his demon, as the Westerner's is hypocrisy. Aziz was seized by it, and in his fancy built a satanic castle, of which the foundations had been laid when he talked at Dilkusha under the stars.[63]

In such a state of mind he even entertains the impossible notion that Fielding had been the one to enter the cave with Miss Quested as if it were a truth, and later manages to persuade himself that the marriage he had fancied as impending between the two had actually taken place.

Satanism, a susceptibility to evil thoughts, is certainly present to a marked degree in Aziz. Here is the darker side ever latent within the mysticism of the heart, the equivalent of the murderous potentiality of a Gino Carella. Aziz stops short perhaps of a capacity for evil action, but of evil thought he is disturbingly capable. This appears not only in his unreflecting readiness to accept gross suspicion for truth, but also in the nature of certain thoughts, especially sexual thoughts, that occur to him. Though direct and uncomplicated sensually, Aziz adopts towards certain women, women unattractive to him physically, an attitude that is to contribute as much as anything else to his eventual estrangement from Fielding. For sexually, he is a snob. In the darkness of the mosque when he first hears the voice of Mrs Moore, he is deceived by it into thinking she is young, and when he finds that she is old, a fabric bigger than the mosque itself falls to pieces.[64] And again later it is as "an excessively aged lady" that he first describes her

[63] *P.I.*, p. 290f.　　　　[64] *P.I.*, p. 23.

to Fielding. In the same way, for all her friendliness, he does not fail to notice with cold antipathy the angularity, the breastlessness of Miss Quested. The sexual snobbery does not amount to much to begin with, but it is always there, and when the Marabar erupts and he finds himself accused of sexually assaulting Miss Quested, it comes rampaging to the surface. After the trial, Miss Quested asks Fielding what Aziz is saying about her, and he cannot reply, for such remarks as Aziz had made had been not merely bitter but foul:

> The underlying notion was, "It disgraces me to have been mentioned in connection with such a hag." It enraged him that he had been accused by a woman who had no personal beauty; sexually, he was a snob. This had puzzled and worried Fielding. Sensuality, as long as it is straight-forward, did not repel him, but this derived sensuality—the sort that classes a mistress among motor-cars if she is beautiful, and among eye-flies if she isn't—was alien to his own emotions, and he felt a barrier between himself and Aziz whenever it arose.[65]

After the Victory Banquet at Dilkusha, lying with Aziz under the stars, Fielding makes the first attempt, if not to reconcile him to Miss Quested, at least to persuade him of her integrity and courage. If an apology is called for, he insists, Aziz has only to dictate one and she will sign it. But the reaction is still the same:

> " 'Dear Dr. Aziz, I wish you had come into the cave; I'm an awful old hag, and it is my last chance.' Will she sign that?"[66]

Fielding protests, "Oh, I wish you wouldn't make that kind of remark. . . . It is the one thing in you I can't put up with", but to no avail, and his continued concern for Miss Quested merely serves to awaken in Aziz the monstrous suspicion that he is interested in the girl sexually. Eventually suspicion, encouraged by malicious gossip, becomes fact and he breaks out with, "So you and Madamsell Adela used to amuse one another in the evening, naughty boy."[67] Startled, and enraged at being called a naughty boy, Fielding loses his head, calls his friend a "little rotter"—a remark from which their already deteriorating

[65] *P.I.*, p. 251.   [66] *P.I.*, p. 263.   [67] *P.I.*, p. 284.

relationship is slow to recover. Ostensibly convinced, Aziz agrees that the rumours to which he had listened were unfounded, but, in due course, as part of his satanic fantasy that Fielding and Miss Quested are planning to marry, they return and are finally credited.

The darker side of Aziz, the obverse as it were of his emotional spontaneity, is there and must be acknowledged. It is present as a perpetual threat of discontinuity in even the most exalted of his relationships, even that with Mrs Moore. That he is able, from heart to heart, to know her instantly and finally, to establish with her from one moment to the next a timeless and unassailable relationship, is the measure of his essential greatness, is to explain and justify Fielding's eventual realisation that he belonged in a spiritual category higher than his own. Yet even here the menace of failure, of discontinuity was never far absent. Aziz could go out with all his heart to the heart he sensed in Mrs Moore, but having done so he could just as easily forget her. When the next time comes for him to meet Mrs Moore, at Fielding's tea-party, we find that he has forgotten her entirely, that the romance at the mosque had sunk out of his consciousness as soon as it was over. While they are present, Fielding and Mrs Moore have strange and beautiful effects on him—they are his friends, "his for ever, and he theirs for ever; he loved them so much that giving and receiving became one".[68] The love however is of the moment and has at every successive encounter to be renewed. At the Marabar picnic Mrs Moore is once again perfection; he would do anything for her, die to make her happy. On the other hand the love that he first felt for her in the mosque is not still with him, it wells up anew "the fresher for forgetfulness". Aziz meets Mrs Moore on three occasions only, and his love for her is thus subjected to a minimum of strain. No demand is made on her to experience and condone those serious defects of character later to become so apparent to Fielding. Had she lived and become involved in the trial and its aftermath, been confronted with Aziz's darker side, she might well have done better than Fielding in the matter of forgiveness and understanding; but it is at least possible that his love for her would

[68] *P.I.*, p. 149.

have ceased to well up with all its original spontaneity. Aziz, we must conclude, has a great capacity for love, a heart that functions at the expense of the head. When Mahmoud Ali grossly deceives him and lies to him about Fielding's marriage, Aziz forgives him utterly, "because he loved me", fails to see any incompatibility between love and untruth. At the last, all the futile and unnecessary misunderstandings cleared up, he is reconciled to Fielding, and on their final ride together the old love, or something very like it, wells up once more; but it will persist on one condition only, that they shall never meet again. Such is the limitation imposed on Aziz by the mysticism of the heart to which he subscribes. He can love Mahmoud Ali and those like him because in relation to them only the heart is involved. Fielding however, attempting to harmonise both head and heart, is to be loved finally in the abstract, in memory only. And it might well have been the same, had she lived, with Mrs Moore. The infection of intellectualism is upon Fielding, inhibiting him to the point where he is spiritually inferior to Aziz, blinding him to Mrs Moore. However, that complex harmony of head and heart to which he aspires is one that enters not at all into the feeling-dominated mind of Aziz.

Detailed analysis of the several other Indians presented to us in *A Passage to India* is hardly called for. Emerging in varying degrees as individuals, they yet partake, like the Chandrapore British, in a collective spirituality, in terms of which they think and act and have their being. Aziz is their spokesman and archetype, his sensitivity to the unseen substantially theirs also. A common Indian identity is thus suggested to us, and our sense of it is of course heightened by the simplifying factor that, with the exception of Professor Godbole, all the Indians made more than passingly familiar to us are co-religionists, Moslems. For this reason Godbole, a Hindu integrated into the unseen with a completeness quite beyond the capacity of any Moslem, has to be singled out for attention.

Godbole, a character so subtly and paradoxically motivated as scarcely to seem one at all, is nevertheless one of the author's most convincing creations, fully and consistently realised in terms of the unseen. With the nature of that unseen animating Godbole at every turn, in other words with Hinduism, we shall

deal presently, relating it to the whole spiritual concept to
which the author seems personally to subscribe; but meanwhile
Godbole himself as an individual in whom life is indistinguishable from religion must briefly concern us. Amid all the
turmoil and tension of Chandrapore he strikes the note not so
much of detachment or indifference, as of an achieved and
unassailable harmony:

> He was elderly and wizen with a grey moustache and grey-blue
> eyes, and his complexion was as fair as a European's. He wore a
> turban that looked like pale purple macaroni, coat, waistcoat,
> dhoti, socks with clocks. The clocks matched the turban, and
> his whole appearance suggested harmony—as if he had recon-
> ciled the products of East and West, mental as well as physical,
> and could never be discomposed.[69]

Godbole's imperturbability may seem at times, at least to the
Western observer, excessive, even incongruous. When the
civilised serenity at Fielding's tea-party has been crassly
shattered by Ronny's intrusion, and when ugliness and nasti-
ness prevail on every hand, Godbole chooses this most unsuitable of moments to sing. No one is in the mood to hear him,
but yet we cannot feel that the song itself or the enigmatic
explanation of it that follows are finally incongruous. What has
it done, after all, but re-establish the lost essence of a serenity,
a moment of civilisation, which had been only temporarily and
in appearance destroyed?

The seeming perverseness of Godbole's reactions to affairs
on the purely human plane, reach a kind of apotheosis
immediately following Aziz's arrest. Fielding, his mind bursting
with trouble, encounters him at the College and is compelled to
listen to a long speech, devoid of basis and conclusion, on a
scandal involving an unpopular colleague. Godbole concludes
fantastically by hoping that the expedition to the Marabar was
a success. Evidently, says Fielding, he has not yet heard about
the catastrophe. But he has. Well, counters Fielding with an
amazed stare, how can an expedition involving such an event
be called successful?

"I cannot say," replies Godbole. "I was not present."

[69] *P.I.*, p. 76.

Then with an irrelevance that Fielding finds quite unbearable, he goes on to mention his impending departure from Chandrapore, his plans to establish a High School at Mau. Perhaps Fielding could suggest a suitable name by which the school could be generally known. Sickened, Fielding can only protest that he has no names for schools in his head, that he can think of nothing but poor Aziz. Does Godbole realise that he is in prison?

But Godbole's answer, totally unexpected as ever, reveals that in fact there has been no irrelevance, that the issue consuming Fielding is what he also has been talking about all along:

> "Oh yes. Oh no, I do not expect an answer to my question now. I only meant that when you are at leisure, you might think the matter over, and suggest two or three alternative titles for schools. I had thought of the 'Mr. Fielding High School' but failing that, the 'King-Emperor George the Fifth.' "
>
> "Godbole!"
>
> The old fellow put his hands together, and looked sly and charming.[70]

But still, with enigmatic evasiveness, Godbole will not commit himself or declare his belief in Aziz's innocence, and the seeming abstractness of his ensuing disquisition on the nature of good and evil once again reduces Fielding to exasperation. In conclusion he relates a legend with no apparent bearing on anything that has gone before, and which might have been acceptable had he told it at the tea-party two weeks previously. Fielding receives it in gloomy silence.

Exactly what goes on in the mind and soul of Professor Godbole, except possibly when we follow him in meditation at the festival of Gokul Ashtami, is seldom made explicit, although the logic underlying his acts and utterances may sometimes be inferred or guessed at. Occasionally however, as with the mysterious explanation of the Marabar caves which Aziz attempts to pry from him and which he refrains from giving, we seem to be brought up against the incommunicable,

[70] *P.I.*, p. 184.

something inexpressible through words. Through silence therefore, through paradox, through the enunciation of the seemingly irrelevant, Godbole seeks to make available his own profound and delicate apprehensions of the unseen. And as with his utterances, so also with his acts, each one premeditated, each one the end product of a precisely calculated spiritual motivation. When, for example he misses the train to the Marabar through miscalculating the length of a prayer, he may indeed have done no more than miscalculate. On the other hand the miscalculation may have been an effect not a cause, the outcome possibly of that incommunicable awareness of what resided within the caves. Godbole himself, or something within yet apart from him, may well have decided that wisdom itself would be better served if he did not go. In the same way his occasional capacity for inaction, as when he fails to come out publicly in support of Aziz, slips off evasively to his new appointment before the impending trial, cannot be explained superficially. Mrs Moore, we must remember, was also at this time being evasive, declining to declare herself publicly, eventually slipping away. In both there may well have been, consciously or otherwise, the realisation that here and now at the human level nothing was achievable, that the time and the place for a higher more effective intervention had yet to come. Also censurable at the purely human level was Godbole's apparent obtuseness towards Aziz, his failure to notify him, though he knew the facts, that Fielding had married not Miss Quested but Stella Moore. His silence, Aziz justifiably protests, has plunged him into a pretty pickle. And Godbole's "Never be angry with me. I am, as far as my limitations permit, your true friend",[71] is disarming rather than explanatory. Yet we must still assume an explanation, look for it beyond the appearance of mere absent-mindedness, of a culpable indifference to material things. Could it be that the misunderstanding was somehow necessary, that in rebound from it Aziz and Fielding would be the more firmly committed to reconciliation—the very purpose, occultly communicated to Godbole, of Mrs Moore? In assessing the mystery that is Godbole, a residue of question marks is left unavoidably on our hands.

[71] *P.I.*, p. 318.

We can infer, surmise, indulge in educated guesses, but must lose ourselves eventually in the intimations of a wisdom that Godbole himself cannot make explicit. Yet he possesses and is possessed of it, and in his strange presence in consequence all lesser mortals must feel themselves as children preoccupied with toys.

The nature of the unseen as presented, explicitly and by implication in *A Passage to India*, and the extent to which it is endorsed by the author personally, must now be defined. Perhaps there is, as we have already suggested, rather less explicitness in this novel than in *Howards End*; for example, the word "unseen" is used only once, in connexion with Miss Quested's resumption of her morning kneel to Christianity. Yet the unseen, though unspecified as such, is once more continuously present, determining character, precipitating and informing from first to last every thought, word, and action. Once again, as in *Howards End*, the existence of an unseen spiritual world has been postulated to us in terms of its various manifestations at the human level, in particular through the medium of the dead. After death, Mrs Moore like Mrs Wilcox before her, exercises a greater rather than a lesser influence upon the living, even to the extent of actually manipulating their lives. Beyond this point, beyond suggesting, and always by implication, that the unseen exists and that the dead inhabit it, the author still does not attempt to go; and to this extent *A Passage to India* is no more than a re-statement of the spiritual position finally attained to in *Howards End*. That position, it will be remembered, involved a few speculative gestures in the direction of Theosophy and of its observations on the life after death and the nature of the unseen. In *A Passage to India* no further reference to Theosophy will be found, but on the other hand India itself is very much the spiritual home of Theosophy, the fountain-head of the two great religions, Buddhism and Hinduism, upon which its teachings depend.[72] Forster himself

[72] Of interest in this connexion is the speculation of Mr Paul Fussell Jr in his article, "Mrs Moore: Some suggestions", in *Philological Quarterly*, xxxii (1953), pp. 381-95, that Mr Forster in creating Mrs Moore may have had in mind some of the experiences of Mme H. P. Blavatsky, founder of the Theosophical Move-

N

does not emerge as an advocate for Hinduism any more than
for Theosophy. Like Ralph and Stella Moore he appears rather
as one who likes Hinduism for its involvement with the unseen
while taking no personal interest in its forms. (This lack of a
personal identification is very apparent in the account of Gokul
Ashtami that Forster gives us in *The Hill of Devi*.[73]) Yet
Hinduism, in particular through Professor Godbole, is allowed
to speak for itself and in doing so might be expected to take us
somewhat further into the unseen than previously. However, it
scarcely does so. Hinduism in fact, as presented to us in *A
Passage to India*, is notably inexplicit on the subject of the
underlying spiritual reality in which it so implicitly believes.
Indeed the point is finally made with reference to the Gokul
Ashtami festival that any kind of explicit spiritual communication is not to be looked for. At the climax of the festival when
the Birth occurs and Infinite Love, taking upon itself the form
of Shri Krishna, saves the world, those involved have at all
events attempted to undergo a spiritual experience. The human
spirit, by a "desperate contortion" has sought to "ravish the
unknown", flinging down science, history, and even beauty in
the process. But has it succeeded? Books written afterwards,
comments the author, will say "Yes":

> But how if there is such an event, can it be remembered after-
> wards? How can it be expressed in anything but itself? Not
> only from the unbeliever are mysteries hid, but the adept
> himself cannot retain them. He may think, if he chooses, that
> he has been with God, but as soon as he thinks it, it becomes
> history, and falls under the rules of time.[74]

The unseen, in other words—the author's own words—existing
only at the level of eternity, may not be transferred thence into
the world of time, but must by its very nature remain incommunicable, indescribable in human terms. Nevertheless, as

ment. Mme Blavatsky also visited India (in 1879), heard ghostly voices in some
caves near Bombay, was addicted to patience. No resemblance in character is
of course to be found, but the parallels between the two women are suggestive of a
continuing interest by Forster in Theosophy. Mr Fussell speculates further on the
extent and nature of that interest in his article.
[73] *The Hill of Devi*, pp. 100-20. London (Edward Arnold) 1953.
[74] *P.I.*, p. 300.

we have seen, the author does in some measure continue his attempt to communicate and to describe, to imply something at least of the nature of the unseen in terms of its observable effects at the level of human events and personality. For example, the identification of the unseen as a source of love is suggested to us not only implicitly, as in previous novels, through the capacity for love observable in those sensitive to the unseen, but now through Professor Godbole explicitly. In his state of partial disembodiment at the festival, splinters of detail from the bodily past, an old woman he had met in Chandrapore, a wasp, a stone occur to the Professor's thinning senses, and he is impelled not only to love them, but to recognise that in doing so he is imitating God. He succeeds with the wasp and the old woman, who is Mrs Moore, and knows that he has thus assumed, however inadequately, a divine attribute.

To this extent, by explicitly associating the unseen with love, *A Passage to India* can be said to have taken a significant step beyond its predecessors. Also new and spiritually significant, and again derivable from Hinduism, are the various passages in the novel where spiritual concern passes beyond man himself to the various kingdoms of nature subordinate to him, with the implication that these too may have to be included ultimately in the divine promise of salvation. In any assessment of the sum total of sadness on the face of the earth, the author now suggests, the pain that is endured not only by men but "by animals and plants, and perhaps by the stones"[75] needs to be taken into account. Hinduism, aware of the divine reality within the illusory appearance, attempts to extend love to all created things, and when Professor Godbole fails to do so in the case of a stone, he recognises this as a sign of his own limitations. In the same way, the two devoted Christian missionaries, old Mr Graysford and young Mr Sorley, challenged by both the Hindu and Buddhist concern with the lower kingdoms, are also represented as attempting in characteristically inadequate fashion to think the matter out. In God's house are many mansions from which no human being regardless of race will be turned away. But will the divine hospitality cease there?

[75] *P.I.*, p. 257.

Consider, with all reverence, the monkeys. May there not be
a mansion for monkeys also? Old Mr. Graysford said No, but
young Mr. Sorley, who was advanced, said Yes; he saw no
reason why monkeys should not have their collateral share of
bliss, and he had sympathetic discussions about them with his
Hindu friends. And the jackals? Jackals were indeed less to
Mr. Sorley's mind, but he admitted that the mercy of God,
being infinite, may well embrace all mammals. And the wasps?
He became uneasy during the descent to wasps, and apt to
change the conversation. And oranges, cactuses, crystals and
mud? and the bacteria inside Mr. Sorley? No, no, this is going
too far. We must exclude someone from our gathering, or we
shall be left with nothing.[76]

A somewhat extended unseen therefore, embracing in love
not only man but all created things, confronts us in *A Passage
to India*—an unseen to which Christianity in its official capacity,
is unable adequately to subscribe. Once again in the final
novel the limitations of that particular religion, "poor little
talkative Christianity" are made devastatingly apparent. The
fallibility of old Mr Graysford and young Mr Sorley, their
ineptitude in confrontation with the cosmic immensities of
Hinduism and Buddhism, need no further elaboration. The
bells of their church, though calling to all mankind, do so feebly
and inefficiently and are ignored. During a famine they
distribute food and make converts, but when times improve are
naturally left alone again, "and though surprised and aggrieved
each time this happened, they never learnt wisdom".[77] Even
less adequate of course is the official Christianity of Anglo-
India, the Public School sort embraced by such as Ronny
Heaslop that "never goes bad, even in the tropics". Perhaps
the criticism here is being directed rather against the limited
exponents of Christianity than against the religion itself. But
we must also remember that Mrs Moore was, to begin with, a
devout and conventional Christian who embarrassed her son by
reminding him of the Christian principle of love. Yet Mrs
Moore, even before the spiritual devastation inflicted by the
Marabar, had already begun to waver. In confrontation with

[76] *P.I.*, p. 40f.   [77] *P.I.*, p. 105.

India, the Christian God, though constantly in her thoughts, began to satisfy her less and less:

> She must needs pronounce his name frequently, as the greatest she knew, yet she had never found it less efficacious. Outside the arch there seemed always an arch, beyond the remotest echo a silence.[78]

In comparison with Christianity, Mohammedanism, the religion of Aziz, is accorded a considerable degree of recognition. Here at least is a living religion, communicating itself not pallidly through the mind, but vividly and instinctively through the blood. Positively, as mediator of the unseen, Islam has much to contribute, is the source of all that is fine and generous in Aziz, the well-spring of his capacity for love. Yet Aziz, in terms of his sensitivity to the unseen, is as we have seen limited, subordinate in particular to Mrs Moore and her children, Ralph and Stella. Like Fielding, he, and Islam along with him, are presented to us as missing something. The shallow arcades of the mosque provide but a limited spiritual asylum, and

> "There is no God but God" doesn't carry us far through the complexities of matter and spirit; it is only a game with words, really, a religious pun, not a religious truth.[79]

Mohammedanism, presented as an instinctive religion, addressing itself to the heart at the expense of the head, thus takes us so far, but in the last analysis not far enough. Aziz, though presented in greater depth and subtlety, is no more finally than a Gino Carella writ large.

In its presentation therefore of the unseen as a positive force, a source of benevolence, *A Passage to India*, in particular through the medium and witness of Hinduism, achieves an extension in depth and, to a limited extent, in range also. An extension at all events in depth and subtlety is also to be found in its assessment of the darker side of the unseen, of its manifestation as evil. That spiritual experiences of two kinds are present in the final novel is evident: those resulting in benevolence and its eventual triumph; and those, as undergone in particular at the Marabar caves by Miss Quested and Mrs Moore, that result in evil. The evil set in train by the Marabar, and later counter-

---

[78] *P.I.*, p. 55f.   [79] *P.I.*, p. 287.

acted in the spirit by Mrs Moore, is represented more explicitly than heretofore as really existing. Even the somewhat prosaic Fielding is made aware following the arrest of Aziz of a mass of madness that "had to be shoved back into its pit somehow", and later conceives of it as an evil propagating in every direction with "an existence of its own, apart from anything that was done or said by individuals".[80] Also, after the trial, when the Indian mob shambles vengefully towards the hospital, it is represented as being possessed by the "spirit of evil", striding abroad over an earth and under a sky rendered insanely ugly. The exact nature of the experiences undergone by Miss Quested and Mrs Moore in the caves is never precisely indicated, but that they were productive of evil, in the one case an explosion of racial hatred and injustice, in the other a catastrophic loss of faith, cannot be disputed. On the other hand the caves themselves and the hills that contain them are not presented to us as being in themselves evil or as the abode of evil spirits. They are by reason of their immeasurable antiquity associated with a kind of primeval nothingness preceding not only good and evil, but also space and time. To the questions posed by Forster himself with reference to Mrs Moore: "What had spoken to her in that scoured-out cavity of the granite? What dwelt in the first of the caves?" the answer is given:

> Something very old and very small. Before time, it was before space also. Something snub-nosed, incapable of generosity—the undying worm itself.[81]

Moreover, and however inconceivably, the "something" in the caves or the hills is represented as being not only older than time and space, but older than spirit itself. The unspeakable hills, "flesh of the sun's flesh", rising abruptly and insanely out of the plain, bear no relation to anything dreamt or seen. However, to call them "uncanny" is to suggest ghosts, and

> they are older than all spirit. Hinduism has scratched and plastered a few rocks, but the shrines are unfrequented, as if pilgrims, who generally seek the extraordinary, had here found too much of it. Some saddhus did once settle in a cave, but they were smoked out, and even Buddha, who must have passed this

---

way down to the Bo tree of Gya, shunned a renunciation more complete than his own, and has left no legend of struggle or victory in the Marabar.[82]

Entrances, we are informed, have been made into some of the Marabar caves, but others, deeper in the granite, have remained sealed up "since the arrival of the gods":

> Local report declares that these exceed in number those that can be visited, as the dead exceed the living—four hundred of them, four thousand or million. Nothing is inside them, they were sealed up before the creation of pestilence or treasure; if mankind grew curious and excavated, nothing, nothing would be added to the sum of good or evil. One of them is rumoured within the boulder that swings on the summit of the highest of the hills; a bubble-shaped cave that has neither ceiling nor floor, and mirrors its own darkness in every direction infinitely. If the boulder falls and smashes, the cave will smash too—empty as an Easter egg.[83]

A nothingness, a quintessential nothingness older than creation, older than spirit, is thus to be sensed by those penetrating into the caves, and is to be suggested to them in particular by the reduction of all sound within the cave to a howling, meaningless, uniform echo—"boum" or "ou-boum". Not all who enter are affected; neither Fielding nor Aziz experience anything out of the ordinary. But for others, those presumably attuned in a particular way to the unseen, the experience is climactic. What exactly "happens" in the case of Miss Quested, is never made clear. As she enters the cave she is thinking of love, realising for the first time that she is about to enter into a loveless marriage, and when she emerges a few moments later the hysterical delusion of a sexual assault by Aziz has established itself in her mind. A certain connexion between the two states may perhaps be inferred logically, but the nature of the intervening experience in the cave, the brush as it were with the incommunicable "Ancient Night" of Professor Godbole, is never indicated. On the other hand, in the case of Mrs Moore, the sudden and catastrophic transition precipitated in parti-

---

[82] *P.I.*, p. 130. The notion that anything can be "older than spirit" is puzzling, to say the least! Spirit, as opposed to soul and body, is surely not subject (to use Forster's own phrase) to "the rules of time".

[83] *P.I.*, p. 131.

cular by the cave's echo, is not only more logically apprehend-
able, but also to some extent familiar. For what after all is this
quintessential nothingness suggested by the echo and witnessed
by the cave, but once again—on a vaster scale—the goblin
footfall, the panic and emptiness detected by Helen Schlegel in
the Fifth Symphony of Beethoven? Once again, by a single
insidious touch, all meaning and purpose is represented to us as
having been drained out of life; infinity itself, along with piety,
courage and pathos, reduced to insignificance. "Everything
exists, nothing has value." In Helen's case, the insidious quali-
fying moment comes and goes; but on Mrs Moore, older than
Helen and so less resilient, the undermining influence persists,
affecting adversely both her thought and conduct, although
with some slight respite, for the limited remainder of her days.

The echoing nothingness of the Marabar caves then,
neither good nor evil in itself and yet clearly productive of evil
in those shattered spiritually by contact with it, may be no more
than an extended version of the panic and emptiness introduced
to us in *Howards End*. And once again, as in that novel, the
author, like Beethoven before him, declines to come to rest in
his own pessimism, and *A Passage to India* like its immediate
predecessor is brought through spiritually to a triumphant
conclusion. At one point though, the pessimism of the final
novel is taken significantly if somewhat enigmatically further
than this and is accorded a kind of ultimate endorsement by the
author. That Mrs Moore and Miss Quested underwent in the
caves some kind of visionary experience, and that the effect of
this experience was, especially for Mrs Moore, profoundly
disillusioning, is made clear enough. The author however is not
now content, at all events in this vital connexion, to allow his
characters to speak for him. In the course of the passage de-
scribing the nature and origin of the voice in the cave he introduces an aside, speaks out to the reader personally. Visions,
he insists, and by implication he himself is no stranger to them,

> are supposed to entail profundity, but—Wait till you get one,
> dear reader! The abyss also may be petty, the serpent of
> eternity made of maggots.[84]

---

[84] *P.I.*, p. 217.

Questioned about this far-reaching observation in later years, Forster has tended to play down its significance, to characterise the whole nightmare experience of Mrs Moore, despite his own personal confirmation of it, as no more than, "a moment of negation . . . the vision with its back turned",[85] and such within the context of *A Passage to India* as a whole it is clearly made out to be. The negation and disillusion of Mrs Moore, even before she leaves India, is shown to be neither absolute nor final, and her experience of the unseen beyond death, while not denying it as a source of evil and negation, certainly proclaims it as productive also of goodness and love. Yet the absoluteness of the author's statement about his own personal experience of the unseen, his apparent insistence that *all* visionary experiences must confirm the undermining nothingness of eternity, remains, and cannot really be counteracted by subsequent second thoughts and reservations. Once again in fact, as in *Howards End*, the ominous note of ultimate doubt is being sounded, the illogical claim made that the universe and all human endeavour within it can be at one and the same time both meaningful and meaningless. In *A Passage to India* however, through the medium of a single aside of devastating import, the author seems to be resolving the contradiction, coming down if anything on the negative side.

Two further manifestations suggestive in some measure of the nature of the unseen, are present in the final novel, as in its predecessors—those conveyed to us through superstition and, more implicitly, through the workings of fate. In relation to superstitions the author is once again equivocal, presenting them, as it were, for what they are worth, neither accepting nor denying. Ghosts, for example, may or may not exist, but then there is the mysterious accident sustained by the Nawab Bahadur's car on the Marabar road, and its subsequent "explanation":

> Nine years previously, when first he had had a car, he had driven it over a drunken man and killed him, and the man had been waiting for him ever since. The Nawab Bahadur was

[85] Angus Wilson, "A Conversation with E. M. Forster", in *Encounter*, November 1957, p. 54.

innocent before God and the Law, he had paid double the
compensation necessary; but it was no use, the man continued
to wait in an unspeakable form, close to the scene of his death.[86]

The Nawab himself, and those to whom he relates the incident,
believe the story; for them it is a racial secret communicable
more by blood than speech. Aziz, however, though a belief in
ghosts runs in his blood also, chooses on this occasion to hold
aloof, to insist that Moslems must get rid of such superstitions if
India is ever to advance. But then there is also Mrs Moore.
When Adela and Ronny tell her of the accident she shivers and
says "A ghost!" although the idea of a ghost scarcely passes her
lips.

 The same equivocal acknowledgement of "festering superstition", occurs also in the final section of the book with the
description of the young Mohammedan saint worshipped at
Mau:

> His mother said to him, "Free prisoners." So he took a sword
> and went up to the fort. He unlocked a door, and the prisoners
> streamed out and resumed their previous occupations, but the
> police were too much annoyed and cut off the young man's
> head. Ignoring its absence, he made his way over the rocks that
> separate the fort and the town, killing policemen as he went,
> and he fell outside his mother's house, having accomplished her
> orders. Consequently there are two shrines to him to-day—
> that of the Head above, and that of the Body below—and they
> are worshipped by the few Mohammedans who live near, and
> by Hindus also.[87]

Aziz, once again, tends to be scornful, and forbids his children
to accept such superstitious nonsense. But, like himself, they
are impervious to logical argument, and continue to say and
believe what their natures suggest. The description of the saint
and his mythical activities is whimsical, affectionately humorous.
We are reminded by it of another saint, Santa Deodata
in *Where Angels Fear to Tread*, whose claims to sanctity are
described with an equal fondness and whimsicality. Once
again apparently, superstition as an existent fact is being called

---

 [86] *P.I.*, p. 103. The "mysterious accident" has its counterpart in reality. See
The Hill of Devi, pp. 89-90.
 [87] *P.I.*, p. 308.

to our attention, not for literal acceptance, but as witnessing perhaps, at least in some measure, both to the existence and nature of the unseen.

On the subject of fate, conceived of as an invisible disposing power, *A Passage to India* has on the surface nothing specific to say. This, in view of the author's preoccupation with Indian religion, is perhaps surprising. Fundamental to both Buddhism and Hinduism is the concept of reincarnation, of the part played by the previous life, or lives, in determining the destiny or Karma of the individual. And yet, neither in *A Passage to India* nor in his autobiographical *The Hill of Devi* does the author make any reference to Karma or indicate any awareness of the totality of its influence on the Indian way of life and thought. Fate in *A Passage to India* is less in evidence than, for example, in *A Room With a View*; but still by implication it is there, in the conveyed sense of events occurring, not haphazardly, but purposefully, so that a predetermined spiritual objective may be achieved. This is particularly evident at the book's conclusion when all those involved in the final process of reconciliation find themselves assembled at Mau with a fortuitousness that they themselves, in terms of their surface reasons for being there, cannot adequately explain. The surface reasons are there and not to be discounted; nor may we oversimplify by insisting that the spirit of Mrs Moore posthumously acting has contrived it all. The first move towards Mau was taken in Mrs Moore's lifetime by Professor Godbole, slipping off to his appointment there in the days preceding the trial. And Mrs Moore herself, it will be remembered, while passing through Asirgarh on her way out of India seems to be vouchsafed a premonition of events later to take place there and over which in the spirit she will preside. Exactly what we are entitled to infer from all this is never precisely indicated. But the implication of an unseen force at work influencing and even precipitating events at the human level has once again been made.

In relation, then, both to superstition and to the workings of fate, we can say once again of the unseen in *A Passage to India*, that any extension beyond *Howards End* has been in depth rather than in range. Thus it may be concluded that the author's final novel, though superior in many ways to any of its predecessors, represents spiritually a marking time. Here finally is a point of culmination, beyond which the author reveals himself as unwilling or perhaps by definition unable to go. That he has not succeeded in doing so, and that the inhibiting doubts featuring so largely in *A Passage to India* have not been overcome, is certainly suggested by the fact that no further novels (over a period now of more than forty years) have been forthcoming.

It now remains, having established as objectively as possible the spiritual position of which *A Passage to India* is the final, definitive expression, to submit that position to critical assessment. Is it acceptable or unacceptable, adequate or limited? Is it indeed a position beyond which, as the author seems to imply, it is not possible for anyone to go?

VIII

Conclusions

IT will be apparent that the concept of the unseen and its manifestations informing the novels and stories of E. M. Forster is one that comes to rest in paradox, in positive and negative assertions and implications that cannot be logically reconciled. The existence of an unseen world, a transcendent spiritual reality, has been at no point questioned or denied; on the other hand entirely contradictory and irreconcilable claims have been made concerning its nature and significance. On the positive side, we have been made aware, by statement and implication, of the unseen as a force active in human affairs, and as a means, irresistible in the long run, to human salvation. Over against it, however, and in total and irreconcilable opposition to it, has been set a negative concept, an unseen that proclaims the ultimate nothingness of the universe and the futility within it of every kind of human endeavour. No attempt is made to reconcile this paradox, to conceive, for example, of doubt itself as a negative spiritual manifestation to be fought and overcome. Instead, we have been tacitly and finally required to accept the illogical—a universe that is at one and the same time everything and nothing, meaningful and meaningless.

We cannot do so, and by way of conclusion to our analysis of stories and novels, it becomes necessary to submit the author's implicit and fundamental paradox to more searching examination. Does he himself really subscribe to it? Or does he in fact come down personally on one side or the other, the positive or the negative? The final spiritual emphasis of the novels and stories has been, as we have demonstrated, predominantly positive. Only in one of the novels, *The Longest Journey*, does the emphasis seem to fall on the side of spiritual deterioration and defeat, and even then not decisively. Otherwise, for those susceptible of harmony, able to connect the seen with the unseen, the head with the heart, salvation on this side of the grave has always been assured. This overwhelmingly is the message of Forster the creative artist, this the interpretation of life in terms of which the created characters and their environment stand before us with unquestionable reality, indeed possessed of a higher reality than would be theirs in everday life. Why then, we may well ask, is the author still unsatisfied, still unconvinced by his own conviction, his own representation of positive and negative, darkness and light, in perpetual conflict, with hope in the outcome always subsisting, and the assurance of redemption on this side of the grave? Why must there always be a final reserve of pessimism, an ultimate insistence not that the universe *may be* after all meaningless, but that, however illogically, it *is*?

On the assumption that the illogical is never acceptable, we must look for its resolution where alone it can be found, in some flaw, some inadequacy in the author's fundamental concept of the unseen. The nature of that concept has been suggested to us so far only through the medium of the novels and stories. Forster, however, confronts us not only as a creative artist, but also more personally and directly, as critic and commentator, through a wide range of essays. If we turn, however, to these critical writings, as we surely have a right to do, for a more specific elucidation of the author's views on the unseen, we shall be strangely disappointed. Even an essay with so promising a title as "What I Believe", will be found to consist of nothing more than idealistic advice on the conduct of human life, without any indication of the spiritual basis from which such idealism must proceed. Equally uncommunicative on the subject of the unseen is, for example, the author's well-known *Aspects of the Novel*. In the chapter of this book entitled "Prophecy", he takes note to be sure of characters and situations that stand for more than themselves and are attended by infinity, and identifies four writers, Dostoevsky, Melville, D. H. Lawrence and Emily Brontë, as alone possessed of the prophetic capacity to create them. But any explicit indication of his own personal concern as a writer with the same kind of

infinity and with the means of its presentation through literature is absent. The occasion for his observations, a series of
public lectures, was perhaps unsuited to the personal note.
Somewhere, however, within the critical writings a place should
certainly have been found for a personal statement, an unequivocal indication of the extent to which he is prepared to
endorse the concept of the unseen of which the novels and
stories are the manifest expression. Yet he does not say, does
not endorse. And there is no doubt that this reluctance, this
virtual refusal to assess his own works in other than purely
humanistic terms, has done much to encourage so many critics
to ignore the spiritual implications within them. A certain
spiritual evasiveness is thus to be detected throughout the
critical writings, a reluctance to go beyond the purely human,
to see the human, as in the novels, *sub specie aeternitatis*.

The external human world of the thirties and forties with
which many of the essays sought to deal, a world menaced and
eventually involved in war, had little enough to commend it;
and it might be argued that Forster by approaching it so
consistently at the human level was seeking to come to terms
with it. In fact, however, as the essays themselves make
abundantly evident, he was not doing so. At a time when, as
seldom before in history, the individual was being required to
take a stand on moral and political issues, to allow his first
principles to be publicly known, Forster, though clearly on the
side of right and decency, was avoiding anything in the nature
of a fundamental spiritual commitment. At no point did he fail
to denounce the evil of the time inherent, for example, in the
Fascist and Nazi tyrannies, on the other hand at no point either
was he prepared to assess that evil on a spiritual basis or identify
himself publicly with those nerving themselves to resist it by
force, or even with those, numerous at the time, proposing the
alternative of non-violent passive resistance. Instead a kind of
personal abdication was being advocated, a retreat into privacy.
The sensitive and the civilised, it was argued, on every hand
menaced and insulted, should silently withdraw, go underground, as it were, with their values and inner resources until
in the fullness of time, the embattled lunacy of the outer world
having finally destroyed itself, sensitivity and civilisation would

again become possible. An aristocracy, in other words, not of power but of sensitivity was to be the solution:

> On they go—an invincible army, yet not a victorious one. The aristocrats, the elect, the chosen, the Best People—all the words that describe them are false, and all attempts to organize them fail. Again and again Authority, seeing their value, has tried to net them and to utilize them. . . . But they slip through the net and are gone; when the door is shut, they are no longer in the room; their temple, as one of them remarked, is the Holiness of the Heart's Affection, and their kingdom, though they never possess it, is the wide-open world.[1]

When the supreme challenge of the war itself finally came, despite an interlude of resentment and disdain savagely expressed in the article "They Hold Their Tongues",[2] Forster rallied in its support, at least to the extent of making, in 1940, three anti-Nazi broadcasts and compiling a war pamphlet "Nordic Twilight".[3] In essence, however, the pamphlet and the broadcasts did no more than recognise that the Nazis were intolerable, and that the war, having started, it would be better, all things considered, if it were won. Of the actual confrontation involved, however, with spiritual forces as evil as any in history, there is still no specific acknowledgement. The underlying aristocratic detachment, product of an absolute unwillingness to come to terms with the horrible world "out there", remained, and up to the present has not been significantly modified.

In *Howards End*, as we noted in our analysis, Forster went as far as he was prepared to go in acknowledgement of the outer world of "telegrams and anger", in recognition of the undoubted fact that houses, though they cannot stand by bricks alone, yet cannot stand without them. Such acknowledgement, however, of the Wilcox world, was always fatally qualified, conditional on the expectation that the civilisation of movement to which it was committed would some day work itself to rest, and the ordered decency of the earth-centred past return. Temporary accommodation with scientific progress

[1] "What I Believe", in *Two Cheers for Democracy*, p. 81f.
[2] *Op. cit.*, pp. 38-40.
[3] "Macmillan War Pamphlets", London (Macmillan) 1940.

might be necessary, but only on the understanding that such progress was in fact regress, a collective movement in the wrong direction during which the earth itself and those still sensitive to it could do no more than withdraw and patiently beat time. In the decades since *Howards End* this rejection of science and all its works has been frequently re-stated, most uncompromisingly perhaps in the essay "English Prose Between 1918 and 1939" published in 1944 at the very heart of the Second World War. There is, he declares here,

> a huge economic movement which has been taking the whole world, Great Britain included, from agriculture towards industrialism. That began about a hundred and fifty years ago, but since 1918 it has accelerated to an enormous speed, bringing all sorts of changes into national and personal life. It has meant organization and plans and the boosting of the community. It has meant the destruction of feudalism and relationship based on the land, it has meant the transference of power from the aristocrat to the bureaucrat and the manager and the technician. Perhaps it will mean democracy, but it has not meant it yet, and personally I hate it. So I imagine do most writers, however loyally they try to sing its praises and to hymn the machine. But however much we detest this economic shift we have to recognize it as an important influence, more important than any local peace or war, which is going on all the time and transforming our outlooks. It rests on applied science, and as long as science is applied it will continue.[4]

Along with this open detestation of what is often called the technological revolution, which has certainly not ceased to accelerate since 1944, has gone in Forster's case a special resentment against the destructive impact of that revolution upon man's natural environment. When the beautiful agricultural setting in Hertfordshire, commemorated in *Howards End*, was finally sacrificed to accommodate a satellite town, Forster can recognise the economic need for the houses, but at the same time cannot free himself from the conviction that

> something irreplaceable has been destroyed, and that a little piece of England has died as surely as if a bomb had hit it.[5]

---

[4] *Two Cheers for Democracy*, p. 278.
[5] "The Challenge of Our Time", *op. cit.*, p. 68.

Such an attitude, as Forster himself recognises, is the product of divided loyalties, towards his working-class friends who need the houses, and towards the irreplaceable in the English countryside that must be sacrificed to provide them. In this instance the loyalties are divided and Forster takes refuge in ambiguity. He cannot, he says, equate the problem. But there is little doubt where his personal sympathy lies. The technological revolution, essentially the conquest by man of his natural environment, will go on, but unsupported by Forster. Instead he will continue to revert to the unindustrial past, glad to have known the English countryside

> before its roads were too dangerous to walk on and its rivers too dirty to bathe in, before its butterflies and wild flowers were decimated by arsenical spray, before Shakespeare's Avon frothed with detergents and the fish floated belly-up in the Cam.[6]

The viewpoint is emotional, and to some extent illogical and unjustified. For example, it takes no cognizance of the fact that the technologists who have in the past so recklessly upset the balance of nature, are now through methods of conservation and preservation actively seeking to restore it, and with some promise of ultimate success. But to this, the positive, beneficial and constructive side of technology, Forster remains indifferent. For his whole antipathy to the modern world, his consistent, and at times petulant, refusal to come to terms with it, is based on no impartial assessment but, as the novels have shown, on a rejection of the intellectual self-consciousness that has brought it into being.[7] In the novels open hostility towards the intellect and self-consciousness in general was directed principally against its exponents in the cultural field, Cecil Vyse, Tibby Schlegel and the chattering monkeys of the London drawing-rooms. But it has also been more forcibly expressed through the medium of the author's preferences, in particular for such as Gino Carella and Italians generally, for Stephen Wonham and Aziz, in whom the conscious intellect is shown to be somewhat

---

[6] "Aspect of a Novel", in *The Bookseller*, p. 1230, 10 September 1960.

[7] It could be argued that the Forsterian rejection of technology and of the kind of intellectuality responsible for it, had already received definitive expression in "The Machine Stops", first published in 1909.

in obeyance, subordinate to unreasoning impulses of an instinctive kind—impulses originating in a spirituality, an unseen rooted far back in time. Not an extension but a lowering, a dulling of consciousness is thus being upheld for us. Not an advance into the modern world created by the intellect, but a withdrawal from it into the primeval spirituality of the ancestral past.

In this respect, Forster has often been compared to D. H. Lawrence, with his belief in the blood, the flesh, the tribal unconsciousness as being wiser than the intellect. And certainly no one has been more passionate than Lawrence in denouncing the headlong advance of the twentieth century into scientific industrialism. Forster, though committed in much the same way to the primeval, the instinctive, does not pursue the logic of his committal to the point attained by Lawrence of denouncing all scientists as liars and refusing on principle to look down a microscope.[8] Nor does he spend much of his life, as Lawrence did, in actual quest for the mindless tribalism in which he claims to believe. Lawrence's creed, his rejection of human consciousness in favour of a return to the instinctive spirituality of the past, is consistent and intelligible, however impractical and mistaken we may consider it to be. And there is no doubt that, up to a point, Forster would like to subscribe to it.[9] However, he finds himself ultimately unable to do so, unable in particular to overlook his own realisation that the instinctive spirituality of the past, the mysticism of the heart as we have called it, though conferring great benefits, does so at a disturbing price. Gino Carella, Stephen Wonham, Aziz have at their disposal a warmth and spontaneity, a redemptive capacity for life denied to the coldly intellectual; but over against this, and recognisable as proceeding from the same spiritual source, must be set their no less remarkable capacity for the brutal, the treacherous, the obscene. Perhaps the primitive unseen, instinctively experienced, does not always demand in return for its benefits so

[8] Aldous Huxley, "D. H. Lawrence", in *The Olive Tree*, p. 208. London (Chatto and Windus) 1936.

[9] The complex of attraction and repulsion felt by Forster for Lawrence as a writer and thinker existed also at the personal level. See Wilfred Stone, *The Cave and the Mountain*, pp. 379-81.

o*

exacting a price. Ruth Wilcox, for example, would seem to derive from it nothing but wisdom and benevolence. Nevertheless by some at least a sufficient price must be paid to render highly questionable not only the unseen to whose influence they are being subjected, but also the state of consciousness, or rather unconsciousness, through which that subjection is taking place.

Inhibited then, by his own realisation of its darker side, from advocating a wholesale return in the D. H. Lawrence manner to the primitive, the unself-conscious, Forster is also held back, despite himself, from an equally wholesale rejection of the conscious modern scientific world by his recognition, as we have seen, of certain spiritual manifestations within it. With the insight of the artist he perceives these manifestations, is made aware through them of an unseen actually present and actively at work in man and his environment. As an artist he perceives and, at all events by implication, seeks to render his perceptions. As a thinker, however, he is unwilling or unable to endorse explicitly what as artist he has implied. According to Forster himself, in his capacity as thinker, the unseen is not to be found in terms of its manifestations within the material, but exists on its own in isolation from it and may not be experienced at all by the conscious mind. This concept of what is involved in the experience of the unseen is made very explicit for us in the meditative processes attributed to Professor Godbole at the festival of Gokul Ashtami. To begin with, it will be recalled, as the images of the wasp, the stone, the old Englishwoman (Mrs Moore) present themselves to him, he remains to some extent immersed in matter; but when the festival achieves its climax and the God is born, it is evident that for a moment at least the material has been set aside, an extra-sensory experience entered into. However, by reason of its nature, of the fact that it has taken place in isolation from the sense-perceptible world, the experience remains incommunicable; it can neither be remembered nor described. Stepping in personally at this point, the author says as much explicitly. The human spirit, he claims, has tried

> by a desperate contortion to ravish the unknown, flinging down science and history in the struggle, yes, beauty herself. Did it

succeed? Books written afterwards say "Yes." But how, if
there is such an event, can it be remembered afterwards? How
can it be expressed in anything but itself? Not only from the
unbeliever are mysteries hid, but the adept himself cannot
retain them. He may think, if he chooses, that he has been with
God, but as soon as he thinks it, it becomes history, and falls
under the rules of time.[10]

A comparison between this view of the mystical experience
and the Romantic view, to be found most explicitly in
Wordsworth, is instructive, for certain resemblances are evident.
For Wordsworth too, the mystical state when we "see into the
life of things" is attainable only when consciousness, the "light
of the sense" goes out, and we become "a living soul". Also we
would seem to find in Wordsworth a confirmation of Forster's
insistence on man's incapacity to retain the mystery he has
experienced. The soul, he says in *The Prelude*, "Remembering
how she felt, but what she felt Remembering not", retains no
more than an obscure sense of "possible sublimity".[11] To this
extent, we might say, the Wordsworthian and the Forsterian
views on the nature of mysticism correspond. Beyond this
point however, there are important divergences. In the first
place it has to be recognised that whereas Wordsworth was
himself a mystic, a philosopher in terms of his own mystical
experiences, Forster makes no claim to be similarly endowed.
Apart from the inconclusive and enigmatic, "Visions are
supposed to entail profundity—but, wait till you get one, dear
reader", he offers us nothing in the way of a personal mystical
experience to justify his intuitions of the unseen. Wordsworth
furthermore, though unable to describe his experiences of the
"Imagination" as he calls it, "through sad incompetence of
human speech", yet derived from them an unassailable conviction of the greatness of man and his ultimate fate. When the
light of the sense was extinguished, but with a flash that has
revealed the invisible world, he knows from then on, that

> . . . whether we be young or old,
> Our destiny, our being's heart and home,
> Is with infinitude, and only there;

---

[10] *P.I.*, p. 300.   [11] *The Prelude*, Book Second, ll. 315-18.

With hope it is, hope that can never die,
Effort, and expectation, and desire,
And something evermore about to be.[12]

By contrast we have from Forster, on the basis presumably of intuitions rather than any direct experience, the concept of an unseen that may indeed proclaim man's greatness and significance, his capacity for love, but equally and at the same time his nothingness. "The abyss also may be petty, the serpent of eternity made of maggots." And to this inhibiting and ultimate qualification we must undoubtedly attribute that alienation from external life so particularly apparent in the critical writings, an alienation for which his underlying theory of the nature of the mystical experience has provided the justification. If the unseen is conceived of as existing in isolation from the seen, and if it can be experienced only by annihilating the seen, then obviously the seen and every form of consciousness linking man with it must be thought of as an obstacle, an impediment that must be eliminated to permit the divine to enter in.

Such a concept of the unseen and of the preliminary process of annihilation that man must undergo in order to experience it, has been extensively presented and argued for us in the creative and critical writings of another twentieth-century author, Aldous Huxley. From the outset of his career as a writer Huxley, in contrast to Forster, whose predominant if contradictory optimism we have noted, has been strongly and consistently imbued with a sense of the total meaninglessness of human existence. In his novels, especially in *Eyeless in Gaza*, we can observe a limited attempt on the author's part to come to terms with external life and endow it with meaning, but the attempt is half-hearted at best and invariably theoretical. Eventually in *After Many a Summer*, published in 1939, Huxley abandoned all attempts to reconcile himself to external life, and on the assumption that meaning and purpose can be attained only in the mystical union with the divine, makes a clean sweep of human consciousness and every kind of activity proceeding from it. Man, in terms of the ultimate Huxleyan philosophy, is a nothingness indigent of God, and only by

[12] *The Prelude*, Book Sixth, ll. 603-8.

reverting to his intrinsic nothingness can he create the necessary vacuum for the manifestation of the Godhead within him. Thus by implication and definition all human activity, even the pursuit of the good, the beautiful and the true, must ultimately be set aside. At the human level inexorably, and all good intentions notwithstanding, nothing but evil can be achieved.[13] The extremeness of the Huxleyan conclusion, logically proceeding from the concept of an unseen totally divorced from matter, is hardly subscribed to by Forster. Yet it must be recognised that the unseen envisaged by Huxley is Forster's also, and only by a break in his own logic, by failing to carry his concept right through, can he escape the Huxleyan conclusion that all life at the human level is an evil nothingness, a barrier between man and God.

Up to a point, right up to the point of that final inhibiting reserve of hypothetical pessimism, Forster does escape. The malignant goblins of ultimate doubt and derision, the total negation witnessed to by the Marabar caves, are given a hearing, but then, like Beethoven, the author steps in, blows with his lips and scatters them, brings back the "gusts of splendour, the heroism, the youth, the magnificence of life and death". On a note, not of panic and emptiness, but of spiritual triumph and hope this side of the grave, the novels, like the symphonies of Beethoven, are thus brought to their conclusion. Triumph, it is true, the full measure of salvation, is reserved for those who in some degree have retained their instinct for an unseen of immemorial antiquity manifesting itself through "Italy", through the English soil, through the spiritual heritages of Hinduism and Islam. Those possessed through heredity with an instinct for the unseen are saved absolutely, no matter the moral aberrations into which by the same spiritual instinct they may be led. On the other hand those who, by venturing too far into intellectuality, into self-consciousness, have lost touch with their own instinct-guided past, are not necessarily on that account quite forsaken. The ancient unseen though disregarded is always there, biding its time, always ready to exert its redemptive influence through a particular place, a particular person.

[13] Aldous Huxley, *After Many a Summer*, pp. 90-122. London (Chatto and Windus) 1939.

The redemption may be partial, for instinct, once supplanted by consciousness, can hardly be resumed; but for those upon whom the ancient unseen in whatever form has impacted, Philip Herriton and Miss Abbott, Stewart Ansell, George Emerson and Lucy Honeychurch, Helen and Margaret Schlegel, Fielding, Miss Quested—for those at least a capacity for truer relationships and a more harmonious way of life will have been assured.

The optimism, the hope held out to the self-conscious, is guarded, limited, and has hardly become less so in the light of Forster's inability, as evidenced in the critical writings, to achieve the promise of harmony in life that he seems to hold out to the self-conscious characters in his novels. But can we accept his judgement and his theory, his insistence on the inferiority of consciousness to instinct? Do not the self-conscious characters, in particular Margaret Schlegel, bravely at odds with external life and winning through to inner harmony—do not these recommend themselves to us finally, in the author's despite, as the true progressives to whom the future evolving out of the trials of the present will belong? Must we indeed renounce them and their spiritual achievements in favour of an instinct-guided past, of a Carella, a Wonham, an Aziz, who when they come to people may love certainly, but are equally liable to betray and even to kill?

A distinction must always be drawn, as already suggested, between the Forster who as creative artist observes and presents life as he finds it, and the Forster who would interpret it in terms of a theory of the unseen. This theory must now be recognised as inadequate, unable to incorporate within its terms of reference all that has been artistically observed. On the face of it the position adopted by Forster in relation to the unseen might appear unexceptionable. If the nature of the mystical experience is indeed indescribable and incommunicable in human terms, and if it can only be entered into instinctively or unconsciously, then indeed the instinctive man, cradled without knowing it within the divine, is superior to the intellectual man who, by becoming self-conscious, has cut himself off from the unself-conscious spirituality of an instinct-guided past. Such a conclusion however depends on the assumption that the nature of the unseen *is* in fact incommunicable, that man cannot by conscious and deliberate thinking come to an understanding of his own spiritual composition and of the way in which, if it does do so, the spiritual manifests itself within the visible world.

In this connexion it becomes necessary to mention, as Forster himself does in *Howards End*, the body of information on spiritual matters summarised within the term Theosophy and representing nothing less than an attempt to render in terms intelligible to the human mind the nature and processes of the spiritual world. Forster it will be remembered, seemed neither to accept nor wholly reject the findings of Theosophy, but they and the considerable extension beyond them represented by Anthroposophy cannot be readily ignored in assessing what can or cannot be consciously known and communicated about the unseen world of soul and spirit. That extensive information on spiritual matters has been made available by Rudolf Steiner, founder of the Anthrophosophical movement, is already widely known, although comparatively few of those who know about it are prepared as yet to accept and make use of it.[14] Nevertheless it is there, communicated to us in a form accessible to the modern logical, scientifically conditioned mind. In Steiner, in other words, we do indeed encounter an individual gifted with mystical powers, able to undergo mystical experiences, and who not only claims that such experiences *can* be communicated through the medium of human speech, but has also succeeded in so communicating them. Steiner, whether we accept him or not, thus stands before us as one able to experience and investigate the unseen, and then to communicate the results of his own extra-sensory research, not in a suggestive language intelligible only to other mystics, but in terms taken exclusively from the world of everyday human existence. Wordsworth, at the beginning of the nineteenth century, could communicate the *feelings* involved in the mystical experience but nothing of its content, and this same incapacity

---

[14] Rudolf Steiner (1861-1925) incorporated the essentials of his Anthroposophy in *An Outline of Occult Science*. London (Rudolf Steiner) 1949; New York (Anthroposophic Press) 1949. Other important works by Steiner available in translation are *Theosophy*, *The Philosophy of Spiritual Activity*, and *Knowledge of the Higher Worlds and its Attainment*.

is to be found whenever we consult the mystical communications that have come down to us from antiquity, all of them fully intelligible only to those who had themselves undergone the experience in question. The conclusion from this, however, apparently supported by the mystical record itself, that spiritual experiences by their very nature must *always* remain incommunicable—a conclusion subscribed to by Forster—is one now to which the claims of Rudolf Steiner and the communications of Anthroposophy have to be referred. Moreover the conclusion itself is one with which Anthroposophy, by recognising a process of evolution in human consciousness, has undertaken to deal. Steiner, even more explicitly than Forster, is aware that the spirituality of the ancient past did not communicate itself to the conscious mind of man, that he had access to it instinctively in a dream-like state, a state of dim clairvoyance. According to Steiner again, this "old clairvoyance", as he calls it, is still, though diminishingly, active, manifesting itself for example in the often questionable extra-sensory powers of mediums, astrologers, fortune tellers, telepathists and so on. It is present furthermore in what is left of the dream-like collective consciousness of primitive tribal communities, and it is certainly no accident that D. H. Lawrence in his quest for such an "unconsciousness" turned to the aboriginal tribes of Australia and the Mexican Indians. In its more subtle form it is to be found moreover wherever an individual, or group, or nation, unable to face the demands and implications posed by self-consciousness, deliberately or instinctively seeks to erase or diminish that self-consciousness by a return to the unselfconsciousness of the past. However, as Steiner points out, and as common sense makes evident, the past can never be returned to. Modern man seeking in every direction for facts and proof, for scientifically verifiable knowledge, can never remain satisfied for long with the old atavistic promptings of instinct, or on the other hand with unreasoned appeals to faith. Self-conscious, he needs to know himself both physically and spiritually, and in both areas logically and scientifically on a basis of ascertainable facts. Anthroposophy, a science of the spirit, a compendium of spiritual facts about man and his environment and of the methods, the techniques of meditation, by which whose facts may be experienced and known, presents, whether for acceptance or rejection, an alternative on the one hand to crass materialism, and on the other to vain and dangerous experiments with the instinctive spirituality of the past. For such experiments, as Steiner frequently insists, are indeed dangerous. Simply to make contact with the unseen, any kind of contact with any aspect of the unseen, is no guarantee of moral and spiritual benefit.[15] And the powers and forces invoked instinctively through the medium of the old clairvoyance, as Forster himself in his own despite is compelled to demonstrate, are highly dubious, beneficial if at all at an exorbitant moral price. The unself-conscious spontaneity of a Gino Carella could express itself in a genius for affection, but equally in a demonic impulse to destroy. Forster's intuition in fact of the unseen as a possible source of malevolence, is one that Steiner on the basis of his own spiritual investigations would certainly confirm. Very explicitly Anthroposophy recognises in both the physical and spiritual worlds an incessant conflict between decadent and progressive forces; indeed many of the terrible demonic impulses that have wracked the twentieth century are logically inexplicable except in terms of a decadent spirituality, an "old clairvoyance" speaking to man's instincts at the expense of his consciousness and empowered in consequence only to mislead and to destroy.

Anthroposophy, barely hinted at by Forster in its primitive Theosophical form, cannot be too readily invoked at the present time in reference to the spiritual implications with which he has presented us in his capacity as a creative artist. Yet it throws light on those implications, resolves the element of the irreconcilable, the paradoxical within them, and in a way moreover that does no violence to logic or common sense.

Thus logic and common sense, no less than Anthroposophy, clearly reveal that we are concerned in Forster's novels and stories with two distinct levels of consciousness. A modern "daylight consciousness" through which man seeks to understand himself and the world about him logically and consciously

[15] It is relevant in this connexion to consider the recently publicised effects, moral and otherwise, of extra-sensory perceptions artificially induced through such drugs as mescalin and lysergic acid.

and an ancient "twilight consciousness" accessible only to those who have not advanced into self-consciousness or who, by reverting to instinct and cultivating the feelings at the expense of the intellect, would deliberately hearken back to a pre-self-conscious past. Forster, increasingly dismayed by the modern world that self-consciousness has made for itself, by the prospect of individuals advanced only part of the way towards civilisation, has tended, as we have seen, to renounce it, to invoke the "twilight consciousness" of the instinct-guided past. Along with this preference, however, this endorsement of the unself-conscious at the expense of the self-conscious, has gone the always scrupulous recognition that the benefits of unself-consciousness may have to paid for in malevolence, and in varying degrees of alienation from external life. The price paid by some of the unself-conscious, Wonham, Aziz, Carella, is a severe one, and even Ruth Wilcox, who alone in this category remains consistently benevolent, yet conveys the impression of one distinctly alienated except in theory from the outside world. The exorbitant price must be paid and the author obstinately and consistently requires us to witness it. In the early Italian novels, he envisages a number of self-conscious characters, Philip Herriton, Miss Abbott, Lucy Honeychurch, George Emerson, who derive from their passing contact with the instinctive spirituality of Italy that intensification of the feelings, that mysticism of the heart of which they stand in need. They achieve wholeness, a harmony of head and heart, and are represented to us in consequence as "saved". We are even invited to believe that Rickie Elliot also might have been "saved" had it only been made possible for him to go to Italy. In the ensuing novels, however, and in confrontation with such characters as Helen and Margaret Schlegel, Miss Quested, Fielding, it is made clear to us that the kind of salvation bestowed by such entities as "Italy" falls short of completeness, and will continue to do so so long as the self-conscious, intellectual element within it is unsubdued. Thus Margaret Schlegel, reconciler supreme of the head and the heart, the seen and the unseen, must see herself finally in relation to Howards End as no more than a guardian and preserver, subordinate to an unself-conscious spirituality to which she herself may never attain. Mrs Moore, perhaps, in comparison with Ruth Wilcox, might be represented as one not explicitly identified with the old, instinctive spirituality and who yet comes to be numbered among the truly saved. But Mrs Moore, though unconnected directly and specifically with an ancestral past, was still very much in herself a Ruth Wilcox, wise and good on a basis of instinct rather than consciousness, and surrounded by an alien world incomprehensible to her intellect.

That the unself-conscious spirituality to which he would have us all return is decadent and productive, if indulged in, of nothing but tragic consequences, Forster himself does not sufficiently realise. He can observe the consequences in the behaviour of his unself-conscious characters but cannot identify their cause. He can observe, for example, in *A Passage to India* and more specifically in *The Hill of Devi* the terrible consequences for that unhappy country of a decadent spirituality that prevents its adherents from coming to terms with external life. But the direct connexion between the spirituality and the tragedy he does not, or cannot bring himself to perceive. That on occasion the unseen itself and a sensitivity to it can be productive of tragedy, a source of decadent as well as progressive impulses, Forster certainly recognises, if only by implication. Unfortunately however, by associating decadence with consciousness and by insisting, at least in theory, that the unseen can be experienced only in a state of suspended consciousness, he has come to identify salvation with a form of spirituality within which it cannot be found. That the unseen can be experienced consciously, indeed through the medium of a consciousness systematically extended and developed, and that the experience itself can be logically communicated even to those who have not yet attained it, Forster, as thinker at all events, has not yet been able to bring himself to believe.

The thinker, however, as we have noted already, is in this case also an artist, endowed with exceptional insight into the facts and realities of human existence—an artist moreover who tends to come up with contradictions and paradoxes that he himself as thinker, cannot satisfactorily resolve. Forster, it will be remembered, in a passage descriptive of the creative process, has called attention to a subconscious element within it. The artist, he claims, on the basis undoubtedly of his own experience, "lets down as it were a bucket into his subconscious, and draws up something which is normally beyond his reach".[16] And when the process is over and the work of art, compounded of the conscious and the subconscious, stands created, the artist will look at it in some surprise, and wonder how on earth he did it. Something of this nature, an involuntary element that he himself cannot consciously account for, may well confront us in the works that Forster has created. As artist he cannot do other than accept the material, the intuitions with which he has been presented; as thinker however he may well fall short in the matter of interpretation. As thinker and by personal inclination he may lean towards his unself-conscious characters, endorse them in preference to their self-conscious counterparts; the paradox, however, of their malevolence, which as artist he cannot fail to perceive, must accompany their presentation. As thinker, and from inclination, he may wish to avert himself from the troubled world created by the conscious intellect, but as artist he cannot at the same time refrain from recognising its positive elements, from bringing back for acknowledgement despite himself, the gusts of splendour, the heroism, the youth the magnificence of life and death, the ultimate assurance of spiritual victory. And when the aversion, the intrinsic rejection of consciousness and the world made by it remains, for all the rhetoric, unexorcised, what can he do but resort to paradox, to the unbearable contradiction of a universe that is at one and the same time meaningful and meaningless, all and nothing? As thinker again, committed to the theory of an incommunicable unseen existing in isolation, Forster is logically precluded from finding within the visible world and at the human level anything in the way of a spiritual manifestation. And yet, as artist, he does indeed find such manifestations, has left us with implication after implication that can be interpreted in no other way.[17]

[16] "The Raison d'Être of Criticism in the Arts", in *Two Cheers for Democracy*, p. 121.

[17] The contrast between Forster as thinker and as artist can be further exemplified. In his *Aspects of the Novel*, speaking as a critic and thinker, he plays down the importance of the story (Chapter II), dismisses it as a necessary nuisance, a "tapeworm". As artist, however, in his own novels, he is, as we have seen, a meticulous

E. M. Forster then, a great artist poised on a spiritual threshold, is one who looks back with preference and nostalgia to a vanishing unself-conscious spirituality, forward with reluctance to a new conscious spirituality as yet tentative, though destined to evolve and grow Wiser as an artist than a thinker, he receives from a subconscious not yet raised fully into consciousness intimations both of the old spirituality and the new, and in terms of them creates for us that higher reality of the material irradiated by the spiritual which is the world of art. As a thinker, he falls short of himself as an artist, cannot get beyond the paradoxes in which, through the logic of his divided spiritual allegiances, he becomes involved Undoubtedly these paradoxes and his inability to transcend them consciously, account more than anything for the dying out of his creative impulses after *A Passage to India*, for his unproductiveness artistically since 1924. The five great novels, however, and the anything but "little" stories that preceded them, are there, a permanent achievement. For a long time yet they will continue to challenge our understanding of what we are now, and what we are in process of becoming.

---

contriver of events with a highly-developed sense of their importance and what causes them to occur. In the novels, in fact, the *story* is recognised as of fundamental significance.

Bibliography

I. WORKS BY E. M. FORSTER

The most recent bibliography of Forster's writings is, B. J. Kirkpatrick, *A Bibliography of E. M. Forster*, listed below § II. 1.

1. NOVELS

Where Angels Fear to Tread. Edinburgh (Blackwood) 1905.
The Longest Journey. Edinburgh (Blackwood) 1907.
A Room with a View. London (Edward Arnold) 1908.
Howards End. London (Edward Arnold) 1910.
A Passage to India. London (Edward Arnold) 1924.

2. SHORT STORIES

The Celestial Omnibus. London (Sidgwick and Jackson) 1911.
The Eternal Moment. London (Sidgwick and Jackson) 1928.
The Collected Tales of E. M. Forster. New York (Knopf) 1947.

3. ESSAYS, CRITICISM, AND OTHER WORKS

Aspects of the Novel. London (Edward Arnold) 1927.
Abinger Harvest. London (Edward Arnold) 1936.
"Nordic Twilight" (a Macmillan War Pamphlet). London (Macmillan) 1940.
Two Cheers for Democracy. London (Edward Arnold) 1951.
The Hill of Devi. London (Edward Arnold) 1953.

II. STUDIES OF FORSTER

1. BIBLIOGRAPHICAL

KIRKPATRICK, B. J. *A Bibliography of E. M. Forster.* London (Hart-Davis) 1965.
GERBER, HELMUT E. "E. M. Forster: an Annotated Checklist of Writings About Him", in *English Fiction in Transition*, II (Spring 1959).

II. CRITICAL

ALLEN, G. O. "Structure, Symbol, Theme in E. M. Forster's *A Passage to India*" in *P.M.L.A.*, LXX (1955), pp. 934-54.

AULT, PETER. "Aspects of E. M. Forster", in *Dublin Review*, No. 439 (1946), pp. 109-34.

BEAUMONT, ERNEST. "Mr E. M. Forster's Strange Mystics", in *Dublin Review*, No. 453 (1951), pp. 41-51.

BEER, J. B. *The Achievement of E. M. Forster*. London (Chatto and Windus) 1963.

CONNOLLY, CYRIL. *The Condemned Playground*, pp. 254-9. London (Routledge) 1945.

CREWS, FREDERICK C. *E. M. Forster: The Perils of Humanism*. Princeton (Princeton U.P.) 1962.

FUSSELL JR., PAUL. "Mrs Moore: Some Suggestions", in *Philological Quarterly*, XXXII (1953), pp. 381-95.

GRANSDEN, K. W. *E. M. Forster*. Edinburgh (Oliver & Boyd) 1962.

HOY, CYRUS. "Forster's Metaphysical Novel", in *P.M.L.A.*, LXXV (1960), pp. 126-36.

ISHERWOOD, CHRISTOPHER. *Lions and Shadows*. Norfolk, Conn. (New Directions) 1947.

MCCONKEY, JAMES, *The Novels of E. M. Forster*. Ithaca (Cornell U.P.) 1957.

OLIVER, H. J. *The Art of E. M. Forster*. Melbourne (Melbourne U.P.) 1960.

SHAHANE, V. A. *E. M. Forster: A Reassessment*. Delhi (Kitab Mahal) 1962.

STONE, WILFRED. *The Cave and the Mountain*. Stanford (Stanford U.P.) 1966; London (Oxford U.P.) 1966.

THOMSON, GEORGE H. "Theme and Symbol in *Howards End*", in *Modern Fiction Studies*, VII, No. 3 (1961).

TRILLING, LIONEL. *E. M. Forster: a Study*. London (Hogarth) 1962.

WILSON, ANGUS. "A Conversation with E. M. Forster", in *Encounter*, Nov. 1957.

WOOLF, VIRGINIA. "The Novels of E. M. Forster", in *The Death of the Moth*. London (Hogarth) 1942.

Index